CLASSICAL MUSIC'S STRANGEST
CONCERTS AND CHARACTERS

CLASSICAL MUSIC'S STRANGEST CONCERTS AND CHARACTERS

Extraordinary but True Stories from over
One Thousand Years of Harmony and Discord

Brian Levison & Frances Farrer

**ROBSON
BOOKS**

First published in the United Kingdom in 2007 by
Robson Books
10 Southcombe Street
London
W14 0RA

An imprint of Anova Books Company Ltd

ISBN-10: 1 86105 938 8
ISBN-13: 9781861059383

A CIP catalogue record for this book is available from the British Library.
10 9 8 7 5 4 3 2 1

Typeset by SX Composing DTP, Rayleigh, Essex
Printed and bound by Creative Print & Design, Ebbw Vale, Wales

This book can be ordered direct from the publisher.
Contact the marketing department, but try your bookshop first.

www.anovabooks.com

Contents

INTRODUCTION

Considering all the mishaps waiting to happen, one of the strangest things about concerts is that more of them are not strange. Thousands take place each year at every level of accomplishment but unusual incidents occur very rarely.

Having between us gone to a good number of concerts, neither can remember being present at a particularly odd one, though Brian Levison was in the choir at a concert where the choir's organist took his bow without his trousers (for entirely understandable reasons explained later in the book).

Musicians are perfectionists and perfection does not come cheap. It is not uncommon to phone an orchestral player and to be politely asked to ring back in several hours as he or she is practising. This and hours of rehearsal time go some way to explain why – unlike sporting events where unpredictability is of the essence – the unanticipated is less likely to happen at a concert.

Inevitably though, where egos, large numbers of people, the complications of travel, the logistics of organisation, quirky personalities, accidents and simple bad luck are factors, strange things will happen.

We have drawn our stories from many first-hand accounts and from a wide range of other sources including books, newspapers and journals of all periods. A large number are, we believe, reproduced here for the first time. Some were happening as we were writing. Philip Heyman updated us on his strange wedding reception concert as it happened over the

1

course of two weeks. A few older anecdotes may be familiar but have been considerably expanded with additional information.

'Concert', 'classical' and even 'music' are not, and never have been, exact terms. Public commercial concerts did not begin until 1672, but there were plenty of people listening to good music in churches or in the courts and houses of the aristocracy long before. So if we came across a story from that period that was unusual enough, we included it. Contemporaries of Beethoven and Berlioz did not think they were listening to classical music, but when we listen to the same music today, that is what we think we are hearing. And whether or not you think that John Cage's *4'33"* of silence is music, the first performance certainly made a strange concert.

We have therefore adopted a common sense rather than formulaic approach and drawn the line at points where we think most readers and music-lovers would instinctively draw it. We have excluded opera both because we did not consider opera performances to be concerts and to avoid overlap with other books, though the odd opera-related incident is included.

It would have been impossible to write this book without the help of many people.

Grateful thanks are offered to Jill Haas, Rip Bulkeley and Andrew Ward, veteran of several *Strangest* titles, for the substantial assistance they gave Brian Levison in differing ways.

Many members of the music profession – conductors, soloists, orchestral players, archivists, librarians, academics and writers – have given very generously of their time, expertise and experiences to both of us.

Brian Levison would particularly like to thank John Amis, Bernard Barker, Cliff Bibby, Anthony Boden, James Brown, Margaret Campbell, David Chesterman, Nikki Chesterman, Suzie Clark, Beverley Davison, Darrell Davison, Jonathan Del Mar, John Dunn, Ian Dust, Sally Groves, Paul Harris, Gavin Henderson, Philip Heyman, Catherine Hodgson, Annetta Hoffnung, Julian Jacobson, Robert Layton, David Matthews, Roy Newsome, Philip Olleson, Claire Ormshaw, Anthony Payne, Ernst Reitermaier, Arne Richards, Jim Scott, Kate Taylor, Frank Villella, Terry Webster and Simon Williams.

For her part, Frances Farrer would like to thank especially David Aspin, Michael Buckley, Simon Chalk, Michael Church, David Curtis, Sarah Davies, Mary Firth, Dounja Gremmelmaier, Richard Hawley, Gavin Henderson, Lindon Jenkins, Beresford King-Smith, David Lister, Stephen Miller, Kathryn Mosley, Anthony Phillips and Joseph Spooner.

We both gratefully acknowledge the wholehearted help of the Oxford librarians in the music and general libraries of the Bodleian, the University of Oxford Faculty of Music and the Westgate Central Library. We also received much assistance from the Colindale Newspaper Archive in London, which is part of the British Library.

The briefest way of identifying who wrote which story is to say that Frances Farrer takes responsibility for the following: Old Bach Pays Tribute (1747), Franz Liszt and the Big Tours (1838–47), Conducting for the Dithyrambic (1905–51), Mad About the Beat (1932), The Frock's the Star (1953), Knowing the Score (1964), Hove Too (1993), Karlheinz Stockhausen Takes to the Air (1995), A Show of Hands (1996), Concert in a Cave (1997), Encore to Start (1997), The Thousand-Year Reverberation (2000), The Grandest Leg-pull? (2004), Beating Up the Festival Hall (2004), The Swan and the Firemen (2004), and What a Turn She Gave (2005).

CAPTIVE AUDIENCE

NAPLES, 64 AD

Although the Emperor Nero is musically best known for fiddling while Rome burned, since the fiddle didn't exist at the time the story can reluctantly be regarded as false. But there may be some truth in hearsay accounts that he sang an ode during the conflagration, accompanying himself on a lyre. He was particularly proud of his singing and took himself extremely seriously as an artist. The citizens of Naples had discovered this to their cost only a short time before when he gave an agonisingly long concert only brought to a close through the intervention of a deity.

Nero was active in most of the performing arts both before and after he became emperor. He was particularly passionate about music, which he studied from his early youth. He sang and played the lyre to a good standard and eventually reached the point where he wanted to perform on stage in public. To his mother Agrippina and his advisers, music was an immoral Greek art unsuitable for Roman nobles, and they brought pressure on him to keep his performances private. Nero bowed to their wishes but continued to practise daily under good tutors. He worked hard and was prepared to suffer for his art. To reduce his weight and improve the quality of his voice, he underwent enemas and severe diets. Some days he ate only chives preserved in oil, and never consumed apples or any other food thought harmful to the vocal cords. To strengthen his diaphragm, he lay on his back with heavy slabs of lead on his chest.

By 64 AD, when he was 26, he was rid of the main restraints on his increasingly deranged behaviour. After several attempts he had finally managed to murder Agrippina. The other important influence on his life, his tutor Seneca, had resigned. Free to do as he pleased, Nero married his mistress Poppaea, executed his first wife Octavia, and decided to break new ground for a Roman emperor by giving a public recital.

He thought carefully about the venue. He avoided Rome, knowing it was likely he would be barracked by the plebs. He also knew that the nobles would disapprove. They thought that the emperor's job was to defend the frontiers and expand the empire, not to give concerts. So he settled on Naples, where Greek influence was strong and his reception was likely to be much more sympathetic.

Just the same, he took no chances. He made sure that news of the concert was circulated throughout the region, then sent secret agents to check who failed to attend. Consequently, so many people turned up that none of the usual theatres were big enough. The concert was switched to the largest space available, an amphitheatre with a capacity of many thousands.

The programme was very lengthy and consisted of items composed by the emperor himself and performed by him costumed and masked. Nero's voice was husky and not very powerful, and the performance dragged on and on. No one dared show any sign of boredom or dissatisfaction. It was well known that spies were everywhere, observing how enthusiastically spectators applauded and even the look on their faces. Anything less than rapt admiration was noted and reported, so each piece was greeted with loud applause. Nero also packed the amphitheatre with a claque of five thousand youths brought with him from Rome to make sure he had a good reception. He was so pleased by the rhythmic clapping of a group of Alexandrian sailors that he sent across to Egypt for reinforcements.

Those who thought they could slip away when they had heard enough were sadly mistaken. No one was allowed to leave before the end, even women about to give birth, and several babies were born during the performance. People tried desperately to escape. Some climbed the wall at the back and risked the long drop to the ground. Others collapsed in a heap and feigned death, hoping to be carted off for burial.

Nero, unable to distinguish between genuine and insincere applause, was thrilled by the tumultuous acclaim, and decided to have a repeat performance next day. The audience, which had thought their ordeal was over, was forced to return. After another rapturous reception, he extended for another day and then another. Mercifully for the audience, the concerts were finally brought to a close by a small earthquake that destroyed the theatre. Even then Nero was unwilling to stop and sang through the first tremors until it became unsafe to continue. The Neapolitans praised Poseidon, god of the sea and earthquakes, for his timely intervention. Back in Rome they said it was a bad omen. Nero, Pontifex Maximus, thought differently: no one had been killed so it was a mark of divine favour.

Nero lived another four years until his regime crumbled and he committed suicide. His final words were, 'What an artist dies in me!' and he meant it. Almost 1,600 years later the Italian composer Monteverdi composed an opera about Nero's second wife Poppaea. *The Coronation of Poppaea* was the first opera to be based on a historical character. Nero, who murdered her as well, might not have appreciated the unflattering plot, but he would have adored the music.

THE WRONG SAINT?

ROME, c. 200

Musical academies and societies throughout the world are named in her honour. Countless compositions are dedicated to her. Her representation appears in innumerable mosaics, paintings and sculptures, clutching a musical instrument.

So it would be reasonable to expect that St Cecilia had written a musical treatise or two, maybe entertained her companions with some mellifluous harp-playing, or at least gone down to posterity as having a tuneful voice. In short, possessed some qualifications for the title of patron saint of music.

But there is no record that she was connected with music as a singer, player, composer or in any way. So the question naturally arises, how did she become universally accepted as music's patron saint?

Cecilia probably lived in the second half of the second century AD or at the beginning of the third. A church dedicated to her certainly existed in the Trastevere district of Rome by the end of the fifth century. The official story is that she was a Christian committed to preserving her virginity who unwillingly found herself betrothed to Valerianus, a pagan nobleman. She coped with this awkward situation with aplomb. First she converted him and his brother Tiburtius to Christianity, and then got her new husband to agree to respect her purity.

In the anti-Christian climate of the day, the three of them were martyred. Cecilia's death was particularly bloody. After

7

she survived an attempt to suffocate her in a steam bath, the authorities decided to behead her. However, the executioner failed to kill her with three strokes. According to William Caxton's *Golden Legende*, 'the fourth stroke he might not by the law smite, and so left her there lying half alive and half dead.' She lived for a further three days, using the time to dispose of her estate to the poor, including leaving her house as a church, thought to be the church in the Trastevere.

Cecilia's only tenuous link with music comes in the account of her wedding celebrations taken from the fifth-century *Acts of Cecilia:* 'The day on which the wedding was to be held arrived and while musical instruments were playing she was singing in her heart to God alone saying, "Make my heart and my body pure that I be not confounded".'

Many centuries passed before she was thought of as the musicians' saint. Even Chaucer in *The Canterbury Tales* in the fourteenth century makes no mention of a musical association. It was not until the end of the following century that she was suddenly adopted by musicians' guilds throughout Europe. Quite why is a mystery. Possibly there were some mistranslations. The Latin phrase for musical instruments, *cantantibus organis*, might have been misunderstood as 'organ', so the phrase 'while musical instruments were playing' became 'while playing the organ'. Whatever the reason, the organ is now Cecilia's recognised symbol, as in the painting of her by Raphael in Bologna.

Since that period, St Cecilia's Day, 22 November, has been regularly celebrated with concerts and new compositions dedicated to her. Handel and Purcell are among those to have composed a piece in her honour, as has Benjamin Britten, who was born on St Cecilia's Day.

But did Cecilia actually exist? According to one scholarly theory, she is simply a pious figment of the imagination. It argues that her first church in the Trastevere was built near the shrine of the Roman goddess who heals blindness. Blindness in Latin is *caecita*, very similar to Cecilia. If that is the case, then music is dedicated to the protection of someone who never existed.

8

Music can claim one saintly composer, however. Hildegard of Bingen in Germany, also the first composer whose biography is known, lived from 1098 to 1179. She was born into a large family and at the age of eight was sent to a religious community where she spent the rest of her life, eventually becoming abbess.

As early as the age of three, she began to have visions, but kept this to herself for many years. The visions were often physically painful and modern medical opinion has suggested that they stemmed from migraine attacks.

If anyone can be called a multi-talented workaholic, it is Hildegard. As well as managing the convent and organising its relocation, she wrote major works of theology and plays set to her own music, which may well have been performed in the convent. After initial doubts, she wrote down her visions and became widely known for her prophecies and miracles. Her fame brought her into contact with popes, bishops and kings, to whom she readily offered advice. She wrote treatises about plants and herbs and encouraged their use as medicines. In one of her works, she discusses lovemaking and gives what is believed to be the first written description of a female orgasm. Unusually for a woman at that time, she travelled widely and spoke in public.

Her musical claims are as strong as St Cecilia's are weak. She regarded music as the sound of the angels on earth and left a substantial body of compositions, settings of her own pious poems. Their pure and ethereal qualities have been widely recorded.

The Roman Catholic Church never quite got round to formalising Hildegard's canonisation. However, she is regarded as a saint in Germany and is the outstanding candidate to be patron saint of music.

SLIP-UP IN THE SISTINE

ROME, FEAST OF OUR LADY, 1515

In 1515 the young Flemish composer Adrian Willaert, on a grand tour of Europe, reached Rome and soon went to hear the music performed in the papal chapel as part of the services.

One of the services he attended was the important Feast of Our Lady. As he sat in the chapel, Willaert would not have known which settings of texts were going to be sung. No doubt he hoped he would hear for the first time Josquin des Prés's famous setting of the motet *Verbum bonum et suave*. It was usually performed on this feast day because the Pope particularly liked it and insisted on its inclusion. Willaert had written a setting of the text himself while in Flanders, and was curious to compare Josquin's treatment with his own.

Josquin was the most highly regarded composer of the time. His works were always eagerly sought after. A visitor to one of the many princely or ducal courts would be sure of a much warmer welcome if he arrived with a new Josquin manuscript in his luggage. Attribution often had to be taken on trust, as many manuscripts were unidentified. This could lead to amusing situations where a court might listen to an anonymous new work and give it the thumbs down, only to discover all kinds of hidden qualities when it was later revealed that the composer was the great Josquin. The reverse was also true. If it was by Josquin it was, by definition, outstanding.

Willaert's wish was granted when the choir began to sing Josquin's motet. But what he felt as he heard the opening bars can only be imagined. Perhaps his mouth dropped open or he blinked in disbelief. For the setting was none other than his own! It was naturally gratifying that the Pope admired it so much. On the other hand, Josquin was getting credit that didn't belong to him. Willaert understandably wanted the recognition that could open many important doors of patronage in Rome, maybe even that of the Pope himself.

As the service proceeded, he must have asked himself how this had happened. Most probably some traveller from Flanders had visited Rome and managed to pass the motet off as Josquin's. He must have thought that the chances of Willaert ever being in Rome on the day the piece was played were about zero.

As soon as the service was over, Willaert approached the choirmaster. There is no record of what he said, but it was probably a brusque comment along the lines of 'I've got a bit of a surprise for you . . .'

If he expected apologies and assurances that the attribution would be rectified, he was sadly mistaken. The authorities weren't interested that Willaert had written it. They were more interested that Josquin hadn't. The motet was promptly dropped from future services, though Willaert had it published under his own name a few years later.

He went on to have a distinguished career at St Mark's, Venice. He was director there for 35 years until his death at the age of 82, and frequently repeated this story. Josquin pre-deceased him, but that didn't stop the Josquin misattribution industry. It became even more active than it was in his lifetime, so much so that it was famously recorded, 'Josquin wrote more compositions after his death than during his life.'

MASOCHISM, MURDER AND MADRIGALS

DON CARLO GESUALDO (c.1566–1613)

To Italian society of the sixteenth century, he was known as His Most Illustrious and Serene Highness Don Carlo Gesualdo, third Prince of Venosa, eighth Count of Conza, fifteenth Lord of Gesualdo, to give about a third of his titles. Less complimentarily, posterity has called him 'murderer' and 'Prince of Pain'. To us he is better known simply as Gesualdo, composer of madrigals of outstanding beauty and originality. The grotesque elements of his life have inspired novels, plays, an opera and even a musical.

He was born in the 1560s, the second son of a noble Neapolitan family. The chores of running the estate and producing an heir fell to his elder brother, and Gesualdo didn't have too much to do other than indulge his passion for music. His father's court employed a group of musicians and he showed a very early, almost Mozartian, aptitude for composing and singing. As he grew up, his wealth, position and talent enabled him to establish his own salon of musicans and writers. He and his friends liked nothing better than to row out into the Bay of Naples and spend the whole night singing madrigals.

Life changed dramatically when his elder brother Luigi died heirless. It now fell to Gesualdo to marry and produce a son. The family estates would otherwise revert to the papacy after his death. Gesualdo may not have been too keen on the idea. He was said to care for nothing but music, and to have leanings towards his own, rather than the opposite, sex. However, family pressure could not be resisted and the following year he married his first cousin, Donna Maria d'Avalos.

Donna Maria, who had already been married and widowed twice, was praised as 'the most beautiful woman in the kingdom of the Two Sicilies'. Her first husband reportedly died from overdoing his conjugal activities.

The marriage was initially very happy in their palace in Naples. When a son, Don Emmanuele, was born, everything seemed to be going to plan. But three or four years into the marriage, Donna Maria, by now probably a madrigal widow, took a fancy to Don Fabrizio Carafa, Duke of Andria, 'the handsomest and most accomplished nobleman of the city'. They began a passionate and not very secret affair, often using Donna Maria's own bedchamber for their love nest, and relying on the discretion of her maids.

Inevitably word got around and reached the ears of Gesualdo's uncle, Don Giulio Gesualdo. He had long (but unsuccessfully) lusted after Donna Maria and had assumed that she was chaste.

Warning was passed to the lovers that their secret was known. Don Fabrizio decided it would be prudent to desist, but Donna Maria soon missed his attentions and requested that they resume. When Don Fabrizio pointed out the danger, she retorted scathingly that 'nature had erred in creating a knight with the spirit of a woman, and in creating in her a woman with the spirit of a valorous knight!' No lover worthy of the name could accept this put-down. 'And so did they continue in their delights.'

In the meantime, thwarted Uncle Giulio had alerted his nephew to the situation. Gesualdo decided he needed proof. Donning his hunting gear, he announced that he was off to kill a boar or two and wouldn't be home that night. Don Fabrizio took the chance to set up a tryst with Donna Maria. It was all a trap, of course. Gesualdo returned at midnight. Bursting into Donna Maria's bedchamber, he found the two lovers asleep after making love and 'slew with innumerable dagger thrusts the sleepers before they had time to waken'.

It was a wonderful scandal. The whole city came to view the corpses. Gesualdo fled to his castle in the country. His flight suited the authorities and no further action was taken.

You would have thought that after brutally murdering Donna Maria, Gesualdo's chances of remarrying were just about nil. However, his father had died and he was now Prince of Venosa and a very desirable match. In 1594, four years after he had killed Donna Maria, he journeyed to Ferrara with three hundred pieces of luggage to marry the Duke of Ferrara's cousin, Eleonora d'Este.

If Gesualdo ever felt ambivalent about remarrying, moving to Ferrara brought one unsurpassable advantage: he now lived in the foremost musical city in Italy. The leading composers of the day gathered there from across Europe and not a day passed without several concerts. In this hot-house musical atmosphere, Gesualdo, who had previously published his compositions under a pseudonym, now published four substantial books of madrigals under his own name, works that established his reputation.

But his music heaven did not last very long. After three years the Duke of Ferrara died and Gesualdo returned to his country castle but without his wife Donna Eleonora. Possibly their newborn son, Don Alfonsino, was not strong enough to travel, possibly she had no urgent wish to live with Gesualdo, who was maltreating her. When she did rejoin him, his violence towards her frequently brought them to the point of divorce.

From this time on until his death, Gesualdo's behaviour became increasingly bizarre, with many symptoms of manic depression, possibly resulting from his feelings of guilt and remorse for the death of Donna Maria. A few years earlier he had built a chapel to house a large painting in which he is shown kneeling asking for forgiveness. Now he resorted to flagellation, employing teams of young men to beat him three times a day, 'during which operation he was wont to smile joyfully'. His case even made the medical casebooks in 1635: 'The Prince of Venosa . . . was unable to go to stool without having been previously flogged by a valet kept expressly for the purpose.'

None of this stopped Gesualdo composing, his music pushing back the boundaries of his art and becoming more and more extreme, reflecting perhaps his own psychological state. His last, most advanced, collection was published two years before he died. He also wrote religious works whose themes of guilt, betrayal and redemption had particular significance for him.

For the man born with a silver spoon in his mouth, everything eventually turned to ashes. Weakened by the constant beatings, he died in 1613. Despite all the careful planning, the Gesualdo estates passed out of the family, for he was predeceased both by Emmanuele, his son by Donna Maria, and by Alfonsino, his son by Donna Eleonora.

Antonio Salieri is sometimes accused, falsely, of poisoning Mozart to death. But it is Gesualdo, uniquely among composers, who truly deserves the unwanted distinction of murderer.

THE HIT AND RUN MAN

ALESSANDRO STRADELLA (1639–82)

The extraordinary life and violent death of the seventeenth-century Venetian composer Alessandro Stradella proved endlessly fascinating to nineteenth-century opera composers in search of a good plot. No fewer than six operas were written about him between 1837 and 1867, the best known being *Alessandro Stradella* by Friedrich von Flotow. All but one of the others were also called *Alessandro Stradella*, so an opera-goer of that period had to be careful not to see the same one twice by accident.

The plots were based on a tale that had been in circulation since the early eighteenth century. Stradella, one of the foremost composers of oratorios, cantatas and sacred music of his era and a well-known ladies' man, is unwisely hired by a Venetian nobleman to teach singing to his fiancée, the beautiful Hortensia. Predictably the pair fall in love and elope to Rome, hotly pursued by two hatchet men sent by the jilted grandee with instructions to kill them both.

The hitmen catch up with their targets at the Church of St John Lateran, appropriately enough on Passion Sunday 1675, where Stradella's oratorio *St John the Baptist* is being performed. Having sharpened their knives and with nothing better to do, they tune in to Stradella's music while waiting for the pair to emerge, and are so overcome by its beauty that they give up their murderous intentions. When Stradella and Hortensia come out, the assassins fall to their knees, confess their mission, and advise the couple to make

16

themselves scarce, which they do by disappearing to Turin the same day.

Not best pleased, the nobleman recruits two more thugs who set upon Stradella one evening as he is walking the ramparts in Turin and leave him for dead. However, he is only badly wounded, and he and Hortensia rapidly move on to Genoa. There, another set of thugs gain access to the lovers' bedchamber. This time there is no escape and they are stabbed to death.

The story's attraction for composers is obvious, but as an account of Stradella's life it contains as much fiction as fact. It was not until 1994, when the scholar Carolyn Gianturco published *Alessandro Stradella (1639–1682): His Life and Music* after over a quarter of a century of painstaking research, that the true story was revealed. Stradella's life was shown to be just as eventful as previously thought, if not more so. Flotow and the others may have chosen the wrong plot.

In 1676 Stradella was in Rome and, short of cash, came up with a marriage-broking scam, involving a woman who was prepared to pay ten thousand scudi for a husband. Stradella thought he knew just the man, a young, not very bright relative of Cardinal Cibo, the papal secretary of state. But there was a problem. The woman was lowborn, old, ugly and not respectable, and no young man in his right mind would willingly have married her. To get round this difficulty, Stradella and a singer friend called Vulpio got Cardinal Cibo's relative drunk – very drunk, one imagines – and the ceremony was carried out.

It was a pointless exercise. The cardinal immediately had the marriage annulled and placed the poor woman in an insalubrious nunnery for the rest of her life. He then set about getting Stradella and Vulpio imprisoned, but Stradella managed to keep one step ahead and escaped to Venice.

In Venice he was appointed to teach music to Agnese Van Uffele, the beautiful mistress of Alvise Contarini, a prominent Venetian noble. The pair became lovers and eloped to Turin where, being unmarried, they were forced to live apart. Agnese took refuge in a convent whose rules forbade Stradella from writing to her. He tried to bypass this obstacle by writing a letter in the form of a cantata, but the nuns were no fools and caught him.

The jilted Contarini was by now in hot pursuit. Arriving in Turin, he accused Agnese of stealing ten thousand ducats. When the charge was proved groundless, he next insisted that she marry Stradella, knowing this was the last thing that the marriage-shy Stradella wanted. Otherwise, he threatened, Agnese would have to remain in her convent and become a nun.

Meanwhile the composer had been trying to get work in Turin as a musician at the court of Maria Giovanna. However, she had no wish to employ someone who could be a source of bad will between her and a member of one of Venice's most powerful families. Stradella began to think that he should get back on good terms with Contarini, even if it meant marrying Agnese after all.

To this end, he went to Agnese's convent on Sunday, 10 October 1677 and signed the marriage contract with the approval of Contarini and Agnese's father, who acted as witness. While his prospective father-in-law lingered behind, apparently to discuss some details with his daughter, Stradella left the convent on his own. In the vicinity of the Church of San Carlo, he was attacked by two ruffians, receiving a number of severe blows to the head. He collapsed to the ground where he was left for dead; his attackers fled to the palace of the French ambassador.

No one was sure who was responsible. Popular opinion blamed Contarini, but the Duchess Maria Giovanna suspected Agnese's father and imprisoned him. She made a bitter complaint to Louis XIV of France about his ambassador and a diplomatic impasse ensued. Eventually the French Ambassador and his family were allowed to leave Turin in exchange for a state official the French had arrested. Much to Maria Giovanna's fury, the two assailants were smuggled out in the same carriage.

Contarini, the prime suspect, returned to Venice where he gave the impression of guilt by going round with an armed guard to protect himself, it was said, from Stradella. With Contarini gone, the pressure was off Stradella to marry Agnese.

When he received an invitation to go to Genoa for the carnival, it was a perfect excuse for him to vanish. He had been in Turin for six turbulent months. In Genoa he had a productive and successful few years as a composer, remaining unmarried and continuing his amorous dalliances. One of these was with the mistress of a nobleman and in February 1682 he was attacked in similar circumstances to Turin. This time the assassins were successful. As for Agnese, her fate is unknown. She may never have left the convent again.

Murders and assassinations are, paradoxically, the lifeblood of opera. In real life, assassinations with musical associations are fortunately very rare. Apart from Stradella, there are only four or five instances. One particularly interesting case occurred in 1729 and involved two prima donnas of the Neapolitan opera, Rosa Albertini and Francesca Grieco. Their rivalry in love and music was so fierce that they ended up fighting each other and Grieco received such bad injuries that she had to retire from singing. Soon afterwards, Albertini was assassinated. The killer was let off with a fine, because he had the all-powerful relatives, whereas Albertini had none.

ON THE FIDDLE

LONDON, DECEMBER 1672

When the thought first occurred to the composer and violinist John Banister, he must have been greatly pleased to find such an original way of raising much-needed cash. Like many ideas of genius, it was so obvious that it was surprising no one had thought of it before. Within twenty years his new concept was commonplace in England and soon spread throughout the world.

Banister hadn't always been short of money. For a number of years he had worked successfully for Charles II as a musician. As director of His Majesty's 24 violins, he was authorised to choose a dozen of the violinists to form the select band that accompanied the king on important missions. At the height of his influence Banister was called the English Lully.

The downturn in his fortunes came when the francophile Charles suggested that French players should be included in the ensemble. Banister knew what he liked and what he liked were English fiddlers, not foreign ones. He is said to have used 'saucy words' to the king, who sent him back to the ranks.

Now that Banister had lost his influence and power, the king's violinists were finally able to pursue him for the wages they alleged he had embezzled over the previous four years. He was found guilty, though he was allowed to stay with the 24 because of his ability as a player. Probably obliged to repay the money, Banister had to find another source of income. Which was when he had his good idea.

In the aftermath of Cromwell's Protectorate, the playing of music was restricted to the private houses of those who could afford musicians, or to taverns, which often had a separate chamber called a musick-house. No charge was made to hear the musicians. The tavern made its profit from sales of ale and wine. The musicians made their money from tips.

Banister had been giving concerts for a number of years, going back to 1660, according to Samuel Pepys. Quite what prompted him no one knows, but on 30 December 1672 the following advert appeared in the *London Gazette*:

These are to give Notice, that at Mr John Banister's House, now called the Musick-school, over against the George tavern in White Fryers, this present Monday, will be Musick performed by Excellent Masters, beginning precisely at four of the Clock in the afternoon, and every afternoon for the future precisely at the same hour.

This is almost certainly the first concert advertisement to appear in a newspaper. But though highly innovative, it is not the main reason for Banister's place in the history books. That was his simple, but previously unheard of, request as each person came through the door: 'One shilling, if you please.'

This concert therefore has a special place in the annals of music as the first time an entrance fee was demanded. It was the beginning of public concerts as we know them today.

There was no published programme. 'Call for what you please,' patrons were told, though Banister's own compositions were probably played. It was reported that, 'There was very good musick for Banister found means to procure the best hands in town,' and there was seldom an empty seat.

Banister had to move to larger premises several times to accommodate the growing audiences. Soon public concerts were taking place in musick-houses all over London and in the provinces. In Islington a surveyor named Sadler exploited the health-giving properties of a well found on his land and set up a musick-room and pleasure gardens. The establishment became known as Sadler's Wells.

Despite his up-and-down career, Banister's reputation remained intact enough for him to be buried in Westminster Abbey the day after he died in 1679.

THE CONDUCTOR WHO BEAT HIMSELF TO DEATH

PARIS, JANUARY 1687

There are a number of candidates for strangest death of a composer. Enrique Granados, the Spanish composer, was crossing the English Channel in 1916 when his steamer was torpedoed by a German submarine. Rescued, he plunged back into the water to save his wife and drowned. Out cycling with his daughter, the French composer Ernest Chausson died in a freak accident in 1899 when his bicycle crashed into a wall on his estate. In 1945, the Austrian composer Anton Webern was shot by an American soldier who mistook him for a black marketeer. The French composer Charles-Henri Alkan was trapped for more than a day by a piece of falling furniture before dying in hospital in 1888.

But perhaps none of these deaths was as strange as that of Jean-Baptiste Lully. Considering his very humble origins, Lully achieved exceptional success and riches. Born in 1632 in Italy, the son of a miller, he went to France as a servant when he was thirteen. Talented as a dancer, violinist and composer, he was only 21 when he achieved his first official post in the court of Louis XIV. Eventually he became the equivalent of Master of the King's Music, one of the most important positions at the Sun King's court. Politically and financially astute, he achieved a virtual monopoly over all the music performed in France, earning royalties on almost all performances that included any music. Perhaps most remarkably, thanks to his friendship with the king, whom he had coached in dancing, he was appointed a Secretary to the King, a senior but non-musical position.

On his way to the top Lully made many enemies. They included the eminent playwright Molière, with whom he collaborated, and La Fontaine, the famous writer of the *Fables*. There were plots to poison him and accusations of sexual scandal. Lully, though married with children, was a member of a discreet homosexual group. He also had mistresses. After an argument, the mother of one mistress wrote to the king stating that Lully was having a homosexual relationship with one of the king's pages. As a result Lully lost some of his influence with the king.

Lully's duties included composing pieces for official royal occasions. In 1686 Louis was operated on for a fistula, a procedure considered so dangerous that the surgeons first practised on a number of paupers to make sure they got it right. To celebrate the king's recovery, Lully composed a Te Deum, first performed in the Church of Les Feuillants in Paris with Lully himself conducting.

The modern practice of conducting with a baton did not become widespread until the nineteenth century. In Lully's time, thick rolls of manuscript, staffs and sticks were commonly used to beat time. Lully occasionally used a billiard cue, but on this occasion he beat time by thumping a long pointed stick on the ground. At some point during the performance his aim went awry and he struck himself heavily on his little toe. He was seen to limp after the performance, which was put down to bruising. In fact it was more serious and an abscess formed, which became gangrenous.

Lully's doctor wanted to amputate the toe but Lully refused. When the gangrene spread, the doctors proposed amputating his leg. Again Lully refused, even though he knew this would mean certain, painful death. He spent his last few days organising the disposal of his substantial estate. He is said to have left 58 sacks of gold and doubloons, as well as silver plate, diamonds and other precious stones, and several properties, equivalent to millions of pounds today.

Lully did not lose his sense of humour on his deathbed.

When his confessor insisted that he destroy the opera on which he was working, Lully willingly threw the manuscript on the fire. When asked afterwards why he had burned good music, he replied, 'I knew what I was doing; I have another copy.'

Lully was the dominant musical personality of his time. Despite his personal shortcomings, there is no question that he worked extremely hard. He wrote and produced an opera a year for fifteen years as well as a huge amount of ballet and religious music. Little of this prolific output is played today. Ironically, he is best remembered for the unique manner of his death – the only musician to have literally beat himself to death while conducting.

THE ORGANIST WHO GOT COLD FEET

DRESDEN, AUTUMN 1717

In 1717 the much-admired French organist and harpsichordist, Louis Marchand, left the service of Louis XIV in highly unusual circumstances. Marchand, reputed to be a wife-beater, had recently split up with Mme Marchand, and the king decided that half Marchand's salary should be paid to her as compensation. The musician, described as haughty and eccentric even in his obituary, took exception to this and one Sunday morning during Mass in the Royal Chapel he abruptly stopped playing and went home.

The king sent for him and demanded an explanation. 'Well, Your Majesty,' Marchand is reported to have replied, 'I am only getting half my pay, as half has been paid to my wife. It therefore seems only fair that if she gets half my salary, she should play half the service.'

A little later he arrived in Dresden looking for a job and played for Augustus II, King of Poland and Elector of Saxony, impressing him highly. A well-paid post seemed on the cards. Unfortunately he soon became unpopular with his prospective colleagues, who decided to try and forestall his appointment.

Accordingly, the concertmaster at Dresden, Jean-Baptiste Volumier, put forward the proposal that Marchand prove his ability in competition against another organist. He suggested a contest between Marchand and a friend of his with a growing reputation at Weimar, a certain Johann Sebastian Bach. The chief minister, Count Flemming, thought this would be an excellent diversion for the court and agreed. It was not the first such contest at Dresden. In the 1650s, Johann Jacob Froberger, organist at the Viennese imperial court, and Matthias Weckmann, court organist at Dresden, had competed for a golden chain.

Volumier wrote to Bach pointing out that this was the chance of a lifetime, and urged him to challenge Marchand. Bach was cautious. He knew that Marchand was regarded as the greatest keyboard player of the time and wanted to know what he was up against before committing himself. So he did not issue the challenge but went to Dresden to see Volumier.

Volumier coped with Bach's reservations brilliantly. He secretly smuggled Bach inside a church where Marchand was playing. Bach's fears were put to rest and he promptly issued a challenge 'to execute extempore whatever musical tasks Marchand should set him'. Marchand accepted the challenge eagerly. A time was agreed and a place, the private theatre in Count Flemming's house.

The contest was eagerly awaited. It was more than just a competition between great keyboard players. It was a battle between the two foremost styles of playing, the French and the German. At stake was a prize of five hundred talers offered by the king.

On the appointed day, a large and distinguished audience attended Count Flemming's home. As the time for the contest approached, the judges seated themselves, then the purpose and rules of the competition were announced.

The contestants were thereupon summoned. Bach stood forward but there was no sign of Marchand. There was a long wait. He still did not appear. Finally Flemming sent to Marchand's quarters to remind him of the contest, not that it was likely he could have forgotten. When the envoys asked for Marchand, they received the most unexpected news. Not only was Marchand not going to attend, he was no longer in Dresden. He had fled the city early in the morning on a special coach.

What had caused Marchand, once so eager for the encounter, to flee?

The story goes that the night before the contest, Marchand had done some surreptitious eavesdropping of his own. Perhaps the crafty Volumier offered him the same opportunity he had given Bach. It is amusing to imagine them crouched in the church gallery with Marchand's eyes opening wide as Bach dashed off a thunderous fugue and Volumier alongside whispering, 'You should hear him when he's really trying!' Whatever the exact details, Marchand seems to have realised that Bach had too many weapons for him in this particular battle and scuttled off to avoid inevitable humiliation.

Though the audience was disappointed that the competition was cancelled, Bach treated them to a virtuoso display in compensation, though he was in for a disappointment too. The servant deputed to deliver his prize ran off with the money.

For Augustus II, the abortive contest must have borne an uncanny resemblance to events of the previous year. While on a long visit to Venice, a competition was arranged in his honour between two celebrated Italian violinists, Giuseppe Tartini, composer of the famous 'Devil's Trill' Sonata, and Francesco Veracini. Before the event could take place, Tartini happened to hear Veracini playing in Cremona, realised that he was facing a hiding and withdrew.

Marchand was next heard of a few weeks later in Paris, and there he remained to the end of his life. As for Bach, he never rubbed salt into Marchand's wounds, but subsequently praised him both for his playing and for his compositions, showing his appreciation in the most genuine way, by performing them.

OLD BACH PAYS TRIBUTE

POTSDAM, MAY 1747

The story of the *Musical Offering* conjures up probably one of the most enchanting pictures of virtuosity in the world of musical legend. It concerns the great Johann Sebastian Bach, and it took place when he was 62 years old, and already known as Old Bach.

The young Carl Philip Emmanuel (CPE), son of J S Bach, held the post of court harpsichordist of Frederick the Great of Prussia at the time of this event. The fame and reputation of Johann Sebastian were of course long established. From deep spiritual conviction, in 1723 he had taken the relatively lowly position of cantor of the Thomasschule in Leipzig, in order to return to church music. His family home in Leipzig, however, was the focus of what amounted to musical pilgrimage.

The king made known to CPE that he wished to meet Old Bach, so in 1747, when CPE had been in his service for seven years, Old Bach set off to travel the 120-plus miles to Potsdam to meet him. He travelled with another of his sons, William Friedemann, and the news of their arrival reached the court just at the time of the king's evening concert, in which Frederick often played the flute. That night, according to custom, the list of strangers was brought to him by a servant. The king read it, turned to the musicians and said excitedly, 'Gentlemen, Old Bach is come!' Old Bach was sent for at once, and he hurried to the palace. According to Johann Nicolaus Forkel, the first biographer of J S Bach, the king did not even give the great musician time to change out of his travelling clothes into his black cantor's gown before going to court.

On his arrival an impromptu concert was given. The king abandoned his regular evening concert arrangements and asked Old Bach to play on his several Silbermann fortepianos. These were in different parts of the palace, and Johann Sebastian went from one instrument to the next, playing improvisations on each of them in turn, attended by the king and all the musicians. Old Bach improvised in this way for a while and then asked Frederick the Great to give him a subject for a fugue, offering to play it at once. When he did this the king was astonished, and asked for the fugue to be played with six obbligato parts. This was done with a different subject, to the continued amazement of all. Further impromptu concerts were given on the following day, when Johann Sebastian Bach played all the organs in Potsdam, and again astonished all who heard him.

When Old Bach returned to Leipzig he also developed the second theme into three and six parts, together making up thirteen new works. They included a trio for flute, violin and clavier. The whole was called *Das Musikalisches Opfer* and J S Bach had it engraved, and dedicated it to the king. It is worth recalling that the word *Opfer* means offering, in the sense of a special gift to an important person, rather than the current meaning of 'offer' as something that can be accepted or declined. It also has a stronger meaning, almost that of a tribute, or a sacrifice.

However, there is another interpretation of this story, with which the word 'tribute' might be said to tie in more closely. This one suggests that the whole thing was an attempt on the part of Frederick the Great to humiliate Old Bach. Some commentators have suggested that the challenge of making the music into a fugue for six voices was intended to trip him up. Frederick is thought to have preferred more modern styles to the intellectually demanding counterpoint of canon and fugue.

J S Bach died in 1750. His journey to Potsdam had been his last. It is said that so little was thought of his original scores that many of them were used to wrap meat.

HANDEL WITH CARE

LONDON, APRIL 1749

The date may not stick in the mind like 1066 but 1748 was important for the ending of the eight-year War of the Austrian Succession, which had involved half of Europe. King George II decided that the signing of the Treaty of Aix-la-Chappelle should be lavishly celebrated and ordered a great fireworks display with new music. The result was the magnificent and lasting *Firework Music*, although on the night of its first performance the spectacle was a damp squib.

When it came to selecting a composer, the king bypassed his own Master of the King's Musick, one Dr Green, as he had 21 years earlier for his Coronation music. On both occasions the king chose the German-born Composer of Musick for His Majesty's Chapel Royal, George Frideric Handel.

Handel's connections with England dated back to 1710 and he had long settled permanently in London. His list of successes over the years included operas, anthems and orchestral works, and oratorios such as the universally admired *Messiah*. One of his four coronation anthems, *Zadok the Priest*, was so perfect and appropriate that it has been performed at every subsequent coronation. The king had little problem selecting the composer for the greatest celebration of peace in the history of the nation.

The fireworks were to take place in April 1749 in Green Park, London, on a specially built wooden edifice. Called The Machine, it was an impressive construction. An engraving of the period shows a colonnade with a frontage of over 400 feet.

31

Its central section was over 100 feet high. It was embellished with figures of Greek gods and one of the king blessing Britannia with peace, and topped by a 100-foot pole that supported an enormous sun complete with rays at the edge and the words 'Vivat Rex' in the centre. An excitable Italian, Chevalier Servandoni, was appointed to design the fireworks display and set them off.

There was huge public interest in the celebrations. Even the rehearsal, which was of the music only, attracted twelve thousand people, each paying two shillings and sixpence. 'So great was the press of carriages,' according to Sir Newman Flower, 'that all traffic was held on London Bridge for over three hours.' No change there, then. To Handel's displeasure, the rehearsal did not take place in Green Park, the site of the performance, but in Vauxhall Gardens. The master of Vauxhall had saved the king £700 by lending various lanterns, lamps and thirty helpers free of charge on condition that the rehearsal took place in Vauxhall.

On the day of the fireworks special arrangements were made to admit an even more enormous crowd. All the usual entrances to the park were thrown open, and an extra entrance almost fifty feet long was cut in the park wall. During daylight hours the Guards paraded and the king took the salute in various uniforms. He inspected The Machine and was so satisfied with the arrangements that he gave a purse of money to the officers responsible for them.

The crowds grew even thicker as the time for the music and fireworks approached. Finally, at six o'clock, Handel's music was played from a special gallery against the background of The Machine, which was outlined in light. The king was delighted. The music ceased and the applause died away. The moment everyone had been waiting for had at last arrived. One hundred and one cannon boomed out a Royal Salute. The crowd roared and Chevalier Servandoni's men got the fireworks display under way.

Thousands of pairs of eyes focused on The Machine expecting a blaze of light and colour, but all they saw were tiny eruptions that quickly fizzled out. The distraught Servandoni thought that maybe the fuses had become damp. After many dry days, rain was in the air. Men with torches were rushed in to light the fireworks by hand. In the confusion, they set fire to the edifice as well. Soon the heat was terrific and the crowd, its disappointment turning to panic, took flight. Women fell over in the rush and were trodden down. The bas-relief of the king, aflame, toppled and burned as the evening turned into a disaster. Servandoni wildly drew his sword on one of the court officials and was arrested.

The fireworks had been a damp squib for the king. Only Handel's music had lived up to the magnificence of the occasion. Realising this, the king subscribed no less than £2,000 when the *Firework Music* was performed the following month in aid of Handel's favourite charity, the Foundling Hospital.

For all his pre-eminence and royal popularity, Handel never became Master of the King's Musick. Although he had been a British subject since 1727, perhaps he was still regarded as more German than British. Whether he ever reflected that being German hadn't stopped the House of Hanover from becoming the monarchs of his adopted country, is not known.

OBOE AND OUT

ESTERHÁZA, HUNGARY, AUTUMN 1772

Twenty-two musicians were fed up and depressed. It was now late autumn and they had been isolated in the palace at Esterháza since February. They longed to go home and be reunited with their families and friends whom they had not seen in all that time.

Gloomily they considered the possibility that Prince Nicolaus Esterházy would keep them there until Christmas. It would not be the first time. The prince, a member of one of the richest and most prominent families in Europe, liked to linger in Esterháza for as long as possible. Despite its remoteness deep in the Hungarian countryside, he preferred it to his family estate in Eisenstadt and even to his winter palace in Vienna. Apart from the occasional courtesy trip to court, there was really no need for him to leave. The estate was a self-contained world that included a hospital and medical staff, and hundreds of servants. To entertain himself and his many visitors, the prince had built a 400-seat opera house and marionette theatre. His guests, such as the Austrian Empress Maria Theresa, were much impressed by what he had raised out of the Hungarian marshes. When they left, they reported that here was a palace outdone only by Versailles.

One of the palace's outstanding attractions was the glorious music provided by the prince's orchestra and choir under the direction of its capellmeister Joseph Haydn. It was Haydn's job to train the orchestra and to write whatever music the prince requested. He produced a stream of operas, symphonies and sacred works. He even wrote 125 works for an obscure instrument that the prince liked to play called the baryton, a member of the viol family.

The despairing musicians brought their problem to Haydn. Could he put in a word for them with the prince? Haydn was sympathetic to their request as he too was keen to leave. Fortunately for him, his seniority entitled him to married quarters, unlike his colleagues. But he didn't get on well with his wife, Maria Anna Aloysia, and couldn't wait to get back to Vienna and see his friends.

Haydn knew that persuading Nicolaus would require delicate handling. The prince was fully aware of the musicians' plight. He had already refused to allow their families to stay or even to visit. Nothing that Haydn could say would be likely to change his mind.

But possibly he might respond to a more subtle approach. It is interesting to imagine Haydn bringing his intelligence and well-known sense of humour to bear on the problem. Supposing his request was posed in the language of music, not in speech? It was a solution that he was fairly certain would avoid offending the prince.

He set to work and shortly informed his patron that he had written a new symphony. He may well have said that it had one or two new features without specifying exactly what they were. The prince was delighted and the first performance was arranged. Nicolaus and his guests settled in their seats in the opera house.

The first of the new features may not have seemed so strange to them as it does to us. The symphony was written in the key of F sharp minor and remains the only symphony ever written in that key. The other strange feature did not occur until almost the end of the symphony. The first three movements were composed in Haydn's usual melodious and inventive style. The fourth movement seemed perfectly normal, if a bit fast, and seemed to be working towards a climax, when it suddenly stopped and a long slow movement began. Even for Haydn, well known for doing the unexpected, this was a surprise, as there had already been a slow movement. A greater surprise followed. Each player, or group of players, was delegated to play a solo. When they had finished, they blew out their candles and tiptoed away, taking their instruments with them. One by one the desks emptied until only the string instruments were left, then only Haydn and Tomasini, the leader of the orchestra. Finally the piece came to a gentle end. The pair blew out their candles and left as quietly as one would leave a sleeping child's bedroom.

Haydn had judged it just right. The prince understood the musical message. If the musicians were leaving, he said, we might as well too. The court left Esterháza very soon afterwards.

The unique ending of the 'Farewell' Symphony, as it is universally known, heightens any performance. Conscientious as orchestras are, it is probably one part of their performance they don't always bother to rehearse. After all, there's nothing to play, you just get up and go. What can possibly go wrong? To judge from the following, perhaps they should have a quick practice.

Valerie Taylor, one of the UK's leading oboists, was principal oboist of the Manchester Camerata from the 1970s for almost 25 years. On one occasion she was playing the 'Farewell' Symphony with the Manchester Camerata in Chester Town Hall. First to leave the stage, she opened a door expecting it to lead backstage. Instead it turned out to be a broom cupboard. One by one the rest of the orchestra faithfully followed her until, as she says, 'we were all crushed in like sardines' – and giggling sardines at that. And there they stayed until it was time to take their bow, when, with relief, they fell out of the cupboard, still giggling, and tumbled to the front of the stage.

LAST CHANCE FOR THE KING

WINDSOR, OCTOBER 1788

Late in 1788 confusing rumours about George III's health began to appear in the London daily newspapers. One day it was reported that he was disturbingly ill, the next that he was on the road to recovery. The illness was a cold, the dropsy or rheumatic gout – you could take your pick. In fact it was the recurrence of a mental illness, today thought to be a symptom of porphyria.

The king had suffered from it once before in 1765. Now it returned in aggravated form, causing him to act very eccentrically both in public and in private. In August he attended a performance of Handel's *Messiah* in Worcester Cathedral as part of the Three Choirs Festival. The public had to pretend not to notice as he ostentatiously beat time from his seat as if conducting the orchestra. He also became incredibly loquacious and often spoke for hours on end, on one occasion for sixteen hours.

It was in the interest of the prime minister, William Pitt (Pitt the Younger), to preserve the illusion that the king was *compos mentis* for as long as possible. If George was declared unfit to govern, power would pass to the Prince of Wales as Regent, and Pitt would be replaced as prime minister.

The best way to maintain the status quo was for the king to be seen in public going about his normal duties. However, his appearances only raised concerns, not alleviated them. For example, on 24 October he had unwisely gone to London for a levee – an official royal reception – dressed very carelessly and with his legs wrapped in flannel.

By the end of October it had reached the stage where there was no point in announcing any public engagements because they were always being cancelled. The king moved from Kew to his favourite residence, Windsor Castle. It was there on 27 October that he attended one of the regular evening concerts in an attempt to show that, even if all was not completely well, at least he retained some semblance of self-control.

The same evening, the king's physician, Sir George Baker, arrived in response to an urgent summons from the queen. Baker was on the defensive in his relations with the king, not for medical reasons, but because he had engaged in some insider trading in government stocks. Knowing that they would fall in value when the king's illness was made public, he had recently sold £18,000. The news had got around and people put two and two together about the state of George's health. The result was an avalanche of sales and a 10 per cent drop in stock value, a serious matter for the government. Baker had owned up to the king, who felt obliged to go to London to put an end to the stories of his incapacity, which was the occasion of the unfortunate levee he attended with his legs in flannel.

As Baker was to witness, the concert was not a good choice to demonstrate the king's mental stability. Music seemed to make him excitable, as the *Messiah* incident had showed. During the playing of the music, a selection from Handel, the king talked the whole time and changed abruptly from one topic to another. It wasn't so much that he talked nonsense. Baker admitted that what the king said was not incoherent or even incorrect. It was just totally inappropriate and bizarre behaviour. The court was obliged to act throughout as if nothing untoward was happening.

The king was aware of the effect that music had on him. 'I feel, Sir, I shall not long be able to hear music,' he told the conductor that evening. 'It seems to affect my head and it is with difficulty that I bear it.'

The writer Alan Bennett depicted this concert in the film *The Madness of King George*. He shows the king entering in disarray, haranguing the orchestra and shoving the harpsichord player off his seat, before finally having an argument with the Prince of Wales and attempting to throttle him.

It was this grave incident with the prince, which actually took place a few days later on 5 November, that probably convinced the queen and Pitt that keeping the king's illness secret was no longer possible. Music, which so much excited the king, was banished from the court, and he was handed over to the not-so-tender mercies of new doctors for various highly unpleasant treatments. Not until the following April was the king well enough to resume his royal duties and music returned to Windsor for him to enjoy.

HOW THE DANES DISCOVERED A NEW COMPOSER

DAG HENRIK ESRUM-HELLERUP (1803–91)

The name of the Danish composer Dag Henrik Esrum-Hellerup was unknown even in Danish musical circles, so when the Danes discovered his entry in the most prestigious musical reference work in the world, they were naturally delighted.

The *Dictionary of Music and Musicians*, or *Grove* as it is always called after its founder and first editor, Sir George Grove, has always been considered the musical bible since its first publication in four volumes in the late nineteenth century.

In 1980, a completely new, updated edition was published. Known as *New Grove*, it was the largest single-subject reference work in the world, according to its editor, the late Stanley Sadie. A massive project taking eight years to complete, it ran to twenty volumes and over twenty thousand entries. Standards of scholarship were rigorous. Editors and subeditors pored over every article and discussed any contentious points with each of the hundreds of contributors. Changes were demanded and made.

However knowledgeable the editors were, in the final analysis they could not hope to match the in-depth expertise of the contributors, who were naturally the ranking authorities in their fields.

For Scandinavian music, that position was held by Robert Layton, the musicologist, writer and broadcaster, who was responsible for the entries of Sibelius, Berwald and a host of lesser-known names. The subeditors were often young, comparatively inexperienced graduates and some of the changes they asked for were too picky for Layton's liking. As time went on, he began to find the editorial process irksome. As a bit of light relief, he thought he would check how well informed they really were.

In a matter of twenty minutes, he concocted the biography of a likely sounding Danish composer. He remembered the nineteenth-century Danish composer Peter Lange-Müller and liked the idea of a double-barrelled name. His friend, the Canadian musicologist and academic John Bergsagel, who had moved to Copenhagen in 1970 and now taught at the university there, had lived in both the Esrum and Hellerup areas of the city. Yes, Esrum-Hellerup sounded good.

Layton began to flesh out the details. Two hundred words later, Dag Henrik Esrum-Hellerup existed, on paper at any rate. In the approved dry, factual *New Grove* style, he was given a career as a composer, flautist and conductor. Smetana, Berwald, Wagner and Quantz's treatise on flute playing were mentioned to give authenticity.

Layton did not expect his creation to get through the system. Indeed, to assist the editors in spotting the spoof, he put in what he thought were a few obvious giveaways.

Surely no one would be fooled by the bibliography: *Esrum-Hellerup: sa vie et son oeuvre* by Andre Pirro. Pirro was real enough, a late-nineteenth, early-twentieth-century French musicologist and organist, but he was an unlikely biographer of Esrum-Hellerup, being a specialist on Bach, Schütz and Buxtehude, composers of a totally different period. A crosscheck with the authors of Pirro's own entry in *New Grove* would have shown no *Life of Esrum-Hellerup* amongst Pirro's almost forty books and articles.

Another clue was the reference to planned performances of *Parsifal* in Esjberg and Göteborg. *Parsifal* had first been produced in 1882 in Bayreuth and, due to the Wagner family's control, was never performed outside Bayreuth until an unauthorised performance in New York in 1903. An informed subeditor might have known this, or at least been alert enough to realise that it was totally implausible for anyone to have been involved in such a project in the 1880s, particularly an old man, supposedly in his eighties, who was simultaneously writing his memoirs (*Musikalische Intryck*, Copenhagen, 1883–6).

The editors might also have been expected to register that there was nothing of substance to back up Esrum-Hellerup's existence. The autobiography was long since unavailable, an opera – *Alys og Elvertøj* – was 'lost', and his speedy rise to fame in the 1850s had been followed by an equally speedy decline. Still, when you have thousands of entries to check and deadlines are tight . . .

Despite the clues, Esrum-Hellerup appeared in *New Grove*. It was a huge joke to Layton's friends, who formed an Esrum-Hellerup society. The joke would have remained private but for a bizarre incident. Someone in the Royal Library in Copenhagen, assiduously trawling through *New Grove*, came across the entry. Thrilled to add a new name to the stock of national composers, the Danes decided to commemorate him with a plaque. Enquiries were made to establish where he had lived and at this stage Layton decided things had gone far enough and revealed the spoof.

Far from being upset, the Danes thought it was hilarious. Articles appeared in the newspapers and an Esrum-Hellerup choir was founded, still going strong today. Inevitably Stanley Sadie got to hear of it, harsh words were exchanged, and for a long while he and Layton were not on speaking terms.

In defence of the editors, they did catch a number of dubious articles. The *Musical Times* published a comprehensive list in February 1981. Most would not have been too hard to spot, such as Genghis Khan't by I. Kidunot; Stainglit, a troubadour who went to the University of Pont de Cam by A.G. Rover; and Verdi, not Giuseppe or Monte, but Lasagne, an entry submitted by Coniglia Gallese, a fine-sounding Italian name which translates as Welsh rarebit. Apart from Esrum-Hellerup, only one other spoof is known to have slipped through the net, the biography of Guglielmo Baldini.

New Grove had recovered its sense of humour by 2001, when the next edition was published. Esrum-Hellerup and Baldini had been excised, but there was an article by David Fallows on

'Spoof Articles' that mentioned them, and also Lasagne Verdi, who apparently almost made it into print. Happily, by then Sadie and Layton were back on speaking terms.

HARD OF HEARING

VIENNA, MAY 1824

Given the uncertainties surrounding first performances, it is not too surprising that they attract more than their fair share of strange concerts. Even so, when you look at how the premieres of some new works from earlier centuries were organised, it is amazing that they took place at all.

The arrangements for the first performance of Beethoven's complex and ground-breaking great Ninth Symphony, the 'Choral', were in complete disarray in the weeks leading up to the concert. Details of soloists, venue, date, time and ticket prices were only finalised at a very late stage.

The venue was originally going to be the Theater an der Wien in March. However, Beethoven had fallen out with the orchestral leader there some years before. He applied to hold the concert in the Large Redoutensaal in April instead, but was offered only the Small Redoutensaal. Finally, on 2 May, with the concert a mere five days off, Beethoven's amanuensis Anton Schindler was able to confirm the Kärntnertor Theatre as the venue after tedious negotiations with officials.

The situation regarding the soloists was equally unsettled. Neither Henriette Sontag, only recently confirmed to sing the soprano solo, nor Caroline Unger, the contralto, knew their parts at all. The tenor had only received his that day. He was Anton Haitzinger, a late replacement for Franz Jäger, who had declined to sing, saying the range was too low for him. Thankfully, the bass, Joseph Preisinger, was more advanced in his preparations. However, he was to drop out in the next day or so: the range was too high for him, he said. He was replaced by Joseph Seipelt, who had only two days to learn the music.

It was a strenuous concert for the soloists. As well as singing the final movement of the Ninth Symphony in public for the first time, they had to sing three movements of the extremely taxing *Missa Solemnis*. Understandably, they found the technical demands very great and asked Beethoven to make some minor concessions to help them out. Except in one small instance, he categorically refused. 'You are a tyrant over all the vocal organs!' Unger exclaimed, probably regretting that she and Sontag had literally begged Beethoven to let them sing. Needing all the practice they could get, they must have despaired when they found that the number of rehearsals was being reduced from three to two when a ballet rehearsal took precedence.

In the end they took matters into their own hands, and at the performance simply omitted notes that were out of their range, aware that Beethoven's hearing was now so bad that he wouldn't know. His deafness prevented him from conducting too, though he did give the tempo at the start of each movement.

During the performance, one of the most famous incidents in musical history took place. At the end of the second movement, there was enormous applause. Beethoven, with his back to the audience, did not hear it and continued to turn pages of the score. Possibly he was out of phase with the orchestra, which had finished, or possibly he was practising the tempo for the next movement. It was Caroline Unger – who had called him a tyrant – who went across and turned him gently round so that he could see the applause, even if he could hear next to nothing.

The chaos associated with the concert's organisation continued afterwards. Although it was artistically a success, Beethoven's financial rewards were very disappointing, and he somehow got it into his head that he had been cheated. He accused Schindler and two others of cheating him, though this was totally untrue.

Chaotic elements had often been a feature of Beethoven's concerts. Back in December 1808, he had given a concert that has claims to be the most astonishing ever. It was in two massive parts, either of which would have made a perfectly adequate concert on its own. Amazingly, except for a concert aria, none of the works had ever been played in public before. What the audience heard were no less than the first performances of the Fifth and Sixth Symphonies and the Fourth Piano Concerto (with the composer as soloist). There were also two movements from the Mass in C, called 'hymns' for the occasion, as the religious authorities objected to church music being heard in a theatre.

That would have been enough for anyone except Beethoven. Maybe he felt the audience was being short-changed, for he rapidly completed his *Choral Fantasia*, a beautiful work in which he tried out some of the ideas which later became part of the final movement of the 'Choral' Symphony.

According to the German composer and writer Friedrich Reichardt, who was present, the concert lasted four and a half hours and took place in dreadful conditions for both spectators and performers. It was late December, freezing, and the theatre had no heating.

By the time the *Fantasia*, the final piece, was played, many in the audience had gone home. As the guest of Prince Lobkowitz, Reichardt didn't dare and wrapped himself in his fur coat to keep warm. The performers weren't so lucky and the soloist in the concert aria 'Ah! Perfido' shivered rather than sang her way through it, according to Reichardt.

The *Fantasia* had been completed very close to the performance and, through lack of rehearsal, some of the clarinets miscounted their parts. Beethoven tried to silence them with angry shouts but failed. Humiliatingly, he was forced to stop the orchestra and restart the whole piece, much to the displeasure of those like Reichardt, who, cold and fatigued, wanted the concert over. Even lovers of Beethoven's music could have too much of a good thing.

THE DISAPPEARING ORCHESTRA

PARIS, NOVEMBER 1833

On 11 September 1827 the French composer Hector Berlioz, aged 23, went to the Odéon theatre in Paris to see *Hamlet* and fell in love twice – with Shakespeare and with Harriet Smithson, the Irish actress playing Ophelia. A few days later he saw her play Juliet in *Romeo and Juliet*. 'I shall marry that woman and write my greatest symphony on the play,' he is reported to have exclaimed, though he later wrote, 'I did both, but I never said anything of the sort.'

So began a sequence of events that was to culminate in one of the worst musical nightmares ever suffered by a composer of Berlioz's stature. Over the months that followed, the infatuated Berlioz did everything he could to attract Harriet's attention. To prove his worth as an artist, he organised a concert of his own music but found out that, engrossed in her own activities, she never heard of it. He wrote to her so often that she instructed her maid not to accept any more letters. He even arranged to have his music played at a benefit performance in which she was appearing, simply to have his name on the same playbill as hers. The obsessive nature of his attentions alarmed rather than attracted her and there seemed no likelihood of his *grand amour* ever coming to anything.

Five years passed during which Harriet left Paris and Berlioz lost track of her. Their paths crossed again when she brought an English theatre company to Paris. But the venture was unsuccessful and she ran up large debts. One evening she was persuaded by Berlioz's friends to go to a concert that he had

47

organised. The programme included the *Symphonie Fantastique* and a sequel called *Lélio*. It was widely known, though not by Harriet, that both works centred around Berlioz's love for her. Certain references in *Lélio* opened Harriet's eyes. She wrote to Berlioz and from then on they were in constant contact. Within nine days of the concert Harriet declared that she loved him and they were married late the following year.

Seeking for ways to repay Harriet's debts, Berlioz organised a benefit concert shortly afterwards. To say 'organised' is perhaps overcomplimentary. There was a change of venue and several changes of date at short notice and the scale of the evening was extremely ambitious. Naturally, there was a large music programme, consisting of several pieces by Berlioz and others. But that was only the second half of the evening. The first half was devoted to drama, with Harriet playing Ophelia in scenes from *Hamlet* and a long extract from another play starring Marie Dorval, a celebrated French actress.

Due to begin at seven o'clock, the concert was delayed by an hour. The hoi polloi in the pit broke into 'songs of a disreputable nature', upsetting the better-off spectators in the boxes. By the time the play extracts had been performed, it was already half past eleven. Harriet's contribution had not been well received. She was not encored even once, whereas Marie Dorval was given an ovation and recalled many times.

Over four hours into the concert, the musical part finally began. Berlioz was conducting but he was inexperienced. In one piece he failed to cue the violins, who missed an entry, and the whole orchestra lost its place. The item had to be abruptly terminated. 'Nothing was going right,' he wrote in his memoirs, adding, 'I felt as if I were slowly sinking into the earth.' If he felt that was bad, much worse was to follow.

Two pieces remained to be performed, first a chorus by Weber, then his own *Symphonie Fantastique*. Berlioz had his back to the orchestra while he conducted the Weber. When he turned round to begin the symphony, he found that virtually the whole orchestra had slipped out during the chorus and gone home. It was midnight and they were not contracted to work beyond then. There remained only a dozen string players and one trombone. Though the audience showed no signs of wanting to go, Berlioz, frustrated and angry, had no choice but to apologise and bring the evening to a close. His enemies were quick to comment that his music drove even the players away. It was small consolation that he made a profit on the evening, helped by the actors and soloists giving their services free.

Berlioz, being Berlioz, picked himself up quickly. Within a month he had organised another much more successful concert. Musically successful, that is. He was still paying off Harriet's debts years later.

THE DIVA WHO INSPIRED CALLAS

MANCHESTER, SEPTEMBER 1836

Rumours had been spreading around Manchester for days that the French mezzo-soprano Maria Malibran was far from well and would not be appearing at the music festival.

Disappointment was intense and the organisers were distraught. Malibran's presence guaranteed full houses. Though many accomplished and popular artists were appearing, she was the star attraction. Her voice was amazing, with an astonishing range of three octaves. Her stage presence was magnetic, she lived life to the full, and her personal life was not free from scandal. In short, she was a diva, possibly not matched till the era of Maria Callas.

Malibran was held in the highest regard by many of the leading musical personalities of the time. Da Ponte, Mozart's librettist, whom she had met in America, described her voice as incomparable. Bellini adapted *I Puritani* to fit her voice, though she never got to sing it. Liszt, Rossini, Donizetti and Mendelssohn all admired her, though possibly not just for musical reasons. 'Mme Malibran is a young woman, beautiful, with a gorgeous figure, a towering wig, full of fire and power and at the same time coquettish.' These are not the words of the susceptible Liszt but, unexpectedly, of Felix Mendelssohn. His father Abraham worried that his son's interest would end unhappily. Felix was less enchanted with her acting. It 'stopped just this side of the ludicrous', he said. Three years later it was Abraham himself who was smitten, though nothing came of it.

Two months before the festival, Malibran, in the early stages of pregnancy, had gone riding in Regent's Park, despite the objections of her husband and friends. Pregnancy wasn't convenient to her career at that moment and possibly she intended to cause a miscarriage. Whatever the reasons, she lost control of her horse and was thrown. She did not lose the baby but her overall health suffered. Despite the accident, she sang at Drury Lane the same evening, convinced that the public would turn against her if she didn't.

Malibran's first Manchester appearance was scheduled for the early afternoon of Tuesday 13 September in the Collegiate church (now Manchester Cathedral), with another concert the same evening. She was also booked to appear in concerts on Wednesday and Thursday.

The concert began at eleven with a complete performance of Haydn's *Creation* in which Malibran was not due to sing. After the interval, there were extracts from a number of other works, beginning with a selection from Mozart's Requiem. After that came the first of Malibran's solos, an aria by Handel.

There was the usual hush in anticipation of the appearance of the soloist. The pause lengthened without any sign of Malibran. It looked as if the rumours were right and that she was not well enough to sing. The conductor, Sir George Smart, uncertain about the situation, turned to the audience and seemed about to confirm this. At the same moment, Malibran appeared. It was clear to the audience that she was very unwell. Her face and lips were pale and she seemed in considerable pain when walking. In fact, the effort was so obviously draining that Smart decided to reprise the quartet just sung to give her time to recover.

When it was finished Malibran rose to sing, but was so unstable that she held on to the front of the choir. She managed to complete her numbers without mishap, but was totally exhausted by the end. Later it became known that she had been barely conscious during the hour before her appearance.

The evening concert followed much the same pattern. According to her friend Mrs Novello, Malibran was in even greater pain. She leaned on the piano for support while she sang a Mozart aria and took part in the sextet from *Don Giovanni*. Afterwards Mrs Novello rubbed her feet for hours to warm them. Malibran was clearly in no condition to sing, yet she never sang better, according to *The Times*.

The following day, still in great pain, she insisted on carrying out her engagements, singing Beethoven, Mozart and Mercadante. According to Novello, she sang beautifully. She even accompanied her husband, a violinist, on the piano while he played Tartini's 'Devil's Trill' Sonata.

The Mercadante piece was a duet sung with Madame Caradori-Allan in a spirit of friendly, or perhaps not so friendly, rivalry. Departing from their rehearsed performance, Caradori-Allan threw in a few impromptu vocal ornaments. The competitive Malibran followed her. The audience was ecstatic and demanded an encore. Malibran turned to Smart and said, 'If I sing it again – it will kill me.'

'Then do not,' he replied, 'let me address the audience.'

'No,' she retorted, 'I will sing it again and annihilate her!' When she returned to the anteroom, she fainted.

On Thursday she got as far as the church but it was impossible for her to perform. She returned to her room at the Mosley Arms, never to leave it again, dying nine days later, aged only 28.

Newspaper interest was intense. Stories of her generous nature began to appear. On one occasion, she had promised to appear in a benefit concert for a young English singer but was summoned to sing for the Duc d'Orléans the same evening. The young singer was worried her star turn would not appear, but not only did Malibran hurry back and sing, she brought with her a hundred crowns donated by the Duc for the young singer. She once sang *La Sonnambula* to raise funds for a financially straitened opera house in Venice. The directors were so grateful they renamed the theatre in her honour and it still exists as an opera house today.

Her death was surrounded by scandal. Medical attention seemed to have been rudimentary and involved bleeding Malibran, cutting her hair off and aborting the baby. Following her death, her husband hurried back to Belgium without staying for her interment, possibly to get his hands on her money. In December, much to the displeasure of Mancunians, who felt great affection for her, her body was disinterred and reburied in Belgium.

Her qualities and early death caught posterity's imagination and she has never been forgotten. The 150th anniversary of her death was widely commemorated and there have been films and plays about her. She was a role model for the modern diva and it is no coincidence that hers was one of only two portraits found in Callas's apartment after her death.

THE VERGERS' REVENGE

LONDON, SEPTEMBER 1837

Sunday evensong had just drawn to a close in St Paul's Cathedral. Ordinarily, the congregation, hastened by some up-tempo organ music, would have made for the doors and disappeared into the autumn evening.

On this particular occasion, much to the vergers' annoyance, the congregation showed no signs of dispersing but remained seated in their pews. 'Service is over, you must go out,' the vergers cried, trying to usher everyone towards the doors, but without success. The reason was simple. It had become known that the voluntary would be played by none other than Dr Felix Mendelssohn, composer of the very popular oratorio *St Paul*, and well-loved piano pieces such as the *Songs without Words*, popular in many households throughout the country. Mendelssohn had given organ recitals in St Paul's before, but chances to hear him were rare and the congregation did not want to miss the opportunity.

Very soon the magnificent space of the cathedral resounded to the mighty chords of a Bach fugue. The vergers appeared to know when they were beaten and disappeared. Everyone listened raptly as the music built towards one of Bach's magnificent climaxes, and they eagerly awaited the next crashing chords.

But instead of the expected fortissimo, the organ suddenly gasped for air and died away like a deflating tyre. Mendelssohn looked around in disbelief as his hands hit the keys but produced no sound. What had happened? Had the organ broken down?

54

The explanation was more prosaic. The cunning vergers had held a private conference and decided to hit the organ at its weakest spot, its air supply. They had a quiet word with the organ-blower and instructed him to stop work. To refuse the vergers might well have cost him his job and he bowed to their authority.

As soon as it was realised what had happened, there was a rush of officials to try to persuade him to continue, but to no avail. Mendelssohn came down from the organ loft bemused. 'Songs without words' were one thing, organs that did not play quite another. The disappointed congregation, robbed of an exceptional experience, departed highly discontented. Everyone was aware that the action was an insult to its distinguished visitor, who would return home with yet more evidence that England was 'a land without music'.

Among those present was Henry Gauntlett, the organist of a nearby church, Christ Church, Newgate Street. Mendelssohn had already played there and declared that the church's organ was the finest he had yet played on in England. So he was amenable when Gauntlett suggested that he give a full recital there to make up for the St Paul's interruption.

Two days later, Mendelssohn performed a substantial programme of six improvised fantasias in a packed church. He also completed unfinished business by playing the whole of the rudely interrupted Bach fugue, possibly with a private twinkle in his eye as he did.

In the audience was the renowned English composer Samuel Wesley. Aged 71, he was frail and in declining health, but had made a special effort to attend, never having met Mendelssohn before. When Mendelssohn had finished playing, he beckoned Wesley forward to perform, which he did with an energy and imagination that was surprising considering his health. On returning home, Wesley said, 'I will never leave the house again,' and he never did, dying a few weeks later.

Wesley was himself the subject of a curious musical story. The *Dictionary of Musicians*, published by John Sainsbury and Co in 1824, reported that he had died in 1815. Possibly Wesley regarded the last 22 years of his life as a bonus.

FRANZ LISZT AND THE BIG TOURS

EUROPE (1838–47)

The dark, feverish, romantic virtuoso pianist and composer Franz Liszt is credited with the invention of the recital, a musical event of great importance in the nineteenth and twentieth centuries. How did the use of a word associated with poetry come to mean a musical performance with a soloist? It was the synthesis of Liszt's musical genius and his charisma, and it comes from a feature of his concerts.

Liszt was a prodigy, and during his childhood his father Adam took care to point up the similarities between the prodigiousness of Franz Liszt and that of his predecessor by sixty years, Wolfgang Amadeus Mozart. Three things a prodigy needs are talent, hard work and ambitious parents. Liszt had all of them. His father was as much a publicist as he was a mentor and seeker of the best teachers. At the age of twelve, Franz Liszt challenged the master Beethoven in a competition for variations set by the music publisher Diabelli. He stands out even in an extraordinary era, in which the virtuosi Schumann and Chopin were among his contemporaries.

Liszt was born in Hungary in 1811, the year of the Great Comet that was said to be astrologically so hugely influential and significant – and which indeed heralded an extraordinarily good wine crop. He was a weak child, prone to fevers and fainting. His father was a fine amateur cellist, pianist, violinist and singer. When Franz was six years old he heard his father playing Ries's Concerto in C sharp minor and was later able to sing one of the themes from memory. Adam Liszt recorded this as the first indication of his son's genius. Afterwards, the boy Franz petitioned again and again to learn the piano, and in the end Adam gave in and taught him. When Franz became feverish yet again (a childhood hazard) the lessons were stopped, but on his recovery they continued and the extraordinary nature of his talent became evident.

By the time the boy was eleven, Adam Liszt had contrived to get him to Vienna to learn with the master Carl Czerny. It was there that Czerny set a composition competition that provoked a remarkable piece of boldness: eleven-year-old Franz Liszt put in a creditable composition in a field that included Beethoven and Schubert. In December of that year, Liszt gave his first public concert. A critic in the *Allgemeine Zeitung* called him, 'A young virtuoso fallen from the clouds'.

The world tour that was arranged by Adam Liszt for his fabulously talented yet sickly son was comparable with the tours undertaken by Mozart. People noticed the similarity, but it seems likely that Adam Liszt had noticed it first. This was a gruelling tour, with long, difficult coach journeys in the middle of winter and usually at night. However, it was the start of a remarkable career. Franz Listz would often wear extravagant costumes and is remembered for having stopped playing because a member of the audience was talking. It was none other than Tsar Nicholas I of Russia who was making conversation. Liszt explained, 'Music herself should be silent when Nicholas speaks'.

During the years 1838 to 1847 Liszt not only toured Europe from the Pyrenees to the Urals, but also established the recital as we know it: the phenomenon of a solo player undertaking an entire performance. And the entire performance was made up not only of the notes: Liszt would walk out into the auditorium during breaks in playing to talk to the audience about the music. Hence the term recital – he actually recited, in the sense of speaking impromptu. He was the first to play an entire programme from memory, the first to open the lid of the piano so that the sound would project into the audience, and the first to play an entire concert unassisted.

He gave more than a thousand recitals in that nine-year

period. He also composed during these years, including the famous *Grandes études de Paganini, Sposalizio, Il Penseroso, Tre Sonetti di Petrarca,* and *Etudes d'exécution transcendante.* Liszt was a deeply philosophical man, and much of his music was inspired directly by the poets and writers he admired, including Byron, Goethe, Lamartine and Senancour.

WITH STRING AND SEALING WAX

One of the problems with inventing a new instrument is persuading other people that it is your original idea and not a rehash of someone else's. Even as recently as 1971, a music magazine suggested that the honour of inventing the saxophone belonged not to Adolphe Sax but to a watchmaker called Desfontenelles. There was little or no support for this opinion, or we'd all be foxtrotting to the Desfontenellesophone.

Sax was born in Dinant in the Meuse Valley in 1814. His father was a successful inventor, who was appointed Instrument Maker to the Court of the Netherlands and won a medal at the 1820 Industrial Exhibition. Sax *fils* worked with his father in his workshop and developed into an even more skilful craftsman. He was an accomplished player of the clarinet and could have become a soloist, but working on instruments, either improving or developing them, was his first love. His display of instruments at the 1841 Brussels Exhibition was so outstanding that the examining committee recommended him for the Gold Medal. The Central Jury thought about it but did not confirm the award, apparently deciding that if it awarded him first prize this year, there would be nothing better to offer him the next. Not surprisingly, Sax was unimpressed and decided to move to Paris.

Once in Paris, Sax, short of capital, set up a rudimentary workshop. He worked hard on designing a new family of valved bugles, the saxhorns. At the same time he began developing another instrument. With its unique tone-colour and wide range, it genuinely broke new ground. It became known as the saxophone.

A further three or four years went by before it was ready to play in public. It was Sax's friend and enthusiastic supporter Hector Berlioz who persuaded him to take the plunge. The Salle Herz was hired and the concert advertised. Berlioz arranged one of his choral pieces, possibly the *Chant Sacré*, for six instruments. Research by Wally Horwood, biographer of Sax, suggests that they were possibly three saxhorns, a bass clarinet and two saxophones.

As is often the case, putting the finishing touches to the new instrument took longer than expected. On the day of the concert Sax was still working flat out on the saxophone he himself was due to play. The starting time of eight o'clock arrived and it still wasn't ready. Nine o'clock came. The audience was getting restive.

Sax was faced with a crisis. He couldn't cancel. The blow to his prestige in this very competitive industry would be enormous and possibly fatal to his business. Desperate measures were called for. He patched up the saxophone with string to secure the keys, and sealing wax to maintain airtightness, and dashed onto the platform.

Berlioz's piece was designed to give each of the six soloists a long section to show off the beautiful tone and dexterity of his instrument. The most beautiful was allocated to Sax, who was last to play. In the middle of one passage, he lingered on one note, causing it to rise and fall, louden and soften, showing off his instrument in every conceivable way for an incredible length of time. The audience was beside itself with admiration and applauded loudly.

One of Sax's colleagues in the audience was less impressed. He suspected that the note had been held so long because Sax had forgotten the fingering for the next note. More likely, Sax was doing emergency repairs on the string and sealing wax, which were coming apart. Better for Sax that he was thought to be an incompetent player than an incompetent instrument maker. He could thank his capacious lungs that he got out alive.

THE MEMORY MAN

LONDON, JUNE 1844

Today we think of Mendelssohn primarily as a composer, but during his lifetime he was regarded as an all-round musician without peer. He was able to conduct, play the piano and organ, sight-read and improvise with equal facility, taking on as many of these roles in one concert as was required.

On top of all that, he had an amazing musical memory. He could recall virtually every note of any piece of music after only one hearing or reading, an ability that was regarded with awe by his fellow musicians. For example, in 1844 he was due to play the solo part in Beethoven's Fourth Piano Concerto. The concert was to take place on the Monday and Mendelssohn arrived for the rehearsal the previous Saturday without a score. Despite not having seen the music for two or three years he played it perfectly from memory. The orchestra were astonished, but incredulous when he extemporised the cadenza in the first movement, not once, not twice, but three times, each time differently. Naturally, he played a fourth cadenza at the concert itself.

In May 1833, he helped out Paganini, who had written a *trio concertante* for viola, guitar and cello. When the guitarist failed to turn up for the first performance, Mendelssohn played the guitar part on the piano, transposing at sight.

During preparation for the first performance in eighty years of Bach's *St Matthew Passion* in 1829, he amazed everyone by accompanying the rehearsals at the piano from memory. There is a scarcely credible story connected with the performance

61

itself, related by Sir Charles Hallé, founder of the Hallé concerts in Manchester.

Mendelssohn, as well as being the instigator of this legendary occasion, was also the conductor and, for good measure, continuo player. According to the story Hallé heard, as quoted in the posthumously published *The Life & Letters of Sir Charles Hallé*, when he opened the score to begin the performance, Mendelssohn discovered it was not the score of the *St Matthew Passion* but a volume that looked like it. It was a difficult situation and his options were few. He could have walked off the platform and got the correct score, assuming it could be found quickly. But that would have been a huge anticlimax in front of the distinguished gathering. Alternatively, he could have closed the score and conducted from memory. However, it was not normal practice at the time to conduct or play from memory, as it was considered impolite and thought to make the performers uneasy, nervous of a memory lapse by the conductor.

Mendelssohn chose neither option. With a piece of quick-thinking and presence of mind remarkable in anyone, let alone a twenty-year-old, he kept the score open to give the impression of conducting from it, even regularly turning its pages, while in fact conducting the whole complicated work by heart (as well as playing the continuo part).

Despite its distinguished source, not everyone considers this story to be authentic. Even if it isn't, it certainly indicates the high regard in which Mendelssohn was held.

One similar story is absolutely reliable because one of the participants, the violinist Joseph Joachim, recorded it.

In 1844, Joachim, a protégé of Mendelssohn's, came to London. He gave a number of successful concerts, but the Philharmonic Society of London refused to organise a concert for him as it had a 'no prodigies' rule and he was not yet thirteen. Thanks to Mendelssohn's influence, the rule was waived and Joachim gave an acclaimed performance of Beethoven's Violin Concerto in May.

A couple of weeks later, he and Mendelssohn and a Mr Hancock were engaged to play at a private soirée organised by a Mr Purdy at Radley's Hotel, Blackfriars, London.

The programme included Mendelssohn's own D minor Piano Trio. Shortly before going on, Mendelssohn discovered that the violin and cello parts had been brought to the hall but not his piano part. He could easily have played from memory but was aware that doing so would draw attention to himself at the expense of his two partners, who would be playing from the score.

His instant solution was a harmless charade. He sent someone off with instructions to find a score, any score, it didn't matter which. The trio then took their places, accompanied by a fourth person to act as page-turner for Mendelssohn. The performance proceeded with Mendelssohn playing his part as though reading from the score, not forgetting to nod from time to time to indicate a page-turn, a remarkable feat of concentration and dissimulation.

THE BATTLE OF THE CHAMP
DE MARS

PARIS, APRIL 1845

A year after his near disaster at the Salle Herz (see 'With String and Sealing Wax'), a chance came for Adolphe Sax to establish his range of instruments as the preferred choice for the French Army.

The French king, Louis-Philippe, and the leaders of the French Army, were concerned that the standard of French military music had fallen behind other nations, particularly the Germans. At the king's suggestion the Duke of Montpensier visited Sax's workshop. This visit confirmed what almost everyone except other instrument manufacturers believed: Sax's instruments were more sonorous, obtained louder volume and stayed in tune better than those of his competitors.

To demonstrate this to ministers and senior officers, a contest was held at the War Office between a band consisting of Sax's instruments and a band made up of current conventional instruments. On the appointed day, the non-Sax band turned up with thirty-two players whereas Sax could muster only nine. Players who had promised to play for him had been bribed or frightened into nonattendance. Despite the unequal forces, it was still agreed that Sax's band was superior.

Now the very top brass had to be convinced. Another demonstration was arranged and the circle of experts was widened to include royal dukes and military personnel of even more exalted rank than on the first occasion. Once again Sax's band was outnumbered nine to thirty-two. Once again Sax's was acknowledged to be finer.

After the demonstration, the royal dukes saw no reason not to reorganise the military bands immediately using Sax's instruments. The military agreed but, wishing to protect itself against accusations of partiality, passed the buck to a commission.

The commission was as thorough as could be. It examined the background to the drop in standards that had so disturbed the king. It noted that a ban on civilian bandsmen in 1834 had robbed bands of good soloists, players and teachers. It showed how military music was organised on regimental lines, each colonel doing as he pleased. It pointed out the variation from band to band in terms of numbers of bandsmen and their instrumentation. The commission ended by inviting manu-facturers to submit sample instruments, though none of any significance was received.

When deciding between Sax's instruments and those of the competition, the commission split into two camps along ideological lines. One group, headed by Michele Carafa, an enemy of Berlioz and therefore of Sax, thought that con-ventional instruments were fine. The other group, Sax's supporters, totally disagreed.

Given the irreconcilable views, it was decided that only another competition between Carafa and Sax could settle the matter. It would take place on a grand scale in the open air on the Champ de Mars. The bands could have 45 players but no more, and the public would be allowed to attend and to register its preference through applause.

Carafa's ensemble included oboes, bassoons and horns, instruments that Berlioz thought sounded weak in the open air. Sax's band had no less than eighteen saxhorns of varying registers, and a couple of saxophones.

Public interest was intense. By late morning, a crowd of twenty thousand people had gathered. The rival bands appeared and lined up in front of the commission. Before the competition proper, various regimental bands marched past showing off their musical skills. Noon arrived and it was time for the confrontation between Carafa and Sax. The respective bands were drawn up 150 yards apart like opposing armies about to do battle.

For the first test, each was to play the same music, pieces by Adolphe Adam, composer of the ballet *Giselle*. Carafa's band was drawn to play first. Thinking no one would notice, Carafa had slipped in four extra players. But the eagle-eyed commission spotted it and instructed him to reduce his numbers to the specified 45. He chose to drop two bugles and two flutes. Even so, his line-up was very strong. He was director of the Gymnase de Musique Militaire where young military musicians were trained, and his band included many of its professors and star pupils.

It was as well that Sax did not have to play first. Once again a number of his players had been bribed and failed to turn up. Not only that, but some of his instruments were incomplete, reminiscent of his problems at the Salle Herz. There were no trumpets or saxophones, and he was short of players in various sections.

While Carafa's band was playing, Sax did the best he could. Humiliatingly, he was forced to add two ophicleides, the very instruments he was trying to make obsolete. He himself carried two instruments in an attempt to cover up his lack of numbers.

Carafa's test piece was received with applause. When Sax started to play, it was the signal for a pre-arranged demonstration. Stones were hurled and Sax was abused as a 'foreigner'. Despite the distractions, and short of seven players, Sax's band received far greater acclaim than Carafa's. The bands next played a march and concluded the first half of the trial by playing music of their own choice. Still the public favoured Sax.

In the second half, the bands were required to play with brass instruments only. The combination of Sax's saxhorns, cornets and trombones produced a far more impressive sound than Carafa's ensemble. The crowd saluted Sax. Victory was his. All he had to do was wait for the official verdict.

But he hadn't reckoned with bureaucracy. The commission treated the Champ de Mars as an experiment, not as conclusive proof. It drew up the profile of an 'ideal' band, which contained 74 instruments. The specification included two saxophones and eighteen saxhorns, which was good news for Sax. Unfortunately, there wasn't a regiment in the French Army that could support a band of that size. A compromise of 55 players was arrived at, with 36 for cavalry bands.

When the Minister of War approved the commission's report, Sax sat back and waited for orders, confident he was about to make his fortune. But fate did not favour him. Less than three years later, Louis-Philippe was forced to abdicate. He and his entourage, which included all Sax's high-placed political supporters, fled the country. The new regime soon reversed the reforms and French regiments promptly reverted to their former instrumentation. Sax's orders were cancelled, and orders already delivered were returned. Sax managed to keep going through this disastrous period, but only because a friend gifted him thirty thousand francs.

Even this gift returned to haunt Sax. After the friend died in 1852, his family came to reclaim the money. Sax was driven into bankruptcy, as he was again in 1873. As the years went on, Sax faced not only financial pressures but the hostility of other manufacturers. On top of bribing and scaring his bandsmen, they ran a financial dirty-tricks campaign, spreading rumours about Sax's solvency with the help of Sax's own book-keeper. They even tried to assassinate Sax on at least two occasions, once murdering one of his employees by mistake.

Sax was professionally successful, receiving honours and awards and running a saxophone class at the Paris Conservatory of Music. But the saxophone never became a regular member of the symphony orchestra in the way he had hoped. Orchestral players in the pay of the competition embargoed it and other of his inventions, thus preventing the famous composers of the time such as Donizetti and Meyerbeer from including them in their operas.

In the twentieth century it has appeared effectively in pieces such as Ravel's *Bolero*, Rachmaninov's *Symphonic Dances* and William Walton's *Façade*, and composers such as Richard Strauss, Vaughan Williams, Bizet and George Gershwin have used it. But it still remains on the periphery of classical music. At least it survives, unlike many instruments that bore the name of their inventor. Its true home was not found till the jazz era. Perhaps Sax would have been content with that.

NAMED AFTER AN ORCHESTRA

LONDON, NOVEMBER 1846

The audience for the evening's promenade concert flooded in as soon as Covent Garden theatre opened its doors. All available space was soon taken, including on the stage. But the box office refused to turn away customers, so people kept pouring in.

The conductor and impresario, Louis Jullien, began the concert with Beethoven's overture to *Fidelio*. With the crowd growing ever more densely packed, people began to feel trapped. In their nervousness, they began to shout, drowning out the orchestra. The music was forced to stop. When Miss Birch sang she was vaguely audible, but Mr Koenig, maestro of the cornet à pistons, might just as well not have been playing.

The music stopped again. Jullien attempted to address the crowd but was hissed at and shouted down. Eventually, he offered dissatisfied customers tickets for the following evening, but they wanted to know why he had taken their money in the first place when the performance was already sold out. The honest answer might have been, 'Because I need the cash', but Jullien smoothly responded that a Full House sign had been displayed. The audience took this with a very large pinch of salt. Police were called to restore order, and from there things deteriorated as truncheons were wielded.

Despite the hubbub, the concert somehow carried on. Finally, the massive musical forces involved in the *British Army Quadrilles* overwhelmed the noise from the audience. The first half ended an hour late. People left in the interval, creating more space, and during the second half there was greater decorum.

Jullien, flamboyant populariser of promenade concerts in England during the 1840s and 1850s, was the first of the personality conductors, precursor of Stokowski, Karajan and Bernstein. His huge concerts at Covent Garden, Drury Lane and other theatres often had a hysterical element to them. On entering, he would mount a red dais and swivel round so that all – especially the ladies – could see how magnificent he looked. His appearance was often greeted with applause lasting several minutes. He dressed outrageously for the times. *Punch* describes how he wore 'his coat thrown widely open, white waistcoat, elaborately embroidered shirt-front and wrist bands of extravagant length, turned back over his cuffs'. His black moustache was 'itself a startling novelty'.

When the commotion made by his appearance had settled down, a servant in livery would appear and present him with a pair of white kid gloves, which he slowly drew on. Most conductors of the period wore gloves, but they put them on offstage. They also brought their baton with them and did not insist on having it presented on a velvet cushion, as Jullien did. When conducting Beethoven, Jullien swapped his usual baton for a jewelled one and changed into a clean pair of gloves handed to him on a silver salver (except for the funeral-march movement of the 'Eroica' Symphony, for which he donned black gloves). For showpiece items like the quadrilles, he would grab a violin or piccolo and 'spontaneously' join in.

Near him was a chair, but no ordinary chair, more a throne of gilt and red velvet. At the end of a piece – which he had conducted facing the audience rather than the orchestra – he would collapse into it, exhausted by the emotional and physical effort of it all.

If Jullien's performance was on an epic scale, he had a name to match. He was born in 1812 in Sisteron in southeastern France, while his family was en route to Paris. When his musician father invited one of the members of the local orchestra to be the baby's godfather, all the orchestra's members claimed the privilege. Louis ended up with 36

Christian names, including two Thomases and one Thomas-Thomas. He must have been glad he wasn't born in Paris, where the orchestra was much bigger.

From the start, Jullien's father prodded him towards becoming a musician, though at first he showed no inclination. Eventually, he grew to like music from overhearing his father giving lessons, and at the age of six was considered a violin prodigy.

When he was about 22, Jullien completed the interrupted trip to Paris, where promenade concerts, devised by Phillipe Musard, were all the rage. Musard had a few attention-grabbing tricks, such as smashing his conducting stool, throwing away his baton, and advancing to the edge of the platform and firing a pistol in the air. No doubt that is where Jullien got some of his ideas.

In 1840, Jullien moved to England, and from then until 1858 gave hundreds of concerts in London and up and down the country. He largely followed Musard's model. Admission charges were low and the programmes were light in content, with waltzes, popular ballades and quadrilles, plus a movement from a Beethoven or Mendelssohn symphony to raise the tone. People could stroll around or dance in surroundings enhanced with flowers, shrubs and fountains. The formula attracted a wide range of audience.

He went to immense trouble to please his public. After fire forced him to leave Covent Garden theatre, he converted the interior of Her Majesty's Theatre into an elaborate artificial garden with reading and refreshment rooms for a season of less than two months.

He was a shrewd exploiter of popular taste and sentiment. During the Crimean War, he concocted the *Allied Armies Quadrilles*. Patriotic tunes of the allies – England, France and Turkey – played by the bands of the Grenadiers, Life Guards, and Coldstream Guards in the national uniforms of the three countries, were greeted 'with vociferous and incessant cheering, waving of hats' and so on.

His admiration for Beethoven notwithstanding, Jullien did not hesitate to beef up the Fifth Symphony with four brass bands, or enhance the thunderstorm in the 'Pastoral' Symphony by rattling a tin box of dried peas to imitate hail, to the displeasure of the critics. On the other hand, he introduced symphonic music to people who otherwise might never have heard any.

His life was full of unusual events. You may wish to take one or two of the following stories with a pinch of salt, as they are Jullien's version, passed on to a trusting music journalist.

When he was about four, an eagle snatched him up into the air and he was saved only because his belt broke before the eagle flew too high. At the age of fourteen, he signed up for the French Navy and fought at the Battle of Navarino, where he received a shoulder wound that permanently restricted his ability to play the violin. He left the navy and joined the army, deserted, was sentenced to death, told the colonel a sob story about wanting to see his mother, and was pardoned. Fighting a duel in Paris, his opponent's sword went right through his breast and out the back. Jullien continued the fight unawares, overcame his opponent and then drew the sword out himself.

On a hectic tour of the USA, where he gave 214 concerts in under a year, he and his band had to cross a frozen river on foot. Everyone was game for the journey except one faint-hearted flageolet player. He was finally seized, strapped to a cello case and pulled across by some of the local helpers.

Although his promenade concerts were financially success-ful, others of Jullien's ventures weren't and resulted in bankruptcy. He returned to France in 1859 to escape his creditors, and signs of depression and mental breakdown became apparent. In July of the following year, he told his fifteen-year-old niece that he was going to kill her so that she could go to heaven and hear the most marvellous music of all, the music of the angels. Quick-wittedly, she asked her uncle to play something beautiful on the piccolo so she could compare his music with that of the angels when she reached heaven. Jullien dashed off to get the instrument and the young girl was able to escape. Jullien was immediately placed in a madhouse and died there a few days later at the age of 47.

A man of prodigious energy and imagination, Jullien was a mixture of showman and musician, with showman taking precedence. His achievement as organiser of promenade concerts should not be underestimated. For over three decades after his death, many tried to follow in his footsteps, including Sir Arthur Sullivan and Jullien's son, but without lasting success. It was not until Sir Henry Wood took them over in 1895 that the Proms again found strong leadership and were established in the format in which they are so popular today.

Jullien was not forgotten after his death. When one of his quadrilles was played at a promenade concert in 1878, it reminded *The Times* of 'old and pleasant times'. He received honourable mentions in a Thomas Hardy poem at the turn of the twentieth century, and his greatest success, the *British Army Quadrilles*, is still performed today.

THE GREAT CHOPINZEE

VLADIMIR DE PACHMANN (1848–1933)

In our own time there have been pianists with quirky mannerisms such as Sviatoslav Richter, who at the end of his career played on a stage lit by a single standard lamp, and Glenn Gould, crouched low over the keyboard, accompanying his playing with a little off-key humming. Such idiosyncrasies pale in comparison with those of the Ukrainian-born pianist Vladimir de Pachmann.

His antics began as soon as he came on stage. When the late Margaret Lyell, mother of the pianist Julian Jacobson, attended a de Pachmann concert, he came onto the platform, probably anything up to half an hour late, and confided to the audience, 'Tonight I will play like a god!'

When Frances Horne went to a recital in London one afternoon, like many other ladies in the audience she dressed as smartly as she could. De Pachmann took one look at her admittedly very elaborate hat, fixed her with his eye and told her to 'Get out!' After a little thought, she did, as the fierce little maestro with the long Liszt-like hair held all the cards and could have refused to play until she left.

Having seen off all distracting millinery, de Pachmann would next fix his attention on his piano stool, adjusting and readjusting it in minute gradations, up, down, backwards and forwards. Inevitably unable to achieve positioning precisely to his satisfaction, he would leave the stage and return with a book to bolster himself on the stool, or perhaps just one page from a book which, placed under the stool, would miraculously make

74

all the difference. In a concert in Boston, dissatisfied with the piano itself, he complained that it was 'lopsided' and the tone came out 'crooked'.

So much for the preliminaries. Now he was ready not only to play, but to begin a commentary, half to himself and half to the front rows of the audience. 'Madame Schumann played this – oh, my God!' he would murmur in a combination of English, French or German. 'Dear God, help me to play this music tonight as You meant it to be played when You sent it into the world.'

'Isn't this beautiful?' he might say as he progressed. If a difficult passage was coming up, he would rally himself, 'Courage, de Pachmann!' If satisfied with his execution, he might exclaim, 'Bravo, de Pachmann!' He would give helpful little pointers to the audience, 'Now the melody,' accentuating the theme so there should be no misunderstanding. Or he would explain that the next passage was very difficult and he had had to practise it at half-tempo, demonstrating how. Then he would move on without actually having played it at the correct speed.

If momentarily there were no verbal asides, there was always plenty to watch, as he acted out the music's emotional content with deep sighs or smiles or winks or by placing his hand over his heart to emphasise a sorrowful section. If playing a waltz, he might sometimes do a waltz step to accompany it. Having played a piece, he would sometimes say, 'Now I play it another way,' and repeat it in a totally different interpretation.

If this was distracting to audiences, woe betide anyone who distracted him. When some ladies annoyed him by following his performance in their score, he upbraided them. 'I make no mistakes. I am de Pachmann. Anyway, I use different edition.' One lady, busy fanning herself on a hot day, was rebuked, 'I am playing in three-four, and you are fanning in six-eight!' If applauded when he considered he had not played well, he would gesticulate towards the audience to quieten it. His reception at the end of a concert could be tumultuous, with women crying and fainting and refusing to leave, so that the management was forced to threaten to lock the hall.

His encores could be works of art in themselves. A Berlin hall had stepped rows where a chorus would be placed in a choral work. After his first encore, de Pachmann went and stood on the first row; after the second, on the second row. The audience soon realised what was going on and determined that he should give as many encores as there were steps. There were fifteen and that is the number of encores he gave. In Glasgow he played an encore after each piece in the programme and the concert took so long that the caretaker put out the lights to get him to stop.

Attending a concert as a spectator did not subdue him. When his friend Leopold Godowsky played – a pianist of the highest reputation and quality whom he much admired – de Pachmann would offer a stream of approving comments to those around him. Very occasionally he differed with his interpretation and once actually went up onto the platform. 'No, Leopold, you moost play it like zo!' he said, playing the passage again before resuming his seat.

But he was capable of the opposite. About to play some Chopin in Carnegie Hall, he stopped, turned to the audience and called to Godowsky to come and play the piece instead, as he was the better interpreter. Godowsky modestly demurred but de Pachmann insisted, so Godowsky had to clamber up to the platform and perform.

Despite the sideshows and distractions, there is no doubt that he was an exceptional pianist. As an interpreter of Chopin, he may well have been unsurpassed. Liszt told the audience at one of de Pachmann's concerts, 'Those who have never heard Chopin before are hearing him this evening.' His playing of Liszt, Mendelssohn, Brahms, Bach, Scarlatti and many others was highly regarded.

He was totally dedicated to the highest standards of piano-playing. In his early twenties – his concert career already successfully launched – he withdrew from public performance for eight years for further study alone, 'beginning with humble finger exercises', and then for a further two years' study a little later.

But somewhere along the line, starting in his late thirties, an element of willed eccentricity appeared in his make-up. He was well aware of this, once saying the fun and games were simply a technique to get the audience's attention. 'Then I begin . . .'

Many found them more of a distraction. George Bernard Shaw called him a 'monkey' and 'pantomimist'. Rachmaninov said he was a 'charlatan' and had to be prevented from walking out in mid-concert. One critic called him 'a professional funny man'. The American critic James Gibbons Huneker invented the nickname for him that stuck – 'The Chopinzee'. Others suffered his eccentricities for the brilliance of his pianism.

He was a collector of precious stones and named them after his favourite composers. A beautiful diamond he called Bach, and an emerald Brahms. Chopin was an opal, Liszt a ruby. He had no stone sufficiently valuable for Richard Strauss. He once scattered his jewels across a table and told a friend, 'Sit down and listen. I will play and reproduce in music all these colours.'

There was a concert in 1912 in St Louis when the conductor, exasperated by de Pachmann's behaviour and the extended, frenzied response of the audience, decided that the pianist was being discourteous to the orchestra, threw down his baton and led the orchestra from the stage. The audience waited for over an hour but the orchestra did not reappear. The list of de Pachmann's strange concerts is virtually endless. More than anyone else in this book, they were his trademark.

TWO INTO ONE WON'T GO

WORCESTER, SEPTEMBER 1848

Edward Elgar used to relate a story told to him by his father. William Elgar was a violinist on the back-desks in the orchestra at the Worcester Festival for a number of years and was playing on the night that two singers got themselves into an extraordinary fix.

The contralto Marietta Alboni and the bass Luigi Lablache were two of the most famous singers of their era. Alboni was the only singer Rossini was prepared to accept as a pupil and was a renowned performer in his operas. Lablache had the honour of being a torchbearer at Beethoven's funeral and sang in the Requiems at both Beethoven's and Chopin's funerals. His bass was described as deeper 'than almost any ever heard' and he had been singing tutor to the young Queen Victoria.

Physically, both singers were heavyweights. Pictures of Lablache show that he would have needed no extra padding to play Falstaff in Verdi's opera (had the part then existed). As for Alboni, she was described by the writer Mme Girardin as 'an elephant who has swallowed a nightingale'.

That evening, as a change from the sacred music that was the staple fare of the festival, both were happy to let their hair down in a concert of miscellaneous pieces. Their performance of the comic duet 'Oh! Guardate che figure' from Gnecco's *La Prova d'un Opera*, a very popular work in its time, was rumbustious. The audience loved the way Lablache imitated Alboni's practice of embellishing a tune with extra notes. They laughed and applauded as Alboni, in her turn, did a creditable job of

78

matching some of Lablache's deep, black, bass notes (she had sung Don Carlo, a baritone role, in Verdi's *Ernani*).

An encore was requested and, after obliging, the two singers stood hand in hand, acknowledging the applause with the usual bows. Still bowing, still hand in hand, they walked off the platform towards the exit, a narrow archway leading to the cloisters. So absorbed were they in bowing that they entered the archway at the same moment. And there they became wedged. For some time the audience assumed they were still bowing. When the real situation became apparent, it took the combined efforts of a number of stewards to release them.

Elgar was still telling this tale towards the end of his life, eighty years after it happened.

Another story about Alboni shows her in a more flattering light. When she went to Trieste to sing Rosina in Rossini's *Barber of Seville*, she was warned that a cabal was being organised against her. Undeterred, she went to the organiser of the cabal and offered to take part in the evening's fun. She was unrecognised by the organiser who gave her a whistle and told her to blow it with all her might after Rosina's aria. 'What, has she done anything wicked?' asked Alboni.

'We know nothing about her,' said the cabal organiser, 'except that she comes from Rome; and we wish to have no singers here of whose reputation we are not the creators. You have but to add to the tempest that will be raised,' she was told.

Alboni made sure that she wore the whistle around her neck for the performance that evening. When some of the cabal blew their whistles before she had begun to sing, she advanced to the front of the stage. 'Gentlemen,' she said, showing off the whistle and smiling, '*we* must not hiss *me*, but the cavatina; you have commenced too soon!'

After a brief silence, thunderous applause swept through the house, and she took eleven curtain calls. Let us leave her here triumphant, rather than jammed in an exit.

MUSIC DOWN THE TUBE

BRITANNIA BRIDGE, WALES, MAY 1849

A most unusual venue for a concert resulted from one of the biggest and most innovative engineering projects of its time, the construction of a rail bridge across the Menai Straits separating the Isle of Anglesey from northwest Wales. The bridge had to be stiff enough to support the weight of heavy trains and high enough to allow the passage of boats at all times. The engineer in charge, Robert Stephenson, son of the inventor of *The Rocket* railway engine, produced a design featuring two huge rectangular tubes, 460 feet long, 15 feet wide and 30 feet high.

Local interest was enormous and large crowds visited the construction site. The quantities of material used were on a huge scale, including one and a half million cubic feet of stone and the production of two million rivets. By mid-May 1849, the main tubes had been constructed and lay alongside the Menai Straits. The next step was to load them onto pontoons, float them into position and lift them into place.

In the short window between the completion of the tubes and their erection in June, the engineering staff of the Chester & Holyhead Railway came up with the idea of holding a concert to celebrate the near-completion of the project. And where better to hold it than in one of the huge tubes itself. Although this presented many problems of acoustics, lighting, seating, ventilation, sanitation and rudimentary decoration of the primitive tube, they held few terrors for the builders of the massive Britannia Bridge, who coped with the difficulties in style.

Between seven and eight hundred people from all levels of society attended. Promenades were provided for the local elite with seats along the sides when they wished to rest. The less privileged had to stand at the far end of the tube at some distance from the orchestra.

Each end of the tube was decorated with branches to resemble a grove and five hundred candles provided lighting along its whole length. The *Examiner* reported that 'the whole effect, to the eye and the ear, was most pleasing.' The sound carried excellently down the whole length of the tube 'with scarcely diminished volume'. Refreshments were also available 'on a scale much more liberal than could reasonably be expected'.

The programme went on for two hours and consisted of marches, glees and solo ballads. There were contributions from the local choirs of Caernarfon and Bangor, but the star of the evening was Master Hayden, son of the music director for the evening, who sang a solo, 'Thy Smile, Dear Maid', set to music by his father. When this was encored, he chose not to sing it again, but began a new piece and, sadly, 'did not sing it as well'.

The concert continued until nine and terminated with the national anthem and three rousing cheers for the Prince of Wales and Robert Stephenson himself.

The evening's entertainment did not end there. Immediately after the concert, a makeshift group of violinists, flautists and a triangle player got together to provide music for quadrilles, polkas and country dances. The dancing carried on until midnight.

The completion of the bridge, however, did not go completely smoothly. In August, part of a hydraulic press fell 84 feet onto the tube it was raising, killing a workman. Eventually the bridge was finished and survived in its original design until 1970, when it was badly damaged by fire.

There is an unexpected musical footnote. One of the engineers working on the bridge with Stephenson was a certain Mr Grove, later Sir George, compiler of the famous musical dictionary that bears his name.

WAITING FOR GOTTSCHALK

ALBANY, NEW YORK STATE, 1862

There was a full house in the concert room in Albany and the audience eagerly awaited the afternoon recital to be given by the celebrated American pianist and composer Louis Moreau Gottschalk.

Just before the start time at four-thirty, the manager stepped forward to inform the audience that Mr Gottschalk sent his profound apologies but, due to circumstances beyond his control, he would be unable to fulfil his engagement. There was a sigh of disappointment and the audience melted away, speculating that he was perhaps indisposed or had suffered a personal loss of some kind. The truth behind his absence was amusingly different, although the audience would not have appreciated the story.

By the time of the Albany concert, Gottschalk calculated that in the previous four months he had given 85 concerts around America and covered fifteen thousand miles by train, often travelling eighteen hours a day. He was suffering from burnout, as he recorded graphically in his diary. 'The sight of a piano sets my hair on end like the victim in the presence of the wheel on which he is to be tortured. Whilst my fingers are thus moving, my thought is elsewhere.'

To maintain interest and concentration on his massive tours, he used to set himself goals. One ambition was to be the first pianist in America to give three concerts in one day. He achieved this in St Louis in April, but was still dissatisfied. It was too easy in one city. Could he do it in, say, three different towns, involving a trip of a hundred miles?

The chance came when he reached New York City. The towns of Newark, Albany and Troy were in easy reach with good rail links. He could leave New York in the morning, give a concert in Newark at noon, catch the one-thirty train to Albany, with a concert at four-thirty, and then on to Troy for the final concert at eight.

The Newark concert was a great success and Gottschalk duly caught the train to Albany. In his carriage were, as he reports in his memoirs, 'a charming young girl and her mother, both hampered with boxes, umbrellas, and other movable utensils'. Gottschalk was 33 and single. He liked women, women liked him and one imagines a little bit of flirting must have gone on with the daughter.

When the ladies rose to get off at the station of Fishkill, Gottschalk did what any young man seeking to impress a pretty woman would have done. He sprang to his feet and leaped out, holding a cage with a canary in one hand, while helping mother and daughter to the ground with the other. The ladies were very grateful and thanked Gottschalk profusely. Gottschalk tried to extend the conversation, no doubt hoping for an address. When it became apparent that none would be forthcoming, he turned to board the train, only to find that it was already a hundred yards down the track and disappearing behind a bend in the road.

He was now marooned in the middle of nowhere with only an hour to go to the performance. No doubt the concert hall in Albany was already beginning to fill with people. His attention returned to the mother and daughter. Perhaps he might salvage something in their company. That slim hope was punctured when he saw that they had been met by husband and boyfriend respectively in a carriage and had already lost interest in him.

There was nothing Gottschalk could do but telegraph his agent in Albany telling him to cancel both the concert there and the later one in Troy. Probably he didn't mind having a free afternoon, but the experience was enough to put him off making another attempt on his record, though it would have taken more than that to put him off flirting.

GOTTSCHALK AT LARGE

SAN FRANCISCO, MAY 1865

Louis Moreau Gottschalk, who we have already met in 'Waiting for Gottschalk', was naturally drawn to large-scale enterprises. *The Siege of Zaragoza*, for example, which he wrote in Madrid in May 1852, was scored for no less than ten pianos. It was wildly popular at its first performance and Gottschalk became an instant favourite of Queen Isabella II. The audience was so enthused it tried to crown him with a laurel wreath but he demurred. Instead the fans were allowed to carry him shoulder-high to his residence, accompanied by bands.

Some years later he arranged Wagner's march from *Tannhäuser* for fourteen pianos. A performance in San Francisco in 1865 was so successful that he immediately scheduled another. A difficulty arose when one of the pianists fell ill on the eve of the concert. Gottschalk, having used up the stock of good pianists in San Francisco, could find no suitable substitute. However, he knew the public would be upset if, having advertised fourteen pianists, he cut down to thirteen. A possible solution appeared when the proprietor of the hall suggested his son as a replacement. He was a first-class amateur pianist, at least according to his father.

Gottschalk did not trust amateurs. 'They are never frightened at anything,' he wrote in his memoirs, 'finding everything that is given them to play too easy, and are offended if requested to study it; in the presence of the audience they stick in the mud, embarrassed, and leave you to extricate yourself as well as you can.' Gottschalk knew where the buck

84

stopped in the event of disaster. 'You alone will be held responsible, and as to them, they know not how it happens that they made a mistake.'

However, he allowed himself to be overruled by the father's enthusiasm and proposed a rehearsal. The son thought this was unnecessary, commenting that the part was very easy to someone who played the fantasies of Liszt. Persuaded that it was only to go over one or two minor performance points, eventually he agreed. Gottschalk had only to hear two bars of false notes to know the worst, though he kept his thoughts to himself.

He was now in a difficult position. Both father and son thought the rehearsal had gone off excellently and had alerted all the son's friends about the concert. Gottschalk, in the meantime, was seriously thinking about calling the concert off, citing illness as the cause. It was his tuner who came up with a solution. Producing a *crochet*, a kind of hook, he took out the whole of the interior mechanism of the son's piano. 'The keyboard remains, but I assure you there will be no more false notes,' he grinned triumphantly at Gottschalk.

The hall was full for the performance. The amateur had specially requested a place at the front where his friends could easily see him, and was given a prominent position near the footlights. Gottschalk knew there was one major weak point in his deception. In those days, when the majority of pianists came on stage they played a few preliminary scales or chords before starting the concert proper as a form of warm-up. If the son were to do that, he would instantly detect that the piano had been muted. Accordingly, Gottschalk prohibited all the pianists from any preliminary practice on stage. The reason he gave was that the pianos would make their greatest impact by a simultaneous grand entrance at the start of the piece.

The piece got under way exactly as planned by Gottschalk. Deafened by the thunderous sound of fourteen – no, thirteen – pianos, the son did not suspect anything. 'He was superb,' Gottschalk noted in his diary. 'He was sweating great drops; he was throwing his eyes carelessly on the audience, and performed with miraculous ease the passages apparently the most difficult.'

At the end there was tempestuous applause and calls for an encore, especially from the young man's friends. An encore was granted and the pianists prepared to begin again. In the excitement of his success, the son forgot the injunction about not playing any preliminary chords and idly attempted a little scale. To his astonishment, no sound emerged. He tried again. Still nothing. 'The stupor which was printed on his countenance is inexpressible,' says Gottschalk. The flabbergasted pianist began to investigate the cause. First he inspected the strings: perhaps his forceful playing had broken them. Next he depressed the pedals a few times to check they were in order, then he tried out his scale again. Finally it was clear he had concluded that the piano was just out of order. Frantically he tried to attract Gottschalk's attention.

Gottschalk, who had followed all this with great amusement, carefully avoided meeting his eyes and gave the signal to play the march again. The young man was in a quandary. Did he get up and leave the platform? Did he just sit there without playing? His pride would not let him do either. He sat there and went through the pantomime of playing, unaware it was the second time he had done so. 'His countenance, which I saw from below,' Gottschalk writes, 'was worth painting, it was a mixture of discouragement and of spite.'

In the greenroom afterwards, Gottschalk congratulated the performers but commented that the effect had been greater the first time. 'The mischief!' cried the son. 'My piano broke all at once!' Gottschalk and the tuner were able to keep straight faces but not the secret, and it was not long before the amateur discovered the truth.

Gottschalk was very soon forced to leave San Francisco, not due to this incident but because he was accused of sexual impropriety with a young woman student, a charge later proved to be false. He fled to South America, where he was highly popular. His taste for the gigantic did not diminish and he organised concerts with as many as 650 participants. He died from malaria in 1869, aged only forty, collapsing onstage in Tijuca, Brazil after playing a piece called *Morte*.

MAN OF A HUNDRED UMBRELLAS

ERIK SATIE (1866–1925)

Honfleur, birthplace of the composer Erik Satie, is a small Normandy coastal town near the mouth of the Seine. Less well known than the town's picturesque harbour or many excellent restaurants is a small jewel of a museum in the house where Satie lived for a few early years. An hour or so spent here will give you a marvellous insight into the quirky and bizarre character of its dedicatee.

One room is given over to a Heath Robinson style merry-go-round. Designed and used by Satie himself, it is powered by a bicycle that visitors are allowed to ride. Another room has been done up like a chapel, recalling Satie's one-time interest in the Rosicrucian sect. In another, Satie's compositions are playing on a white piano, its keys rising and falling without visible assistance. A small bedroom contains some of his famous velvet suits and a collection of his large number of umbrellas, many never used. The very first exhibit in the museum is a giant pear with wings, a reminder of a well-known story.

When Claude Debussy, a great friend, once complained that Satie's music lacked form, Satie reacted by bringing him a seven-part composition called *Three Pieces in the Shape of a Pear*. The bemused Debussy asked what the title meant. It was called that, Satie said, so Debussy could no longer complain that his music was formless.

Debussy was also the butt of another Satie witticism. At the 1905 premiere of *La Mer*, one of whose movements is called 'From Dawn to Midday on the Sea', Debussy received the usual post-performance congratulations. Satie's deflating comment was, 'Ah, my dear friend, there's one particular moment between half past ten and a quarter to eleven that I found especially stunning!'

Satie specialised in strange titles and odd instructions to performers. One piece was called *Shrivelled Embryos*. A pianist would come across directions to play 'light as an egg' or 'dry as a cuckoo' or, in *Sonatine Bureaucratique*, 'as if you are thinking of promotion'. Another work, *Vexations*, has to be repeated 840 times, expanding what is basically a two-minute piece into one of up to 24 hours. Performances are said to be a life-changing experience, as will be seen in 'The Grandest Leg-pull'. Some pieces have short, evocative titles like *Simplement*, *Tendrement* or *Je te Veux*.

Satie was a rebel against received ideas and conventions and especially rejected the pervasive influence of Richard Wagner and his massive operas. Satie's pieces are more often two to three minutes long, not two to three hours. *Trois Gymnopédies* is a good example. Composed when he was only 21, it is probably his best-known work. The first and most famous of the *Gymnopédies* lasts only three minutes, yet Satie creates a spacious, limpid atmosphere that seems timeless.

Unwilling to compromise by taking a nine-to-five job, Satie adopted a Bohemian lifestyle – poverty for the sake of art. In his early days, he lodged in a room so small that, after squashing in a bed and a piano, it was impossible to open the door. It was unheated and he used to wear seven shirts to fight off the cold. At one point he and his roommate Contamine de Latour had only one pair of trousers between them. De Latour would wear the trousers to work in the daytime and Satie would put them on in the evening to go to his job in Montmartre as pianist in one of the cabarets.

Any money that did come Satie's way usually didn't last long. He had a gourmet's taste for good food and drink, and loved taking his friends out to dinner. He never did things by halves. On inheriting seven thousand francs, he went out and bought seven identical velvet suits, the start of his 'Velvet Gentleman' period when he never wore anything but one of those suits. One evening he was about to go to the theatre with a friend when he insisted on going home to change. When he returned his outfit was indistinguishable from the original, 'only with the velvet in a very slightly better condition'. By the time the seventh suit wore out, he said he never wanted to see velvet again.

In 1898, aged 32, he economised by moving out of Paris to Arceuil, some ten kilometres away, where he lived until his death 27 years later. He established a daily routine, walking into Paris with frequent stops for refreshment at favourite cafés and bars along the way, often taking out his notebook to compose. In the evening he would try to catch the last train back at one in the morning. But if he stayed on drinking with friends and missed it, he would walk. Occasionally he would accept a lift part of the way but never as far as his house, possibly to avoid asking the driver in. The whole time he lived in Arceuil he never invited anyone inside his apartment, not even his landlady if he was ill. Friends thought he was involved in some secret liaison, but this was not the case, as became clear after his death. In fact he is reputed to have had only one affair, with the artist Suzanne Veladon, which ended after six months. Satie seems to have been too distressed to contemplate another relationship and remained unmarried.

In 1906, as he moved into his forties, Satie changed from 'Velvet Gentleman' to the look by which he is best remembered: 'Bourgeois Functionary', dressing identically day after day in black suit, bowler hat, white wing collar and immaculate white shirt. He always carried an umbrella and almost always, whatever the weather, a heavy overcoat wrapped round him like a dressing gown. He had a neatly trimmed goatee beard and a pair of pince-nez he was constantly re-adjusting. He remained stuck in this image for the rest of his life, 'ageless, neither old nor young', as he was described by Valentine Hugo, the young artist, designer and musician. She knew Satie well for many years and he used to call her affectionately his '*chère grande fille*'.

He was a temperamental friend and over the years had ructions with almost everyone of importance in his life such as his brother Conrad, Debussy and Ravel. About Ravel he said acidly, 'Maurice Ravel refuses the Legion d'Honneur . . . yet the whole of his work accepts it.' He broke up with one friend because he thought he had deliberately punched a hole in one of his precious umbrellas.

For many years Satie's music was not widely known, though Ravel admired it and played it at concerts. Debussy was another admirer and orchestrated *Trois Gymnopédies*. Satie's main success was with songs written for cabaret stars such as Pauline Darty, the Queen of the Slow Waltz, for whom he wrote the enchanting *Je te Veux*.

In 1917 he finally made a breakthrough into public awareness when the impresario Diaghilev, director of the Ballets Russes, asked him to write the music for the ballet *Parade*. His collaborators were of the highest stature – Jean Cocteau, Pablo Picasso and Léonide Massine – which indicates how highly Satie was regarded.

Parade, with its combination of talents, its cubist scenery and exotic effects such as typewriters and car horns, was a *succès de scandale* in much the same way as Stravinsky's *The Rite of Spring* had been in 1913. At one point the arty section of the audience was yelling, '*Vive Picasso*' while Satie's friends were bawling out his name.

Satie died in 1925 from cirrhosis of the liver caused by decades of overdoing the calvados. Notoriety had not brought him financial stability, as his friends discovered when finally they were able to enter the forbidden territory of his apartment.

'What a shock we had on opening the door!' the composer Darius Milhaud wrote later. 'It seemed impossible that Satie had lived in such poverty.' He had no belongings of value. In every corner were piles of old newspapers, old hats and walking sticks. The broken-down piano, which he had never played but kept all his life, was there of course, covered in dust. In the wardrobe were his famous velvet suits, and perhaps a hundred umbrellas, some still in their shop wrapping. Along one skirting board were hardened lumps of excrement. There was a parcel delivered several years previously, still unopened, and, in his exquisite calligraphy, the manuscripts of compositions that had long been thought lost. There were other important manuscripts that no one knew existed. Completely black from the dirt, the friends left to clean themselves up.

Yet out of this squalor every evening, Erik Satie had emerged like a butterfly from a chrysalis, dapper in his bowler and suit, to begin his ten-kilometre walk to the bohemian delights of Montmartre. His last words were 'Ah, the cows,' a suitably enigmatic farewell from someone who had made enigma into a musical art form.

Posterity has been kinder to his music than the public of his era. This odd, idiosyncratic, principled individual is now regarded as a most progressive and highly influential composer of the twentieth century.

LIEBLING, LOOK WHAT THEY'VE DONE TO OUR TUNE!

TRIBSCHEN, SWITZERLAND, DECEMBER 1870

Preparations had been going on for weeks in Zurich and Lucerne, then at the lakeside villa itself as unobtrusively as possible. Richard Wagner was anxious not to arouse Cosima's suspicions and spoil the surprise, the performance of a piece of music written specially for her 33rd birthday.

But Cosima could sense that something was up. Her husband was being coyly secretive, and Richter, his closest musical associate and an able horn player, was learning the trumpet. He was making so much noise about it that she scolded him several times, and he was forced to take to a rowing boat in the middle of the lake to practise.

Early on Cosima's birthday, which fell on Christmas Day, 1870, a small orchestra of fifteen players assembled on the staircase leading to the still-sleeping Cosima's bedroom. At a signal from Wagner, the violins started very softly to play a lovely theme. The gentle melody slowly intruded into Cosima's consciousness. At first she was unsure if she was awake or asleep but, as she wrote in her diary, 'It grew louder. I could no longer imagine myself in a dream. Music was sounding and what music!'

When the sound died away, Wagner came into her bedroom and handed her the music he had written. Whether Cosima had guessed the nature of the secret activities isn't known. She always said she didn't, but perhaps she was being tactful. It wouldn't have been surprising if she had worked it out, because she had started the idea of giving musical presents, having woken Wagner one year with Richter playing Siegfried's horn call, and later organising a performance of a Beethoven string quartet.

The present was played twice more during the day. Cosima saw that Wagner had chosen themes with a strong personal significance for them both. The opening theme came from the opera *Siegfried*, which Wagner had recently finished, itself based on music Wagner had composed with her in mind a few years earlier. There was also material from an unfinished string quartet inspired by her, and a lullaby to symbolise their young son, Siegfried, born the previous year and nicknamed Fidi.

Because of all these intimate associations, the composer and his wife decided that, despite requests, the piece should never be published or played in public. However, seven years later, money problems forced them to change their mind and they sold it. Ever since then, the *Tribschen Idyll with Fidi's Bird Song and Orange Sunrise* has been one of the best-known and most popular pieces in the repertoire, under its usual title, the *Siegfried Idyll*.

Once beyond their control, Wagner and Cosima knew the *Idyll* would have good, bad and indifferent performances. But what happened to their beloved work in a concert in Blackpool just before World War I would have been beyond their worst fears.

As a young man, the master-bassoonist Archie Camden passed several summers before and after the war playing in an orchestra on the town's North Pier. One season he and a couple of his colleagues, bored by the daily orchestral grind, decided to have a bit of harmless fun at the expense of a naive young viola player called Harry.

Concerts were often disturbed by the comings and goings of the concertgoers and by the vendors calling out 'Programmes here' as they tried to sell programmes to the newcomers, even when a piece was in progress. This was a source of great annoyance to the orchestra's conductor Simon Speelman.

Through a bit of play-acting, Camden and his two colleagues managed to convince the gullible Harry that he was a born ventriloquist. They persuaded him to 'throw' his voice during the evening performance. The plan was that when Camden signalled, Harry was to call out 'Programmes' the way the programme girls did. When Harry was dubious, Camden told him that the more of these kinds of interruptions there were, the more likely the pier authorities would be to accept Speelman's complaint and get the girls banned from selling programmes during performances. So really, Camden persuaded Harry, it was all to help Speelman and was a perfect use of his amazing ventriloquistic gift.

Harry spent the concert with eyes glued anxiously on Camden, waiting for his cue. Camden made no move until it was time to play the *Siegried Idyll*, then, right in the middle of the quietest section, he nodded at Harry. Seated with the other violas only feet from Speelman, Harry called out, 'Programmes, penny each!' The three conspirators were in fits. The rest of the orchestra quickly cottoned on and began to laugh, so much so that the furious Speelman could hardly finish the piece. 'You're fired!' he hissed at the bemused Harry, who couldn't understand why Speelman was directing his ire at him instead of the programme girls.

Aware that his joke had overstepped the mark, during the interval Camden got his colleagues to explain to Harry what had been going on, while he dashed round to see Speelman in his room. Camden told the still apoplectic conductor exactly what had happened, apologised, and asked him to reinstate Harry. 'You are very naughty,' Speelman said, smiling, 'but I can see it is just high spirits. OK, Harry is reinstated. But you might have chosen a different piece, not the *Siegried Idyll*!'

No doubt the long-dead Richard and the still-living Cosima would have thought the same.

JUST ONE CORNO DI BASSETTO

LONDON, 1889–90

The newly promoted music critic of the *Star,* a lanky 32-year-old Irishman with a thick black beard, was considering what by-line to use for his twice-weekly column. Rather than use his own name, which he said 'meant nothing to the public', he decided on a pen name. Feeling playful, he went for something to make him sound like an exotic foreigner with a title. After considering Count de Luna, a character from Verdi's *Il Trovatore,* he settled on Corno di Bassetto.

In his first article under this name in February 1889, he announced with tongue in cheek to a bemused public, 'The Di Bassettos were known to Mozart, and were of service to him in the production of several of his works.' This was perfectly true, if not quite in the way the reader would have understood it. Corno di bassetto was simply Italian for basset horn, an instrument used by Mozart in his Requiem. Adding, 'We are a branch of the Reed family,' was a rare example of Corno pushing a joke too far.

For the next fifteen months or so, Corno produced some of the most trenchant, witty and well-informed music criticism ever written in the English language. He had been brought up in a musical family in Dublin in which almost everyone played an instrument. A close family friend, Vandeveur Lee, exposed him to so much music that by the time he was fifteen, he could sing and whistle complete works by Handel, Haydn, Mozart, Rossini and many others. By the age of twenty he was earning money as a music critic in London, ghosting a column for Lee.

95

Today, Corno is best known as a Nobel Prize-winning playwright. But it was his music criticism for the *Star* that first brought him to public attention. He took it seriously though not solemnly, and wrote about music for most of his very long life in a highly entertaining and informative way. What he learned about musical structure strongly influenced his plays. Characters are specified as being a contralto or tenor and so on. His dialogues are the equivalent of duets, trios and quartets. At a rehearsal of one of his plays a director said, 'Ladies and gentlemen: will you please remember this is Italian opera.'

In keeping with his socialist principles, Corno reviewed everything from grand opera at Covent Garden to a school concert in southwest London to an American lady whistler at Her Majesty's Theatre. His love for music and his energy in its pursuit were inexhaustible. He often attended two events an evening, sometimes leaving an opera halfway through to go on to a concert.

Corno was no respecter of reputations. He criticised the German Hans Richter, one of the most famous conductors of his era and first conductor of many of Wagner's operas, for performances before they had taken place. As Corno logically pointed out, 'If criticism is to have any effect on concerts, it must clearly be published before they come off.' He advised Richter to play a lot better than last year, admonishing him, 'I remember one scramble through the "Ride of the Valkyries" which would have disgraced a second-rate military band.' It would be interesting to know what Richter, the expert on Wagner, thought about this criticism.

He was equally blunt about a woman pianist who retired from playing when she married. 'I counted it as the first genuine artistic act in her career,' he commented. He was a little kinder when she returned to playing in public a few years later. The renowned violinist Joachim was described as 'making a sound after which an attempt to grate a nutmeg effectively on a boot sole would have been as the strain of an Aeolian harp'. But, though it sounded personal, it wasn't. He could also describe Joachim's playing of Beethoven as being 'as fine a piece of playing as any mortal has a right to expect'.

Sometimes he surprised with his praise. At a concert where a baritone solo of a song by Sir Arthur Sullivan turned out to be a duet with a crying baby in the audience, it would have been easy for Corno to have switched off. Instead he stayed with the performer and wrote, 'Great and deserved was the applause elicited by his fortitude and his artistic singing under exceptionally trying circumstances.'

Humour at his own expense was never far away. During one concert, a storm suddenly broke with such ferocity that everyone thought it might be an earthquake. Not many critics would have confessed, 'I refrained with difficulty from crawling under the seat.' And would anyone else have admitted that he went to one concert solely because the name of the performer, Adrienne Verity, appealed to him, or that he fell asleep during another?

Corno was disarmingly quick to admit to errors of judgement. On one occasion at a private gathering, he took pity on a quiet lady of about forty who was on her own and politely made conversation with her. At the end of the evening a hopeful call went out from the hosts asking if anyone would like to play the piano. When no one stepped up, the quiet lady offered to play. Corno was horrified and prepared himself for the worst. Patronisingly, he offered to turn the pages for her, expecting something banal like 'The Maiden's Prayer'. 'I felt I was being very good to her,' he says. Instead she played something she had written herself. After the first two bars he sat up. 'Has anyone ever told you that you are one of the greatest pianists in Europe?' he said to her naively at the end. Her reply was a put-down such as he rarely encountered in his life. 'It is my profession. Perhaps you will hear me at the Philharmonic. I am to play Beethoven's E flat Concerto there.' Her name was Agatha Ursula Backer-Grondahl, and Corno described her as: 'A great artist – a serious artist – a beautiful incomparable unique artist.'

He was not the sort of person to turn up his nose because a piece of music was popular. Responding emotionally to the stirring 'Hungarian March' from Berlioz's *The Damnation of Faust*, he said, 'I felt towards the end that if it were to last another minute I must charge out and capture Trafalgar Square single-handed.'

Given the number of musical events he attended, it was not surprising that Corno had his fair share of strange musical experiences, which he enjoyed passing on to his readership. On one occasion he went to hear Verdi's *Aida*. After beginning his review with the comment, '*Aida* filled the house at Covent Garden on Saturday quite as effectually as *Il Trovatore* emptied it earlier this week,' he moved on to the events of Act IV.

At the beginning of this act, the State barge containing Egyptian notables approaches the Temple of Isis along the Nile. Directing the craft in this production was an Egyptian oarsman, positioned on the prow. He brought the craft to a halt and the notables behind him exited onto dry land. This loss of ballast caused the prow to suddenly shoot up into the air, dislodging the oarsman, who flew out of the barge. Corno reported how the aria that followed 'was received with shrieks of laughter'.

At another concert he attended, a singer was hissed off the stage before he'd even sung a note, because the audience was worried there would not be time to hear the main attraction, the Belgian violin virtuoso Ysaÿe, play again. As for the lady whistler, he felt he could do better himself and dedicated part of the article to different techniques of whistling.

On 16 May 1890, Corno announced that he would no longer be writing for the *Star* or, as he expressed it, 'Friday will no longer be looked forward to in a hundred thousand households as the day of the Feast of Light.' Refused a raise from two guineas a week, he had decided to resign. He moved to another newspaper where he felt free to sign his columns, if not with the full majesty of George Bernard Shaw, at least with the famous initials.

SEVERAL STRINGS TO HIS BOW

ENNIO BOLOGNINI (1893–1979)

The gifted Argentinian cellist, Ennio Bolognini, had such a diverse range of interests that he has strong claims to be called the most multi-talented musician of all time. As well as being an exceptional cellist, he could box, wrestle, scull and fly stunts. He spoke many languages, including Hebrew, Greek, Japanese and Hungarian, and fifteen different Italian dialects. A habitual gambler, he had a formidable reputation as a ladies' man and was notorious for his short temper. His is a long way from the standard image of a string player, forever worried about protecting his hands. Sometimes his musical and non-musical interests overlapped in amusing ways.

Bolognini was born in Buenos Aires in 1893. His father was an amateur cellist and his mother a well-known opera singer. Toscanini, a friend of the family, was his godfather. At the age of fifteen, he won a cello as first prize in a cello contest and while still in his teens was so highly regarded that Saint-Saens and Richard Strauss were happy to be his piano accompanists in performances of their own music. In the summer of 1942 in Chicago, where he was playing for the NBC orchestra, he had gambled through the night and cleaned out the other players. His final opponent, desperate for a last hand to recoup his losses, had nothing to bet but his dog, a magnificent Great Dane. Bolognini agreed to the stake and won the hand, but was faced with a problem as he had to go straight to the local radio station to play. He had no choice but to take the dog with him and tied it to his chair leg while he played a piece by Massenet.

What happened next had all the elements of high farce. Startled by the strange sound, the dog took fright and began to pull the chair around the studio with Bolognini on it. The cellist was unconcerned and continued to play with consummate skill. The real problem belonged to the programme host, because the sound was getting weaker as Bolognini was dragged further and further from the studio microphone. Eventually he was forced to grab the microphone in a desperate attempt to keep up with the runaway chair.

Another overlap of his musical and non-musical interests involved flying. Bolognini flew his own private plane to a high level of skill. Before World War II he had helped found the American Civil Air Patrol and during the war trained pilots to fly B-29 bombers. He was once due to be the soloist at an outdoor performance at the Ravinia Festival, an amphitheatre near Chicago. The afternoon rehearsal did not go well, Bolognini had a row with the conductor and was either fired or stormed out. The evening concert went ahead as scheduled without him. As the performance took place, and much to the audience's annoyance, a plane appeared, drowning out the music. The audience waited for it to pass overhead, but it continued to circle low above the concert arena, completely disrupting the performance. It was Bolognini getting his revenge.

Eventually he landed in a nearby parking lot where he was arrested by police, though not without landing a few blows, another example of skills overlap. Before coming to the USA, he was a champion boxer who had left Argentina for New York to be Luis Firpo's sparring partner prior to his 1923 world heavyweight boxing championship fight with Jack Dempsey.

There is another Ravinia flying story, according to which Bolognini cut his engine while whistling the Siegfried horn call from Wagner's *The Ring*. The audience expected him to crash, but he restarted his engine and disappeared. Both stories are equally well attested and perhaps both are true. After a little acquaintance with Bolognini, one gets to feel that anything was possible.

Bolognini seems to have been a complete virtuoso. He was able to play violin concertos on the cello in the violin range and could play flamenco music using the cello as a guitar. By adding a sound box to the cello, he could imitate dive bombers, racing cars and bird calls. One winter evening, he and three colleagues, one of whom was a Russian singer, were due to give a concert in Waukegan, north of Chicago. Snow, which developed into a major storm, delayed the arrival of the singer, so that the rehearsal had to take place without him. He still hadn't arrived by the start of the performance and Bolognini kept deferring his numbers, hoping that he would arrive. Finally, the end of the programme was reached without sign of the Russian. Rather than omit the items, Bolognini asked the audience if they would like him to sing the songs. When they agreed, he sang them in Russian in a beautiful deep bass voice, accompanying himself on the piano from memory. In his memoirs, *An Orchestra Musician's Odyssey*, Milan Yancich, one of his colleagues that night, called it 'a feat of remarkable virtuosity and musicianship'.

The famous German conductor Hans Richter was another versatile musician. He could play every instrument in the orchestra, excepting only the harp, and once sang as an emergency soloist in a performance of Wagner's *Die Meistersinger*. But it is the relatively unknown Englishman John Liptrot Hatton (1809–86) who perhaps comes closest to matching Bolognini's range of abilities.

Hatton came from Liverpool and wore many musical hats as a composer of popular Victorian ballads, conductor, accomplished pianist and singer. He once incurred the wrath of *The Times*, which complained that he published songs under the name of Czapek instead of using his own perfectly good English name. *The Times* did not realise it was Hatton's little joke – *czapek* is Hungarian for 'hat on'.

Hatton's most remarkable achievement occurred one weekend in Boston, Massachusetts, where he was music director of the Handel and Haydn Society from 1848 to 1850. On the Saturday he was soloist in Mendelssohn's D minor Piano Concerto, following this by singing comic songs. The next day he was due to conduct the oratorio *Elijah*, but on arriving for the performance discovered that the bass due to sing the title role was ill. So Hatton/Czapek took over the part himself as well as conducting, turning round to face the audience for Elijah's numbers. Bolognini would have approved.

WAS THE CONDUCTOR DRUNK?

ST PETERSBURG, MARCH 1897

The orchestra and pianist play the thunderous last chord. The packed audience barely allows the sound to fade before beginning enthusiastic and long-lasting applause. The conductor and soloist exchange warm handshakes. Calls for the composer fill the air. A tall, lugubrious-looking figure advances to the platform and takes several bows.

This, or something like it, was the scene at the end of the first performance of Sergei Rachmaninov's enduringly popular Second Piano Concerto in Moscow in 1901. Today it is hard to imagine Rachmaninov's music being anything other than well received. Some of his most famous themes have featured in films such as *Brief Encounter* and *The Seven Year Itch*. The fiendishly difficult Third Piano Concerto was the central piece in the recent film *Shine*. *Rhapsody on a Theme of Paganini* is universally loved. But three years before the first performance of the Second Piano Concerto, it was a very different matter.

Rachmaninov, at 23, was one of the up-and-coming talents of Russian music. His career received a significant boost when he was commended by Tchaikovsky himself and his First Symphony, which had taken him two years to write, was accepted for performance by the highly influential St Petersburg conservatory. The event was an appalling experience for Rachmaninov. 'When the indescribable torture of the performance had at last come to an end,' he wrote afterwards, 'I was a different man.' The impact was so profound that it was some years before he could compose again.

The blame for this can be attributed to the symphony's first conductor, Alexander Glazunov, himself a distinguished composer. Problems began prior to the performance. Rehearsal time was inadequate as two other new works were also competing for Glazunov's attention. Worse, he seemed totally uninterested in the new symphony, standing motionless on the conductor's stand and waving the baton apathetically. Nothing Rachmaninov did could rouse him from his state of indifference. With such a lack of proper rehearsal, Rachmaninov feared a humiliating outcome and decided not to take his place in the auditorium for the performance. Instead he hid on a spiral staircase within earshot of the music but also handily placed for a quick exit should the worst happen.

The performance was indeed the disaster he had feared. Glazunov again conducted like a zombie. The result was cacophonous and all over the hall the audience reacted indignantly. Rachmaninov slipped out from his hiding place and fled into the street without taking a bow. His cousin Lyudmila was emphatic that it was Glazunov's fault – 'He wrecked it!' she wrote later – but it was Rachmaninov who got the blame. The following review gives an example of the critical lambasting he received:

> If there were a conservatory in Hell, and if one of its most talented students were asked to write a programmatic symphony about the Seven Plagues of Egypt, and if he were to compose a symphony such as the one written by Mr Rachmaninov, he would accomplish his task brilliantly, and give cause for great rejoicing among the inhabitants of Hell.

Rachmaninov could never work out why Glazunov, whom he regarded as a musician of great talent, had treated his music so shabbily. His wife was quite sure of the reason and said so: Glazunov had been drunk.

Distraught, Rachmaninov thought about destroying the score of the symphony but instead locked it in a desk in his study and never allowed it to be performed again. Shattered by the experience, his confidence totally destroyed, he decided to give up composing. Only the support of his family brought him through. They directed him to a Dr Nikolai Dahl, who specialised in hypnosis. Under Dahl's treatment, Rachmaninov started to compose again and after three years produced the famous Second Piano Concerto. One can imagine how intense his feelings were that triumphant evening in 1901. From that point he never looked back.

And had Glazunov really been drunk? The popular verdict is yes: he was known to warm up with shots of vodka before a performance. It is also possible he could have wanted the symphony to fail because it was too advanced for his taste.

However bitter the memory of that first performance, Rachmaninov never forgot his First Symphony. Over forty years later he included a wistful remembrance from it in his last work, the *Symphonic Dances*.

There is a happy ending though. The score that Rachmaninov locked in his desk disappeared after he moved to America. But two years after his death in 1943 the individual instrument parts were discovered in Leningrad. The missing score was re-created and 48 years after its disastrous first performance, the symphony's second performance was given in Moscow. It was a great success. Subsequently it received the greatest accolade of all: it was used as the introductory music for the BBC's current affairs programme *Panorama*.

A TIMELY DISAGREEMENT

MANCHESTER, NOVEMBER 1899

Who sets the tempo – the conductor or the soloist? It is one of the perennial conflicts in music. Usually it is not an insurmountable problem. The conductor is aware that the audience have come to hear the star soloist play his or her interpretation of a concerto and allows the necessary leeway. He knows that in the second half he can do what he likes with the symphony.

There is a bottom line, however. Conductors reserve the right not to be involved in anything they consider unmusical. If it reaches that stage, there are discussions and usually a compromise is negotiated. Very rarely, the conductor withdraws from the concert rather than be associated with a performance.

A problem of this nature arose in 1899 when the Spanish composer and violinist Pablo Sarasate was on one of his many concert tours of England. He was engaged to play the well-known Mendelssohn Violin Concerto with the Hallé Orchestra in Manchester under Hans Richter, who had just become permanent conductor.

Sarasate and Richter were pre-eminent in their respective fields. Violin works by Bruch, Saint-Saens, Lalo and Dvorak had been dedicated to Sarasate. Richter was closely associated with Richard Wagner and had been involved in the first performances of many of Wagner's operas.

In the audience, excited at going to his first real professional concert, was an eleven-year-old boy, already besotted by music and hoping for a musical career. When the lad got home, his father commented on his luck in hearing two such great artists as Richter and Sarasate. The boy agreed but added that one or two aspects of the concert had surprised him. 'What do you mean?' asked his father.

'Well, the violinist was playing in one tempo and the orchestra in another,' the young boy replied.

His father laughed and pooh-poohed the idea. This was Richter, Sarasate and the Hallé Orchestra after all! Rather than pursue his opinion and risk upsetting his father, the child let the matter drop.

The boy in question was the legendary Archie Camden (already encountered in 'Liebling, Look What They've Done to Our Tune!') who, by the end of a career spanning almost 65 years, was regarded as the foremost bassoonist of his era.

Years passed. Camden, who was also a talented pianist, was one day accompanying Arthur Catterall, leader of the Hallé, at a recital and began reminiscing about this incident. Catterall had played in the concert as a young man and remembered the circumstances very well.

At the rehearsal, he told Camden, Richter's tempo was too slow for Sarasate's liking, and at the first violin entry he doubled the speed. Inevitably there was chaos and the rehearsal ground to a halt. A confrontation followed between conductor and soloist, each insisting it was his right to set the tempo. Both were unyielding. In the heat of the argument, Sarasate threatened to go back to Spain, Richter to Germany.

James Forsyth, manager of the orchestra, tried to mediate. He begged them to reconsider for the sake of music. Neither would budge an inch. For the sake of their reputations? Under no circumstances. For the sake of the Hallé Concerts Society? Absolutely not: a principle was at stake. Well, what about the members of the orchestra, who would go hungry if the concert was cancelled?

This finally struck home. They would not place their fellow professionals in such a situation. Grudgingly they came to an agreement. When Sarasate was playing, the orchestra would play at his tempo; when playing on its own, at Richter's.

And this extraordinary, unmusical compromise is what

Camden had heard. As Arthur Catterall commented, he had not been so silly as his father had said.

Camden came to take up the bassoon as a result of a wonderful, creative accident with interesting links to this concert.

One Thursday, aged fifteen, he saw an advertisement offering a scholarship for a 'beginner on the bassoon' given by an anonymous 'Gentleman interested in the bassoon'. The examination was the following Monday. Camden had never even handled a bassoon, let alone played one. However, the idea appealed to him and he dashed out, borrowed an instrument and spent the intervening days trying to learn the rudiments, hiding his activities from his father whom he suspected would have disapproved.

The examiners were senior teachers from the Royal Manchester College of Music. When they asked him to play, he offered the only thing he could manage, a rising eight-note scale. They nodded gravely and asked him to play something else. This was something Camden hadn't foreseen and he was at a loss as he had already played his entire repertoire. All that came to mind was to play the same scale, only going down. But this was technically far trickier than he anticipated, and he ended up with a series of squawks, which caused a good deal of mirth among the examining board. In his very amusing autobiography, *Blow by Blow*, Camden adds, 'I also noticed that a screen placed across a corner of the room was rocking dangerously.' Despite this, his all-round musical ability was so evident that he won the scholarship.

He didn't find out the full story behind the scholarship until a few years later, though he often wondered about its donor. In 1910, when he was 21 and second bassoon at the Hallé, he received a better offer to become principal bassoon of a Glasgow orchestra and sadly prepared to resign. He told Richter, who expressed his regret. Camden hadn't yet signed the Glasgow contract when he was summoned to see the manager of the Hallé, James Forsyth. Forsyth wanted to tell him more of the circumstances behind the scholarship. He revealed that the donor was Hans Richter himself. Richter had become fed up with importing German bassoonists because there were no English players able to play the German version of the instrument. It had also been the portly Richter who had been hidden behind the dangerously rocking screen trying to stifle his laughter.

Camden was overcome. Realising what he owed Richter, he cancelled his plans to go to Glasgow. It was not long before he became principal bassoon of the Hallé anyway, when its existing principal became trapped in Austria on the outbreak of World War I.

In April 1962 in New York, serious tempo differences became apparent when Leonard Bernstein, conducting the New York Philharmonic, and Glenn Gould, the famously eccentric Canadian pianist, were rehearsing Brahms's First Piano Concerto. In this instance a different solution was found.

Bernstein, whose tempi were often considered very slow, found that Gould wanted to take an even slower speed, so slow that Bernstein felt it was unacceptable. Gould and Bernstein were still musically at odds when the time came for the concert. Bernstein could have withdrawn, but he respected Gould too much. He came up with a diplomatic, but highly unusual, compromise.

Taking his place on the rostrum, he must have surprised the audience by turning to address them. He explained that, in his view, the performance they were going to hear was – one can imagine him picking his word with extreme care – 'unorthodox', so unorthodox he felt he should mention it. In fact, he went on, there were great 'discrepancies' between him and the soloist. The audience must have been all ears, for it is virtually unheard of for behind-the-scenes wrangling to be made public.

Bernstein raised the question as to who is the boss in a concerto – the soloist or the conductor? He said that he had not come across this situation since – why, since the last time he had collaborated with Glenn Gould!

In this good-humoured atmosphere, the 'adventure', as Bernstein called it, went ahead at Gould's very slow tempi. The audience seemed to like it, but the critics were scathing. And the issue of who is the boss? That, like the 'chicken and egg' conundrum, remains to be settled.

THE MISSING SOPRANO

GLOUCESTER, SEPTEMBER 1904

Until it was superseded by *The Dream of Gerontius* by local hero Edward Elgar, Mendelssohn's oratorio *Elijah* had for many years the honour of beginning the Three Choirs Festival. The festival takes place in rotation in Gloucester, Worcester and Hereford cathedrals and is the oldest surviving music festival in Europe, dating back to the early years of the eighteenth century.

In 1904 it was Gloucester's turn to be host. The festival opened with *Elijah* and the principals included the three sopranos Mmes Emma Albani, Daisy Hicks Beach and Luisa Sobrino. *Elijah* is in two pj112
arts: in Part One, Sobrino was first soprano; in Part Two, which took place after the luncheon interval, Albani became first soprano and Sobrino second soprano. Hicks Beach was not required for the second half and was free to disappear.

When the soloists reassembled for Part Two after lunch, Sobrino, whose singing in Part One was described as 'rather painful', was absent. The conductor Herbert Brewer began anyway, while a search party went off to locate her, and also Daisy Hicks Beach, in case a replacement was needed. Hicks Beach could not be found, but Sobrino was traced to the Bell Hotel where she had gone to have lunch. It soon became clear to the search party that Sobrino had been lubricating her tonsils with a few glasses of wine, perhaps to give a better account of herself in the beautiful trio 'Lift Thine Eyes'.

Concerned that Sobrini might sing 'Lift Thine Glass' instead, the search party left her in the hotel. They hurried back to the cathedral, aware that 'Lift Thine Eyes' was fast approaching. Without Sobrino or Hicks Beach, they faced an embarrassing situation. Then they had a brainwave. In Part One, the small but important role of The Youth, whom Elijah sends to see if there is any rain in the offing, had been sung by one of the boy choristers. His name was Ivor Gurney, aged fourteen, and he had been recognised as outstandingly musical for some years.

Gurney was dragged out of the choir to sing second soprano. It was asking a lot of him. He would be singing unrehearsed and would have to hold his own against Mme Albani, a fixture at the festival since 1877. Known as the 'Queen of Song', Albani had several idiosyncrasies. When singing *Elijah*, she would quite often not come onto the platform until Part Two was about to begin. Then she would enter with her copy of the music tied in ribbon and hold up proceedings while she kneeled for a moment in prayer.

Gurney's mother proudly recorded that he coped with the pressure and sang well. His talent developed and he eventually studied at the Royal College of Music under Stanford, who described him as a young Schubert. Gurney developed into a fine composer of songs and also wrote poetry that is increasingly highly regarded. His later life was sad. Gassed and shell-shocked in World War I and unable to find work, he spent the last fifteen years of his life confined to a lunatic asylum. He died aged 47 in 1937.

Mme Sobrino made it out of the Bell Hotel in time to sing in the evening concert, though *The Times* commented that her high notes in Stanford's Te Deum 'have scarcely the ethereal purity so urgently required in the fine last phrase'. Perhaps she was still hung over.

111

CONDUCTING FOR THE DITHYRAMBIC

LEONARD CONSTANT LAMBERT (1905–51)

Composer, raconteur, alcoholic, Leonard Constant Lambert was born on 23 August 1905, and his many childhood illnesses, which included appendicitis, double mastoid and osteomyelitis, caused him to have eighteen operations. He had to take a quantity of morphia, and during childhood was put on a diet of champagne and burgundy.

Some observers attribute his later alcoholism to this. These experiences left him in continual pain, and he could never put either foot wholly to the ground, walking on his toes with a gait described by the painter Michael Ayrton as bird-hopping.

However, the long period of illness gave him time for reading, and his interest in music was formed very young. He was composing while still at school, writing a short operetta for a house concert when he was sixteen. The music master was horrified when Lambert requested to conduct the school orchestra, and made him a laughing stock over it. He won a composition scholarship to the Royal College of Music where he was taught composing by Ralph Vaughan Williams and conducting by Malcolm Sargent. His instrument was the viola, which is often regarded as less than mainstream.

The dancer, choreographer and entrepreneur Ninette de Valois noticed Lambert and influenced his appointment to conduct what became the Sadler's Wells Ballet. This followed exciting events surrounding the Diaghilev production of *Romeo and Juliet* to music written by Lambert at the young age of twenty.

The rehearsals took place in Monte Carlo, where Diaghilev sacked the original designers and brought in Joan Miró and Max Ernst, 'two tenth-rate painters from an imbecile group called the surrealists', Lambert said. Miró contributed a big blue disc to represent the moon, Ernst asked for two drop curtains, and Diaghilev wondered about abandoning décor altogether. Lambert had written the score for original choreography by Bronislava Nijinskaya, but Diaghilev interpreted it so liberally that Lambert tried unsuccessfully to withdraw the score. There were small riots in Monte Carlo and Paris, and finally also at the premiere in London, which brought useful notoriety, and the work was a success. When it reached London, the *Daily Telegraph* said of it, 'One would not be surprised to learn that to Mr Lambert the whole setting was antipathetic, that as a youngster he had done his bit, so to speak, in an operation over which he had no control'.

Constant Lambert also set poems to music, notably Sacheverell Sitwell's *Rio Grande* in 1928. (Lambert had himself been one of the speakers in *Façade* two years earlier.) But his main career was conducting. He was associate conductor of the Proms in 1945 and 1946. After the last night of the 1945 season he wrote to Michael Ayrton, 'rarely have spectators been so dithyrambic . . . You have possibly read of the wild orgy in which the conductors were pelted with flowers'.

Lambert's reputation with women was not always to his credit. His affair with the young ballerina Margot Fonteyn was supposed to lead to marriage but he stood her up at the registry office, becoming one of the first of a series of men who abused her in one way or another.

The alcohol consumption that had been a feature throughout his life – he said it had no perceptible influence on his work, but others disagreed – began to cause serious problems when Lambert was working on the rehearsals for Purcell's *The Fairy Queen*. He was drinking so much that he was nearly sacked. At the time he was sharing a flat in All Souls Place with Michael

Ayrton, who rallied the company behind him, and all of them threatened to stop work unless he was reinstated.

Other rescues began to be needed for the work of Constant Lambert to reach its public. Four composers had to be brought in to write the orchestration for the ballet *Tiresias*. (One of them, Alan Rawsthorne, later married Constant Lambert's widow, the painter and designer Isabel Lambert.) *Tiresias* was a disaster, and Lambert died at the age of 46 in 1951, the year of its production.

During the 1920s and 1930s, Lambert was also a music critic, with a reputation for sharpness. Of the Cello Concerto written by the pianist and musicologist Donald Tovey and played by Casals at a BBC concert in 1937 he wrote:

. . . I am told by those who had the moral, physical and intellectual stamina to sit it out to the end that Professor Donald Tovey's Cello Concerto lasts for over an hour. This I cannot vouch for as, like several other musicians, I was compelled to leave at the end of the first movement, which seemed to last as long as my first term at school . . .

Lambert lived in the boozy, shiftless bohemia of Fitzrovia, mixing in the Fitzroy Tavern with the arts elite of the day, and there is no doubt that his *bon viveur* reputation was to his detriment, despite the Fitzrovian imperative to behave volcanically.

FOLLOW MY LEADER

NORWICH, OCTOBER 1911

There are certain fortunate musicians who find playing or composing as natural as breathing. The French composer Camille Saint-Saens said that he wrote music as easily as an apple tree grew apples. The Belgian violinist Eugène Ysaÿe, regarded as one of the greatest violinists of his time, commented about himself that he 'played the fiddle as the birds sing'.

A secure memory is a professional necessity for soloists and several stories testify to Ysaÿe's excellence in that area. In 1896, he was due to give the first performance of the French composer Chausson's *Poème*, which was dedicated to him. Beforehand, he played it through once with a pianist, studied the score during a train journey and had one orchestral rehearsal. Such limited preparation was enough to allow him to play from memory and give a perfect performance.

Another first performance of a piece of music dedicated to Ysaÿe took place in more unusual circumstances. A few days prior to Ysaÿe's marriage to Louise Bordeau in September 1886, a celebration banquet was held in Luxembourg attended by friends, including many musicians. At the end, Ysaÿe was presented with a very special wedding gift on behalf of the composer César Franck. It was the score of his Violin Sonata, now part of many violinists' repertoire. Ysaÿe was so excited that he wanted to play it there and then and asked the pianist Léontine Bordes-Pène to accompany him. As Margaret Campbell records in *The Great Violinists*,

'The two proceeded to sight-read the sonata and moved the guests to tears.'

Three months later, the pair gave the first public performance of the sonata in the Musée Moderne de Peinture in Brussels. The concert was running late and by the time Ysaÿe and Bordes-Pène began to play it was growing dark. No artificial lighting was allowed in the museum and it soon grew too dark to read the score by natural light. But it took more than that to faze such accomplished musicians. They were able to finish the performance by playing from memory, despite their limited acquaintance with the work.

But there was one occasion when Ysaÿe's memory failed him catastrophically. At the 1911 Norwich Festival, he was performing the Beethoven Violin Concerto, which he had played on countless occasions. Sir Henry Wood was the conductor and he became increasingly concerned as Ysaÿe faltered badly in the slow movement, hardly able to remember the next note. In fact it was going so disastrously that Wood wasn't sure whether the performance could continue.

The leader of the orchestra, Maurice Sons, saved the situation. He led Ysaÿe through the rest of the performance by playing the soloist's part softly enough for Ysaÿe, but not the audience, to hear. Ysaÿe managed to complete the performance, but Wood said later that it was 'easily the worst I ever directed'.

It is probably true that all soloists suffer memory lapses from time to time. But Ysaÿe was unique in being given such a fortunate solution.

ASSAULT AT THE OPERA

HAMBURG, DECEMBER 1912

By the end of his long life in 1973, the German conductor Otto Klemperer had undoubtedly achieved the status of living legend. Klemperer's Beethoven, or Brahms, or Mahler, were trademark renditions. You knew they would be austere, monumental performances that felt as if they were carved out of rock.

By then Klemperer was a physical wreck. His face was twisted into a permanent scowl, the result of a brain tumour operation, which also hampered movement on the whole of his right side. To attend his concerts, as I did on two occasions, was to be filled with wonder how this crippled giant would ever reach the podium, let alone conduct Mahler's Second Symphony, an hour and a half long.

His was an extraordinary history, the key to which lay in his manic-depressive mood swings, probably inherited from his mother. Throughout his life he acted in bizarre and unpredictable ways. His behaviour was sometimes so extreme that he only just escaped incarceration in a mental institution, and from time to time he entered remedial clinics voluntarily. His escapades often brought unwelcome publicity. The *New York Times* once reported, 'Klemperer gone: sought as insane'. A typical example of his strange behaviour happened early in his career.

In August 1910, aged 25, he began work at the Stadttheater in Hamburg, personally recommended by the composer and conductor Gustav Mahler, probably the most influential musical figure of his time. He soon won glowing praise. One review described him as 'a musician of the utmost sensibility, of thrilling temperament and natural dramatic instinct . . .'

An outstanding future was predicted. But that did not take into account his volatile mental state. Although he appeared an imposing, confident figure, when Klemperer was depressed he lacked self-belief and worried about failure, to the extent that he considered giving up music to become a bookseller. When he was hypermanic, the consequences, as will be seen, could be startling.

The theatre staff included two promising young sopranos, Elizabeth Schumann and Lotte Lehmann. Both later became world-famous singers but at this time they were still making their way in opera. Lehmann fell instantly in love with the new conductor, but Klemperer wasn't interested. He was drawn to Schumann. A charming picture of her as Susanna in *The Marriage of Figaro* shows how attractive she was.

Preoccupied with his new post, or maybe in the down cycle of his illness, Klemperer did not pursue an interest in Schumann during that first season in 1910. Two years passed, during which there were two developments. Schumann married a young Hamburg architect, Walther Puritz, and Klemperer's depression lifted. He now felt buoyant and elated. In this mood, he also felt sexually very alive.

Matters came to a head during rehearsals for *Der Rosenkavalier*. There were many intimate, private rehearsals as Klemperer coached Schumann in the role of Oktavian. Oktavian is a passionate young man in love first with the mature Marschallin and then with the young, beautiful Sophie. No doubt it became necessary to rehearse the physical as well as the vocal side of the role. Fingers entwined, lips met, all in the name of art. Richard Strauss's luscious music was an irresistible invitation to fall in love, and they did.

Despite all the rehearsals, Schumann's Oktavian was not well received at the first and, as it turned out, last night of that particular production on 28 November 1912. Her voice was thought to be too girlish, her personality not strong enough to sustain the illusion that she was a boy. The next night she went to hear Lehmann's debut as Elsa in *Lohengrin*. Afterwards she was due to meet her husband and friends for supper. But she never turned up. When her husband went home to look for her, the maid tearfully told him the astounding news that his wife had eloped with Klemperer.

A week later the couple reappeared in Hamburg. Puritz challenged Klemperer to a duel with pistols. Klemperer was not keen and declined. Fearing Puritz's anger, he kept a low profile and took to travelling in cabs with the blinds drawn. He even cancelled a performance of *Il Trovatore* at short notice.

Puritz was determined to satisfy his honour and waited until Klemperer conducted *Lohengrin* again on 26 December. After the second interval, Schumann, who was in a box, noticed that her husband and his friends had moved to some empty seats in the front row of the stalls immediately behind the conductor. It was clear something was being planned. She tried to attract Klemperer's attention to warn him but without success. Puritz waited until almost the end of the opera before he acted. Rising from his seat, he leaned across the orchestra pit and struck Klemperer twice on the face with a riding crop. Klemperer fell into the pit and tried to retaliate but was prevented by friends who led him away.

Lawyers became involved; statements were issued. Klemperer hotly denied any physical impropriety with Schumann. Unlikely though it seems, that might have been the truth, for years later Schumann swore that they only became lovers subsequent to that evening.

Life now became hard for Klemperer and Schumann. Both lost their jobs and could not get new ones as Puritz warned off all potential employers. They fled from Germany to Vienna, then to Prague, and eventually to the sanatorium where Klemperer sometimes went for treatment for his illness.

Perhaps the clinic triggered off something in Klemperer, or perhaps he had been elated too long and it was time for the cycle to change. His euphoria waned. As it did, the full extent of their unemployable predicament became apparent and his depression returned. This in turn caused his feelings for Schumann to diminish until, by early March, barely three months from their first elopement, he was totally out of love with her.

Unwilling to confront her with the bad news himself, he persuaded the owner of the sanatorium to do so. The abandoned Schumann had few options and chose to return to her husband. She bore Klemperer no long-term bitterness. On her deathbed in 1952, she spoke to him on the telephone. When the call was finished, she remarked to a friend that he had been one of the great loves of her life.

NOT ALL RITE ON THE NIGHT

PARIS, MAY 1913

The first tumultuous performance of Igor Stravinsky's *The Rite of Spring* has passed into legend. English-speaking wits called it 'the Riot of Spring'. French journalists called it not *Le Sacre du Printemps* but 'Le Massacre du Printemps'.

The Rite was the third of nine ballets that Stravinsky wrote for the Russian impresario Diaghilev's Ballets Russes. The first of these was *The Firebird*, composed in 1910, which was such a success that Stravinsky became Diaghilev's composer of choice, though he was far from being Diaghilev's original preference. Three other composers had all let him down for one reason or another before, almost in desperation, he had turned to Stravinsky.

Petrouchka followed in 1911 with *The Rite of Spring* planned for the following year. Stravinsky told how the germ of inspiration for *The Rite* came when he was finishing *The Firebird*. 'I saw in my imagination a solemn pagan rite. Sage elders, seated in a circle, watched a young girl dance herself to death. They were sacrificing her to propitiate the God of Spring. I heard and I wrote what I heard. I am the vessel through which *Le Sacre* passed.'

The 39-year-old Frenchman Pierre Monteux, regular conductor of Ballets Russes, was to conduct the premiere. Stravinsky played through the score for him on the piano. 'Before he got very far I was convinced he was raving mad,' Monteux said later. 'The very walls resounded as Stravinsky pounded away, occasionally stamping his feet and jumping up and down to accentuate the force of the music.' Monteux anticipated trouble from the critics and conservative audiences.

When rehearsals began, it was found that the music and choreography were too difficult and additional rehearsals would be needed. *The Rite* was postponed for a year and replaced by Ravel's *Daphnis and Chloe*. Finally, in May 1913, the first night arrived. When the ballet started, the fashionable audience was taken aback. It knew what ballet was and it certainly wasn't the grotesque shapes those young women were making. It had also grown accustomed to the ravishing tones of Ravel and the Chopinesque lyricism of *Les Sylphides*, and very much disliked Stravinsky's dissonant and crude, jagged rhythms. It had already heard the melodious *Les Sylphides* that evening, ironically enough in an orchestration by Stravinsky done at Diaghilev's request.

Soon the theatre was in uproar. Fighting broke out, insults were hurled. The police were called but didn't arrive until the interval. The din made it impossible for the dancers to hear the orchestra. In the wings Nijinsky, the choreographer, stood on a chair shouting out numbers to keep them in time. Diaghilev turned the lights off and on to restore order. Stravinsky rose from his seat in the stalls and went backstage, disgusted. Somehow or other, dancers, conductor and musicians managed to carry the piece through to the end. Amid applause and protests, Stravinsky, Monteux and the other principals took curtain calls. There has been no musical scandal to match it before or since.

Over the years, ears became attuned to the dissonances and wild rhythms that so stunned the first-night Parisian audience. *The Rite* has long been accepted as a masterpiece. It became so accessible it even featured in Walt Disney's *Fantasia*. In 1963, inspired by the happy chance that its principal conductor was none other than Pierre Monteux, the London Symphony Orchestra decided to give a concert performance of *The Rite* fifty years to the day from its first performance. Monteux was 89 at the time, and two years earlier, he had signed a 25-year contract with the orchestra, playfully insisting on a 25-year option as well. The occasion would have been incomplete without the presence of the composer and Stravinsky was invited. At first he declined the invitation, then changed his mind, arriving late.

According to *Orchestra*, the history of the LSO by Richard Morrison, the performance is best forgotten. Monteux hadn't conducted the work for twenty years. 'He didn't like the piece,' said Barry Tuckwell, then the LSO's chairman and principal horn player, adding, 'he was actually sick of it.' Monteux also brought along his own orchestral parts. They were significantly different from the orchestra's regular parts, and were difficult to read as they were covered in cigarette burns and stains, so the orchestra decided to revert to their own familiar parts. 'The performance was nearly a train wreck,' said Tuckwell.

But that was almost incidental. The key to the evening's success was the presence of *The Rite*'s composer and first conductor. The audience went wild at the end. Monteux gestured towards Stravinsky, inviting him to take the applause. All eyes turned to the box where the composer was sitting. He rose and acknowledged the crowd with a benign smile.

Monteux was not finished yet. Despite his great age, he set off to climb the steps to Stravinsky's box to add his personal congratulations. Madame Monteux, worried he might fall, asked one of the LSO's players not involved in the performance to go with him. 'But he was leaping up the steps almost two at a time,' says Ossian Ellis in Morrison's account, 'and I had great difficulty keeping up with him.'

Beneath his smile, Stravinsky was far from happy. He made derogatory comments under his breath about the performance, which dismayed his companion in the box, Ernest Fleischmann, the LSO's general secretary. The audience would surely have been equally as dismayed. It was ungenerous behaviour towards a man who had gone to the trouble of relearning a piece he no longer much cared for solely to honour its great composer.

MAD ABOUT THE BEAT

MANCHESTER, SEPTEMBER 1932

Words and Music is a revue by the legendary playwright/
performer/actor Noël Coward. Produced in 1932, it contains
two songs that have lasted: 'Mad About the Boy' and 'Mad
Dogs and Englishmen'. Despite them, Coward thought it was
not 'quite as good as it should have been'.

It opened in Manchester in late August before transferring to
London. During the show's three weeks in the north, the
musical director became ill, and Coward decided to conduct
the orchestra himself. Noël Coward, though an accomplished
writer of light musical ditties for theatregoers, was not a trained
musician. By his own admission he had only one key in which
he felt confident. This was not, as might be expected, C major
– 'the only key on the piano that has none of those tiresome
black notes in it' – but E flat. The Master did not explain why.

Coward wrote that a conductor 'must be able to recognise
accurately every confusing little squiggle on the manuscript and
issue instructions to his instrumentalists in the complicated
jargon that they alone can understand', and he admitted that he
could not do this. Before taking up the baton for the overture
to *Words and Music*, therefore, he put in two hours of musical
rehearsal with a lady called Elsie April in his suite at the
Midland Hotel, Manchester. Then they set off for the theatre,
where Miss April kindly positioned herself in the orchestra pit,
somehow wedging herself so she was facing him and at his feet.
When Coward took his place on the podium, 'the front-of-
house limelight operator, whom I could willingly have

garrotted, flung a dazzling pink and amber spotlight onto me and I was forced to acknowledge a cheerful round of applause.'

'God Save the King' took him by surprise. He raised his arms to conduct the anticipated start of the overture and heard a loud roll on the drums. Elsie whispered that it was the national anthem. 'Just a straight four-four all through,' she confided from the pit. 'Take it nice and slowly.' During the overture she whispered, 'That's right, dear – just go on like that for thirty-two bars – look out, here comes a modulation into three-four – that's right, you're doing fine, nothing to worry about now until you get to the six-eight, just two in a bar, dear, nice and steady.' And so on throughout the performance.

Coward recalled in his autobiography, 'Those were two of the most alarming and enjoyable hours I have ever spent. The next morning I was unable to move my right arm, but after having it massaged several times during the day I was able to conduct the show again in the evening. I conducted every performance for two weeks.' He did not record whether Elsie April, who after all was central to the whole exploit, stayed with him for the fortnight. He only recorded sorrowfully that at the end of this interlude, 'I was forced to relinquish that lovely little white stick with the knob on the end.'

A SPANNER IN THE WORK

TORONTO, DECEMBER 1937

The third of the Toronto Symphony Orchestra's (TSO) Christmas Box Symphony concerts in Massey Hall was unusual for a number of reasons. Although there was plenty to heighten the Christmas mood, the conductor Sir Ernest MacMillan also included a piece from a country that was officially atheist.

The Iron Foundry was written by the modernist Russian composer Alexander Mosolov. It was popular enough to have been performed at the Last Night of the Proms in 1932, and was obviously a favourite of MacMillan's, who had played it at a TSO concert the previous year.

Written in the 1920s in the spirit of socialist realism fashionable at the time in the Soviet Union, it went to great pains to recreate the noise of heavy machinery at work. Other pieces in this genre included *A Power Station on the Dnieper* by Meytus, which celebrated a new hydroelectric dam, and *Symphony of Factory Sirens* by Avraamov, reportedly so loud that it could be heard over vast stretches of Azerbaijan.

Mosolov's piece, part of a lost ballet, *Steel*, was more modest in scope. Though lasting only four minutes, its sound effects were on a grand scale and included using a large piece of sheet iron to re-create the effect of clashing iron and steel. Despite its brevity, the TSO and its conductor went to considerable trouble to capture the spirit of the piece. MacMillan appeared on the platform dressed in overalls and conducted with that most proletarian of instruments, a monkey wrench. In keeping

126

with the Soviet work ethic, the orchestra did not leave its workplace during the interval but stayed and ate sandwiches from lunch-buckets.

Mosolov's future was less amusing. In the late 1930s, the modernist movement fell out of favour with Stalin. Some composers were executed. Mosolov was sentenced to eight years' hard labour but, thanks to the intervention of his fellow composer Glière, served only one.

Heavy realism and programmatic music have also fallen out of favour with audiences. Honegger's *Pacific 231*, which recreates a heavy locomotive on the move, has only occasional excursions today. Another Honegger piece, *Rugby*, has long since been kicked into touch by programme compilers.

Richard Strauss wrote a good deal of programmatic music. He prided himself on being able to reproduce any sound in music, no matter how trivial or domestic, such as teaspoons in the *Domestic Symphony*. His *Alpine Symphony* is a detailed description in 22 sections of typical alpine incidents with titles such as 'The Ascent Begins' and 'Moments of Danger'. One moment of danger Strauss was probably not expecting occurred when he was conducting the symphony in London in November 1926. He had reached the noisiest part of the piece, the outbreak of the storm, when the thunder machine, there to provide the climactic effect, toppled slowly over and crashed into the middle of the orchestra below.

The TSO's Christmas Box concerts continued to be original and entertaining for many years, with turns such as the Sumvak Sisters. The 'sisters' were Elie Spivak and Harold Sumberg, who dressed up in a large gown as if Siamese twins, and played on a single violin, one fingering, the other bowing.

The concerts came to an end shortly after MacMillan's resignation in 1956, though the TSO has not lost its taste for the unusual. In 2004 it performed a programme complete with jugglers, which they called *The Flying Karamazov Brothers*, and published a cookbook.

Wrenches have not been entirely lost to music either. *Adjustable Wrench* is the work of a contemporary composer with the appropriately mechanistic name of Michael Torke.

THE FRUSTRATED CELLIST

LONDON, JUNE 1939

The thought must have passed through the mind of many opera- or balletgoers as they enjoy a performance: what must it be like for the poor orchestral players hidden away in the pit? They provide the beautiful music but never see any of the action going on just a few feet above their heads. Great singers and dancers come and go, appearing in highly acclaimed productions, but the indispensable players rarely get a glimpse of their performing magic.

It was a thought that certainly occurred to Anthony Pini during the visit of the Covent Garden Russian Ballet to London in 1939. He was principal cellist of the London Philharmonic, the accompanying orchestra for the season. Stuck away in semi-darkness, he became increasingly frustrated during the opening week. He heard enthusiastic comments about the wonderful performances of Anton Dolin, Lichine and Baronova. There were mouthwatering reports of the enchanting corps de ballet. But no matter how hard he twisted his neck, he was unable to see anything.

Pini took this as a challenge and did some lateral thinking. He was an active cyclist and came up with what he thought was an excellent solution. Removing the side mirror from his cycle, he took it in to Covent Garden. After a bit of trial and error, he was able to attach it to his music stand at an angle that gave him an excellent view of all the artistic delights he had been missing.

His enjoyment of the next performance was as enhanced as he had hoped. But an eagle-eyed high-up in the Royal Opera

House management spotted his hardware addition. No doubt others noticed it too. Most probably saw the funny side of it, but the suit took exception, and reported Pini. The ROH could have simply suggested that he remove the contraption, but it took a hard line and immediately fired him.

It was the LPO's loss. Pini was one of the finest cellists of his generation. At fifteen he had applied for a position with the Scottish Orchestra, but his application had been rejected by Sir Landon Ronald on the unusual grounds that he was too talented. He had been principal cellist with the LPO since he was thirty, a very young age for such an important post. The incident did not harm his career as the BBC Symphony Orchestra soon snapped him up. Much later he returned to the Royal Opera House as principal cellist of the orchestra. It is not known whether there was a 'no wing mirror' clause in his contract.

ALEXANDER'S SAD TIME GRAND

NEW YORK, JANUARY 1940

The demanding piano recital that Alexander Kelberine gave at the Town Hall, New York on 27 January 1940 included two pieces by Bach and one by Beethoven. Nothing too startling there. All three works were in so-called 'sad' minor keys, which perhaps lacked variety, but was not that uncommon.

Alert listeners might have pricked up their ears when the pianist also played Liszt's *Bénédiction de Dieu dans la Solitude* and *Consolation*. Three works in minor keys, solitude, consolation – was there a subtext?

For his grand finale, Kelberine played Liszt's massive *Todtentanz* (Dance of Death), based on the Latin *Dies Irae* plainsong tune. During the recital he had gone from sadness to solitude to death. What did it all mean?

Whether the audience felt its spirits falling as it sat and listened, we will never know. The critic of the *New York Times* did not seem unduly affected. In his review the following day he was concerned with musical values only, commenting that the programme was difficult and weighty, and complimenting Kelberine on his 'wide range of dynamics' and 'kaleidoscopic variety of colour effects'. A few technical slips were referred to, as well as an 'extremely eccentric rhapsodic method of treatment'. It was a standard if mixed review of its type. He didn't look behind the programme at its content, comment on its emotional similarity or wonder whether the strange choice of music carried a hidden message.

The concert finished, Kelberine went back to his apartment. When the caretaker of the building did not see him around for three days, he became anxious and called the police, who broke into the apartment. They found the pianist dead in his pyjamas. He was 35 years old, apparently living apart from his wife, and had died from a drug overdose. A suicide note addressed to a friend was found. He appeared to have been depressed for some time.

Kelberine was a well-known pianist and minor composer, particularly praised for his interpretations and transcriptions of Bach and Respighi. Recordings of his playing and compositions still exist, and include his transcription of Bach's *Komm, Susser Tod* – Come Sweet Death.

THE DAME WHO DEFIED
THE BOMBS

LONDON, OCTOBER 1940

As soon as World War II started, the British Government banned large meetings for safety reasons and introduced the blackout. With theatres, cinemas and concert halls closed, Myra Hess, aged fifty and a concert pianist of international reputation, felt that a cultural blackout had also been imposed. Living in London, she was convinced that music had an important part to play as people sought relief from the stresses and disruption of war. The BBC was doing little to fill the gap, broadcasting a mixture of government emergency orders, recorded music and Sandy MacPherson at the theatre organ. Dire indeed, and she wrote a trenchant letter to the BBC's director-general to complain. Taking the initiative herself, she decided to introduce chamber music concerts to Londoners, something she had long wanted to do.

She began to make plans in detail. Because of the blackout restrictions, the concerts couldn't take place in the evening, but lunchtime was convenient for many people. But where to hold them? A friend mentioned the National Gallery, home of the national art collection. Hess thought she was joking and retorted, 'Or why not St Paul's, or Buckingham Palace?'

But it was not such a bad suggestion. The Gallery, with its pictures removed for safekeeping, lay depressingly empty and without a role. When Sir Kenneth Clark, its director, was approached, he was enthusiastic and obtained the consent of the trustees. But there were other difficulties to overcome. The permission of the Home Office and the Office of Works was needed, and they also had to agree to waive the ban on concerts. Exemption from entertainment tax had to be obtained from Customs and Excise, and so on. The bureaucracy could take months.

Committees were set up to deal with the many issues. Was there a big enough room with adequate acoustics? Yes, the octagonal room on the second floor under the glass dome. What time would the concerts take place? One o'clock (later changed to one-thirty), with repeat performances on Tuesday and Thursday afternoons. Ticket price? As low as possible – one shilling. Payments to musicians? A small flat fee. Profits (if any)? To the Musicians' Benevolent Fund. Tone? Informal. No booking. People could walk in and out between movements, or stroll around in the adjoining galleries, or lounge on the floor and listen.

Such was the will to go ahead that, amazingly, on 10 October 1939, only a month or so after the idea had been mooted, the first of the daily lunch-hour concerts took place.

Expecting no more than a small group of friends to turn up, Hess played the first concert herself rather than ask another artist in order to avoid embarrassment in case it flopped. She need not have worried. One thousand people queued around the block and filed in to occupy a space intended for four hundred.

During the war, the National Gallery was an easy target for enemy bombers and was hit on several occasions. In one period of the Blitz, when London was bombed for 57 consecutive nights, each day Hess wondered what she would find as she turned into Trafalgar Square. Would there still be a concert room (or even a National Gallery)? Or an audience? As she trudged through the rubble and glass after one raid, she was convinced there would be only a small audience. Over five hundred attended.

An eight-day period in mid-October 1940, when the building was hit four times, was particularly difficult. On 15 October a time bomb struck and no concert was permitted. Hess was determined that the continuity should not be broken, which it never was, and arranged for the recital to take place in nearby South Africa House, the only occasion when the concert did not take place in the Gallery. Only three days later, a thousand-pound unexploded bomb was discovered. But 214 people still attended the concert. The climax came on 23 October when it was announced that another time bomb had fallen on the Gallery. Don't worry, the audience was advised, a bomb disposal unit had arrived. Even if the bomb went off, the blast would go in the opposite direction. So 251 people stayed to listen to hear the Stratton Quartet perform Beethoven. Faithful to the traditions of the British working man, the bomb disposal unit took an hour's lunch break, roughly coinciding with the concert. So the unit wasn't around at one-thirty when the bomb went off with an almighty explosion. Though shaken, the audience refused to be frightened off, and the Stratton Quartet, said Hess, 'continued playing . . . missing neither note nor nuance'. At various times enemy action forced the recitals downstairs to the well-protected, though leaky, basement shelter or to a more remote part of the building.

The Blitz came to an end on 11 May 1941, and the recitals returned to their original site under the dome. They remained there until the arrival of the flying bombs in 1944, which drove them once again to the basement shelter.

On 21 July 1944, Hess was playing Schubert's B flat Impromptu when she heard an unmistakable sound. It was a V-1 flying bomb, a pilotless aeroplane that flew at high altitudes and descended so quickly that there was no warning of its target, just an enormous, destructive explosion. Hess decided to do battle with it, or at least with its disruptive noise.

Though she should have been playing piano (softly), she conjured up a tremendous crescendo, so loud it completely masked the increasing noise of the bomb. When she judged the danger had passed, she reduced the volume to piano again – though by now she should have been playing forte (loudly). The recital continued, the audience unaware of her inauthentic interpolations.

To Hess's bitter disappointment, the concerts finished on 10 April 1946 after exactly six and a half years and an unbroken run of 1,698 concerts, of which she had played in 146. For organising them and her contribution to national morale, she had been made a DBE (Dame of the British Empire) in 1941.

During the war the Luftwaffe had presented the most obvious obstacles for the concerts, but it was other enemy activities that were indirectly responsible for resolving a typically British dispute.

The nearby church of St Martin-in-the-Fields always rang its bells for five minutes each afternoon at 1.25, which happened to fall in the middle of the concert. The clangour forced the musicians to stop playing. When approached, the vicar could see the problem but did not feel that musical priorities were more important than calling people to prayer. He offered to reduce the ringing to three minutes, but this was of no real help as it proved impossible for the concert intervals to coincide with exactly those moments.

Hess was inadvertently rescued by the Germans. Having taken France in June 1940, they were expected to invade the British Isles at any time. The government announced that the ringing of church bells would signal enemy landings, and bell-ringing for any other purpose was declared illegal. The bells of St Martin-in-the-Fields were silenced. Dame Myra would ordinarily have nothing good to say about Hitler, but she might have been grateful to him on that one occasion.

THE CAMP WHERE TIME ENDED

GORLITZ, SILESIA, JANUARY 1941

It is six o'clock on the evening of 15 January 1941. The place is Stalag VIIIA, a prison camp for 30,000 mainly French prisoners of war in Gorlitz, a small town in Silesia (now in Poland). The temperature is twenty below freezing. In one of the huts, four of the inmates are about to give the first performance of a piece of music that one of them, Olivier Messiaen, has composed.

Gathered to hear them is an audience of four hundred officers, guards and prisoners. The piece has been written for the only instruments available, the rare combination of violin, clarinet, cello and piano. 'The cold was excruciating,' Messiaen described later. 'The Stalag was buried under snow. The four performers played on broken-down instruments. The cello had only three strings, the keys on the piano went down but did not come up again.'

In these circumstances and with these meagre resources, *Quartet for the End of Time*, one of the acknowledged masterpieces of twentieth-century music, was first performed.

Messiaen, aged 32, was a gifted French musician who had won many prizes as an organist, pianist and composer before the war. He had been conscripted on the outbreak of war but was unfit for active service due to poor eyesight and became a medical orderly. Soon he met a cellist, Etienne Pasquier, and a clarinettist, Henri Akoka. In June 1940 the three of them were captured and imprisoned in Gorlitz. On entering the camp, Messiaen managed to retain several favourite scores, refusing to relinquish them even when threatened with a gun. Akoka also kept possession of his clarinet, which he took everywhere, the only personal instrument in the camp.

Their lives in the camp were made easier because German officers respected musicians. They called Messiaen 'the French Mozart' and he was encouraged to compose. He was even assigned to the quiet early-morning watch so he could have time to reflect on the music he was writing. One officer, Hauptmann Brull, who was helpful to many prisoners, obtained pencils, erasers and manuscript paper for him, as well as extra bread.

Just before his capture, Messiaen had written a short piece, 'The Abyss of Birds', based on birdsong, and this became one of the movements of the quartet he was beginning to compose. Using the latrines as his workroom, he added a further seven sections over the next few months. The total of eight movements, according to Messiaen, a devout Roman Catholic, represented the six days of creation, the Sabbath and eternity. The title came from the vision of the Apocalypse in the Book of Revelations: 'And (the Angel) swore by him who liveth for ever and ever saying, "There shall be time no longer".'

With the arrival of Jean Le Boulaire, a violinist who had known Messiaen in their Paris conservatoire days, the group had grown to four. However, they still had only one instrument between them, Akoka's clarinet. It was the camp's commandant who came to their aid, allowing Pasquier to go into Gorlitz under escort to buy a cello, bow and rosin. They also obtained a violin. This enabled them to begin rehearsing, but only those movements not needing a piano. Eventually a broken-down piano was found and the quartet of players and instruments was complete.

They rehearsed the complex, demanding music four hours a day for two months in the camp theatre, a barracks set aside for activities such as plays, concerts and films. Hauptmann Brull provided wood to warm the barracks and thaw out the musicians' fingers.

The performance almost never took place. Akoka was intent on trying to escape, though he could never persuade Messiaen to join him. On one occasion, he managed to go 350 miles before being recaptured only thirteen miles from the Czech border. On his return to Gorlitz, he charmed the commandant with a little jaunty playing on his clarinet, and was handed a relatively light punishment. Discipline in the camp was not always that relaxed: some inmates were executed for stealing three potatoes.

The date for the first performance was fixed for a Wednesday, so that it did not clash with other entertainment activities usually held on a Saturday. The commandant thought the occasion was so significant that he instructed that programmes should be printed. They were used as tickets and demand was very great.

On the evening of the performance the camp was under sixteen to twenty inches of snow and it was desperately cold. Warmth in the hut was provided mainly by the body heat of the audience. Messiaen gave a short lecture to introduce the work, then the performance, which lasted about an hour, began. Drawing on birdsong, plainchant and Hindu rhythms among other influences, it created a world of sound totally new to everyone there. 'Everyone listened reverently,' said an observer. At the end there was 'an awkward silence', and then hesitant applause began. For many, the sheer fact of the performance was enough, 'an act of revenge' against their captivity.

Several myths have grown up about the evening. Messiaen always said there was an audience of five thousand, though the barracks could not have held more than four hundred. And the cello did not have three strings as he described, but the regulation four. Pasquier, who should have known, said, 'The part was impossible to play on three strings.'

The performance changed the lives of the musicians. Within a month the Germans liberated Messiaen, Pasquier and Akoka on the grounds that they were musicians and noncombatants, though this wasn't strictly the case. Le Boulaire was not released though he later escaped; Akoka was pulled off the train at the last minute because he was Jewish. Undaunted, he later escaped to Marseilles in the Free Zone – with his clarinet, of course.

Later that year, Messiaen returned to teaching and composition in Paris, subsequently influencing many important musicians. *Quartet for the End of Time* is regularly played today and has been described as 'the most significant piece of music to come out of World War Two'. Messiaen died in 1992. Of the quartet's first performance that bitterly cold night in Gorlitz he once said, 'Never have I had an audience who listened with such rapt attention and comprehension.'

A MATTER OF LIFE AND DEATH

AUSCHWITZ-BIRKENAU CONCENTRATION CAMP, POLAND, FEBRUARY 1944

Musicians always take concerts seriously but they are unlikely to treat each one as a matter of life and death. For the women's orchestra in Birkenau it was very different. Its members lived and played in constant fear that an unpleasing performance would lead to the gas chambers.

This fear was heightened even more in February 1944 when it became known that a very high-ranking Nazi official, as yet unnamed, would be touring the camp. His itinerary would include a visit to the music block, where the orchestra would be expected to play for him.

The orchestra had been formed the previous year by Maria Mandel, *SS-Oberaufseherin* of the women's camp at Birkenau. Sadistically brutal, Mandel, who was executed as a war criminal in 1947, had a great fondness for music. She hoped that organising an orchestra, similar to the men's orchestras in both Auschwitz and Birkenau, would raise her profile and improve her career prospects. The orchestra knew that if it performed badly in front of the high official, Mandel's prestige would suffer and she would make sure the players paid a severe penalty. If the performance was truly a disaster, the visiting official himself might order the orchestra to be disbanded and the artists sent to their deaths.

The responsibility for preparing the concert fell on the conductor, Alma Rosé. Rosé, aged 36, had an impeccable musical pedigree. Her uncle was the composer Gustav Mahler, and she had been named after Mahler's wife. Her father, Arnold Rosé, was an exceptional violinist who had played chamber music with Brahms. He had been the leader of orchestras such as the Vienna Opera and the Vienna Philharmonic for 57 years until ejected by the Nazis in 1938. In the 1890s he had led the orchestra of the Bayreuth Festival, founded by Wagner to perform his operas. It was an irony that Hitler, who frequently attended the festival, would not have appreciated. Rosé herself was a virtuoso violinist who, before the war, had formed her own women's orchestra that toured throughout Europe. She and her father had actually reached the safety of Great Britain in 1939. Her father remained there but, needing work, Alma ill-advisedly returned to mainland Europe. She was captured in Dijon in late 1942, while trying to escape to Switzerland. She was sent to Birkenau and was initially assigned to the infamous Block 10 where sterilisation experiments on women were carried out.

She was soon recognised by a fellow inmate at whose house she had once played. Word got out and reached Mandel. Mandel, who wanted only non-Jewish players, could not afford to ignore a player of Rosé's calibre if she wished to improve the standard of the orchestra. She transferred Rosé to the music block, placing her in charge of the orchestra, and obtained a good-quality violin for her from among the instruments confiscated from the deportees.

When Rosé joined the orchestra, its average age was nineteen and its repertoire consisted of a few German marches and Polish tunes, which it did not play particularly well. 'We were playing and we tried hard,' said one of its members, 'but we were like monkeys to an organ grinder.'

Through hard work and an insistence on musical standards, Rosé soon changed that, bartering to improve the quality of the instruments and to acquire musical scores. These she reorchestrated for the available instruments. She also improved the standard of playing by recruiting better players from among the new arrivals. Places in the orchestra were much sought after. Players were largely protected from the threat of the gas chambers and received double food rations and special treats such as extra bread after a concert. Rosé had a private room, though it was tiny. Such privileges did not make them popular with the other inmates.

As well as concerts, the orchestra had many other duties. Each daybreak it was in place at the camp gates to play marches for the departing work details. In the evening it did the same when the work parties came back, the returning prisoners forced to keep in step to the music, though sometimes carrying a comrade who had died during the day. When new transports arrived, the orchestra had to play background music during the fateful selections. Players could be called on at any time to provide music for any of the SS who wished to relax after a day's hard work. It was hateful and almost intolerable but there was no alternative, if they were to survive.

Rosé's discipline was so strict it reminded some of her colleagues of the Nazis themselves. She insisted that the orchestra rehearse ten hours a day. The orchestra was made to stand when she appeared for rehearsal and she threatened players with eviction if they did not work hard enough. In the main they understood that her regime of hard work and discipline was imperative. 'If we don't play well, we'll go to the gas,' was her constant refrain.

But Rosé also protected them. She obtained extra bread and margarine for them and even an extra sleep period during the afternoons. If a player became ill with typhus, as many did, and the SS suggested that she should be gassed, Rosé would protest that the sick player was one of her best violinists, thus saving her life.

For the visit of the Nazi bigwig the orchestra rehearsed as much as twenty hours a day. It now had a repertoire of two hundred orchestral and operatic pieces, including Beethoven, Berlioz, Schubert, Brahms's *Hungarian Dances,* and Schumann (also Dvorak and Mendelssohn, both technically forbidden composers).

In January 1944 a new member of the orchestra, Fania Fénelon, arrived who was a great help to Rosé. Although primarily a singer, Fénelon had an excellent memory. She could recall a wide range of music and orchestrate it for the available instruments of mandolins, violins, guitars, cello, banjos and drum.

Fénelon is a controversial figure, parts of whose 1976 book about her experiences with the orchestra, *The Musicians of Auschwitz*, have been disputed by other members of the orchestra. For example, according to Fénelon the unknown Nazi leader for whom the orchestra was preparing the concert was the inventor of the camps himself, Heinrich Himmler. In her book there is a complete chapter about his visit, containing many specific details. She quotes Rosé as saying, 'Do you realise the implications – Himmler, an absolutely top-rank man!' However, Himmler only visited Auschwitz-Birkenau twice, the second occasion being in July 1942, long before the orchestra was formed. The Nazi high-up was probably the infamous Adolf Eichmann, chief of SS Jewish Affairs.

On the day of the concert the whole camp was in a state of extreme tension awaiting the visit of such an important personage. Rosé's instructions to the orchestra were very specific and covered non-musical matters. They must not look at Eichmann, must sit up straight and mustn't talk amongst themselves. She carried out an inspection to check their appearance was satisfactory. On their platform in the sun, they waited for Eichmann to appear. An hour passed. They grew hot and thirsty but dared not move. Finally the official group appeared, Mandel among them. Rosé, according to Fénelon, snapped to attention, and gave the sign for the orchestra to play the first piece, a medley from Lehár's *The Merry Widow*. Next it played *Twelve Minutes* by Peter Kreuder, with a solo by Fénelon, who recalled her throat being almost too dry to sing. She prayed that she would not be ordered to sing from *Madame Butterfly*, one of Mandel's favourites.

Before long Eichmann moved off. There was no indication whether or not he was pleased. According to Fénelon, Rosé took this as a very bad sign and began criticising the orchestra for playing out of tune. 'Of course he didn't like it. He'll gas us all.'

Back in their block, the women continued to argue and bicker. Suddenly Rosé appeared, carrying her violin. Her mood had changed. To the orchestra's surprise, she announced she was going to play for them. She did this only very rarely as a treat. The message had been passed to her that the eminent visitor had not been displeased by the concert.

Less than two months after the concert Rosé was dead, dying in one of the medical blocks, despite all the assistance that Mandel could provide. It has been suggested that she was poisoned by a jealous inmate who thought Rosé was being released to entertain German soldiers.

Rosé was succeeded by Sonya Winogradowa, but she did not have Rosé's abilities and by October 1944 the orchestra ceased to exist. The Jewish women were sent to Belsen and the non-Jews were returned to the main camp at Auschwitz. A number survived the war and paid tribute to Rosé. Though she was sometimes unpopular, they acknowledged that her willpower, discipline and musical ability had helped to keep them alive.

GONE WITH THE WIND

BRISTOL, AUGUST 1944

If you happen to know any wind players, ask them if they've ever played Malcolm Arnold's Wind Quintet. They are very likely to answer along the lines of, 'Oh, you mean the *Sea Shanties*? Only last week in Cardiff, as it happens . . .' You can then shake your head knowingly and tell them the following story.

The composer Sir Malcolm Arnold, who died in 2006, was very prolific and his output very varied. Symphonies, concertos, overtures, suites and marches tumbled from his pen. He wrote many film scores such as *The Inn of the Sixth Happiness, Whistle Down the Wind,* the Oscar-winning *The Bridge on the River Kwai* (written in only ten days) and many others.

Back in his very early days, when his opus numbers were still in single figures, he wrote two pieces for wind quintet. One of them, an arrangement of sea shanties, has never left the repertoire. The other disappeared off the face of the earth in mysterious circumstances after only one or two performances.

In August 1944, the London Philharmonic Orchestra (of which Arnold himself was principal trumpet) was giving a series of concerts in Bristol. Charles Gregory, the principal horn, came up with a profitable way to use some of the wind section's limited spare time. He arranged with the BBC to give the first performance of Arnold's quintet on the Overseas Service on Wednesday morning, together with a piece by Hindemith. This was long before the days of recorded broadcasts so it would be a live performance. The LPO wind quintet had briefly looked at the Arnold piece but never played it through, anticipating that Tuesday afternoon would be plenty of time for rehearsal.

On Tuesday morning, the LPO had a general orchestral rehearsal. It had only been going for a few minutes when suddenly Charles Gregory appeared in the wings, frantically gesturing the other members of the quintet and Malcolm Arnold to come off immediately, which they did. The rest of the orchestra were much amused by their instant departure, though not the conductor Basil Cameron, suddenly faced with a rehearsal without many of his principals.

Gregory hurriedly explained to Arnold and the four others that the broadcast was not the following day as thought, but that very morning. The six of them piled into a taxi and dashed off to the BBC studio, arriving about 45 minutes before programme time.

At this point they were almost totally unfamiliar with the piece they were shortly to perform live on air. While the sight-reading skills of British orchestral players are second to none, even they would agree that a little rehearsal of a new piece is preferable.

The players were fortunate in two ways. Firstly, the composer was there. As he was the only person who knew the work thoroughly and it was an emergency, it was agreed that he should conduct, though it is not normal practice for chamber works to be conducted. Next, it was a relatively short work, only about twelve minutes. They had time for a quick read-through and to go over the tricky bits a second time – then they were on.

Afterwards, winding down with a drink or two in the pub, the six – Gregory and the quintet – let out huge sighs of relief. At least the performance hadn't broken down, in fact it had gone very well. The incident was quickly added to the anecdotes that musicians like to tell.

It was only a little later that it occurred to someone to ask who had collected the music after the broadcast. The story goes that they looked at each other and realised that none of them had. They rushed back to the studio but there was no sign of it.

Sod's Law dictated that Tuesday was rubbish-collection day and it began to look as if the cleaners had been super-efficient and binned the papers. So, very embarrassingly, the Wind Quintet was gone for ever – its first and last performance. To this day, you will find 'untraced manuscript' if you look up Arnold's Opus 2 on his official website.

The story does not quite end there. In 2004 Stephen Waters, the quintet's clarinettist that day, died. When his papers were sorted, the score and parts came to light. Reconstructing what had happened, it seems that Waters, who was the librarian for the quintet, had retained them for safekeeping, occasionally playing the piece with the Dennis Brain Quintet of which he was also a member. Bit by bit, the music sank to the bottom of his large pile of scores and was lost to sight. His executor immediately sent the parts off to Malcolm Arnold, and subsequently the work was published by Queen's Temple Publications. So the little piece has come back to life after all these years and is available for performance, though it's about time someone told the website.

THE TONE-DEAF DIVA

NEW YORK, OCTOBER 1944

The concert at Carnegie Hall was the hottest ticket in town. It was sold out weeks before the performance with two thousand people turned away disappointed.

On the night of the performance expectation was intense. The queues stretched around the block and you had to prove your identity to get in. Clearly an exceptional singing talent was going to perform.

The cause of all the excitement was a recital by the coloratura soprano, Florence Foster Jenkins. At the age of 76, when most singers have passed their prime and are giving masterclasses, she was making her debut at the Mecca of concert venues.

But Jenkins had never passed her prime, for the simple reason that she never had one. Of all the musicians in this book, including the elephants of the Thai Elephant Orchestra, she was easily the worst. Her voice resembled a squeaky door. When she 'sang', notes were scattered about haphazardly, before wavering, faltering and finally disappearing into the cracks between other equally wrong notes. She has gone down in history as 'The First Lady of the Sliding Scales'; in 2003 Naxos CD of her singing was entitled *Murder on the High Cs*.

So why was Carnegie Hall full? Because people like a good laugh, and nothing is funnier than someone who is unintentionally funny. Jenkins genuinely never seems to have realised that no one went to her concerts for a sublime musical experience but for their amusement value.

Jenkins had musical ambitions from her youth – she gave a piano recital as early as the age of eight – but was a late starter as a singer, only able to pursue her aspirations in her forties when her father died, leaving her independently wealthy. She immediately moved to New York and became very involved in the social and music scene there, counting Enrico Caruso among her contacts and founding the Verdi Club to advance the careers of American artists and musicians. She also financed benefit concerts for charities and it was at these that she first began to sing in public. She gave a limited number of concerts each year in places like Washington, Newport, Boston and New York for which she sold the tickets herself to ensure that only genuine music lovers attended, little realising the spectators' true motives.

Once a year she gave a private concert at the Ritz-Carlton Hotel for a selected group of eight hundred friends, colleagues and admirers. Having gained a large cult following over thirty years, and needing somewhere bigger than a hotel ballroom to satisfy public demand, she had taken the plunge and hired Carnegie Hall.

It wasn't only Jenkins's execrable singing that amused audiences. They also laughed at the appalling bad taste of her productions. On this particular evening, the stage was heaped with exotic flowers and greenery, because Jenkins thought their beauty and the beauties of her voice naturally complemented each other.

The large audience took a long time to settle down. When she finally appeared, her reception was so enthusiastic that another five minutes went by before she could begin. She started with a group of English pastoral songs. Jenkins always dressed in keeping with the period of the songs and acted out their meaning with arch gestures. For this first selection, she appeared as a shepherdess complete with winsome Bo-Peep crook. Later on she sang other songs dressed in an outfit she called The Angel of Inspiration, complete with tinsel, tulle and massive wings worthy of the Archangel Gabriel.

A matronly figure, she never had any sense of how incongruous she looked or that she was being laughed at, attributing laughter or ironic applause to jealous rivals. She sincerely believed she was an artist in the same league as the great divas of the age, Tettrazini and Galli-Curci, if not better.

As the concert proceeded, the audience could hardly wait for their favourites. There was the fiendishly difficult 'Queen of the Night' aria from Mozart's *The Magic Flute*, Adele's 'Laughing Song' from Johann Strauss II's *Die Fledermaus*, and 'The Bell Song' from Delibes's *Lakmé*. Each was exquisitely mis-sung and brought forth barely stifled gusts of laughter.

Probably the highlight of the evening for her fans was her Spanish encore, *Clavelitos*. Having changed yet again, she reappeared out-Carmening Carmen, in a high comb, mantilla and Spanish shawl, carrying a basket of carnations. After dancing a fandango, she tossed the flowers one by one into the audience, accompanying each flower with a shout of 'Olé!' The flowers gone, she flung the basket itself. Enraptured, the audience demanded an encore of the encore, which she willingly granted, though first the flowers and basket had to be retrieved from the audience, so that she could fling them out again. This time the large Carnegie Hall audience joined in with rhythmical handclapping and a boisterous shout of 'Olé!' with each toss of a carnation into the auditorium.

The concert was everything that she and the audience, with their differing expectations, had hoped for. Florence had no greater heights to scale and died a month later of a heart attack. One can imagine that, arriving in Heaven, she immediately applied for a place in the sopranos of the Heavenly Choir. If it is hard to see her passing that audition, no doubt she was allowed to take her place as the Angel of Inspiration.

BRASSED OFF I

PLYMOUTH, SUMMER 1952

Brass bands are forever dashing from place to place, trying to meet unforgiving concert schedules. Given unpredictable travel and weather conditions, it is not surprising that they don't always arrive on time. This is the first of three stories that illustrate the sort of difficulties they can encounter.

In summer 1952, Munn and Felton's band, based in Kettering, were giving a concert one Saturday evening on Plymouth Hoe. As Jim Scott – a long-time cornet player with the band – vividly remembers, the weather was terrible, with heavy wind and rain. He was grateful that the concert was under cover, though a bit worried whether the marquee was strong enough to withstand the gale, which it just about did.

Immediately the concert was finished, the band got straight into the coach for an overnight trip to another concert the following afternoon in Peasholme Park, a mere 300 miles away in Scarborough. Even that was less than the 400-mile overnight trip they once made from Edinburgh for an afternoon concert the next day in Eastbourne on the south coast. On such long journeys, favourite jokes often make an appearance:

Q: How can you tell which kid on the playground is the child of a trombonist?
A: He doesn't know how to use the slide and he can't swing.
Q: What's the difference between cornet players and government bonds?

151

A: Government bonds eventually mature and earn money.

Any jokes would have been cut short on this trip when there was almost a very unpleasant accident. The coach's brakes failed approaching Exeter and it was only quick thinking by the music director, Stanley Boddington, that saved the day. He instructed the driver to slow the coach down by repeatedly driving into the high grass bank at the side of the road. This did the trick, but the coach was a write-off.

Munn and Felton's managing director, Bertie Felton, was following in his Rolls-Royce and drove off to Exeter to find another coach. However, so much time had been lost it was unlikely they could reach Scarborough in time for the concert the next day. It was a point of pride for the band not to miss a concert and Felton tried everything he could to make up the lost time. He even went so far as to try and hire a plane, but some things are impossible at midnight on a Saturday in Exeter.

Desperately tired, the band headed off to a hotel for a few hours' sleep before the replacement coach arrived, only to find that the hotel had no spare beds. The best it could offer was use of the dining room floor, where the bandsmen made themselves as comfortable as they could, only to be up early for a dawn departure for Scarborough. Despite all their efforts, they never did make it in time for the afternoon concert. It was just as well they weren't due to play again in Plymouth. Overnight, their marquee on Plymouth Hoe blew away and ended up in the sea.

THE SOUND OF SILENCE

WOODSTOCK, NEW YORK, AUGUST 1952

Imagine yourself a member of the audience in the Maverick Concert Hall in Woodstock, NY at a concert in aid of the Benefit Artists' Welfare Fund. You know the programme will have a strong avant-garde element, music at the cutting edge. However, you are sympathetic to new music and it is in a good cause. You do not know, as you take your seat, that you are about to be present at the first performance of one of the most notorious and controversial compositions in all music.

Glancing at the programme, you see it includes a new piece by John Cage called *4'33"*. 'Well,' you think, 'if I don't like it, at least it won't last long!'

Towards the end of the concert the moment comes for *4'33"* to be performed. The open piano stands waiting. The soloist enters to polite applause and sits. He puts the score on the stand and then places a watch on the piano. Unusual! Does he have a train to catch? To your surprise, he now proceeds to close the keyboard lid. Then he presses a button on the watch and sits without moving. Occasionally he checks the stopwatch and turns a page of the score. After exactly thirty seconds he raises the lid. Shortly he shuts it and sets the watch again. He turns a few pages. After precisely two minutes and twenty-three seconds he opens the lid. A brief interval, then he closes it. The pianist turns a few more pages. Another one minute and forty seconds pass. Then he raises the lid, gets up and leaves the stage.

153

Instantly there is angry uproar. 'Let's run these people out of town,' someone shouts. You have just 'heard' the world's first piece of silent music.

The piece was not a stunt or a joke, though Cage knew it might be taken as such. That mood was later caught in a review headlined, 'You Could Have Heard a Piano Drop'.

In fact, *4'33"* was part of Cage's serious investigation of the properties of silence, which in turn sprang from his deep interest in Zen Buddhism. The previous year he had visited a chamber at Harvard University specially designed to absorb all sounds. Expecting to hear 'silence', Cage could still hear two sounds, one high, one low. The engineer explained that the high was his nervous system in operation, the low his blood in circulation.

From this experience, Cage developed a theory that there was no such thing as total silence. During *4'33"* he was asking the audience to listen to the ambient silence, the background noise at any particular moment. In his view this could be considered music. During the first performance, the background noise in the first two movements was the wind in the trees and rain blowing onto the roof. In the third it happened to be the sound of baffled members of the audience muttering to each other or walking out. No two performances can ever be the same.

Despite its deep philosophical concepts, earthier elements can intrude into *4'33"*. During a performance at the University of Illinois, elsewhere in the building someone was practising Beethoven on the piano. Over and over he played a particular passage without getting it right. As he grew more frustrated with himself, he vented his annoyance in terms clearly audible in the concert hall and best represented by asterisks. The audience applauded wildly and Cage was said to be delighted.

As with all his scores, Cage took the score of *4'33"* to be stamped as his copyright. Returning the next day to collect it, he found that the administrator, having seen only a blank page, had innocently stamped it in the corner. Cage was furious. 'You've put it on the music!' he shouted angrily.

For the rest of his life, Cage continued to write provocative music requiring unusual instruments such as water containers, decks of cards, birdsong, radios (with newsreader) and much else. Ten years after *4'33"*, he published a sequel called *0'0"*, described as a 'solo to be performed in any way by anyone'. Cage himself performed it by eating a carrot with a contact microphone on his Adam's apple.

In 2002, there was a bizarre sequel. The musician Mike Batt, best known as the creator of The Wombles, wrote an album *Classical Graffiti* containing a track called 'A Minute's Silence'. 'A Minute's Silence' did exactly what it says on the tin. Batt, tongue firmly in cheek, credited the composition jointly to himself and to Cage, who had died in 1992. However, the John Cage Trust, representing the interest of Cage's estate, sued Batt for infringement of copyright. Batt countered by saying his silence was his silence, and that he wasn't quoting from Cage's. It was also a much better piece, he pointed out, as he had been able to say in one minute what Cage could only say in over four and a half. At the end of the day, Batt paid the Trust a six-figure sum donation in an out-of-court settlement, a pricey minute's silence.

THE FROCK'S THE STAR

ATTINGHAM, SHROPSHIRE, AUTUMN 1953

Mary Firth, pianist and music teacher, used to give weekend courses at Attingham Park in Shropshire. This was one of the colleges of adult education that were opened after World War II to provide 'enlivenment' to a nation that had spent many years under siege and, more or less, under fire. The weekend courses took different forms, but during the music weekends there was always a concert on the Saturday evening at which Mary Firth would play, sometimes accompanying a violinist or a cellist.

One such occasion in the autumn of 1953 was open to the general public, which meant the audience was composed of people from the town of Shrewsbury, about seven miles away, as well as students from the course.

The first item on the programme was a piece for piano and violin by Schubert, and Mary Firth accompanied the violinist. The audience assembled and the concert began. A few minutes into the piece, Mary Firth noticed that the owner of the house, Lady Berwick, was sitting in the front row with her head bowed and her eyes closed. Lady Berwick still lived in one wing of Attingham Park, the rest of the house having been leased to the local education authority for use in the cause of adult education. One or two other members of the audience were similarly positioned, heads bowed, in an attitude that, though it seemed attentive, averted its gaze. Had they all fallen ill? Meanwhile, some of the students in the audience were helpless with laughter.

Mary Firth, facing the keyboard, was at right angles to the audience, so that both piano and pianist were in profile. The violinist stood at her right shoulder, and a large standard lamp was between them. The violinist was a young woman wearing a pretty concert frock in one of the new synthetic fabrics. Rayon and nylon were fairly revolutionary materials at the time, and the very height of fashion.

The interval was to follow the first work and at the end of the Schubert the musicians left the stage and the audience was hastily ushered out of the hall as the electrician and carpenter hurried onto the platform to rearrange the position of the light. It turned out that it was the concert frock the young violinist was wearing that was causing all the consternation. The dress was made of thin, flimsy material and the light was so positioned as to render it transparent: it was as though she was totally naked. Happily (for some) the lighting was changed successfully during the interval and the second half was entirely decent.

During October 1955 Mary Firth had to stand in for a pianist who was ill and could not make it to an Arts Council concert in a tiny, out-of-the-way place: Campbeltown, in Scotland. Mary was the wife of George Firth, then head of the Scottish Arts Council, and she didn't generally deputise in this way as she thought it wouldn't look right in view of her close connection with the Arts Council. On this occasion, however, she flew at a day's notice from Renfrew to Glasgow Prestwick and made her way to Campbeltown to find an upright piano and a concert platform so rickety that the instrument rocked forward and back when she played it. She explained that this was early days for the Arts Council concerts, and that later the convention became that they were all given by professionals, and at proper venues. However, the Campbeltown audience was 'enraptured and vociferous' when they discovered that she was the wife of the head of the Scottish Arts Council, and full of praise for her valiant command of the mobile instrument.

CONCERTO FOR HOSEPIPE AND HOOVER

LONDON, NOVEMBER 1956

It was obviously a musical occasion of importance for it had attracted some of the best-known musicians in the country. Surely that was Dennis Brain, the virtuoso horn player, and weren't they the conductor Norman de Mar and the composer Malcolm Arnold?

But what was Brain doing clutching a length of garden hosepipe instead of his horn? And why was Arnold keeping a close eye on some floor-cleaning equipment the cleaners had obviously forgotten to put away?

Also looking ready for action were Donald Swann (of Flanders and Swann fame) and the actors Sam Wanamaker and Yvonne Arnaud. And there was a jolly-faced, rotund tuba player, grappling with an enormous six-feet-tall tuba, like Groucho Marx making love to a matronly socialite in one of his films.

The audience knew it was in for an eventful evening. That was why it had snapped up the tickets within three hours of the box office opening. Possibly their hearts sank as they saw Ernest Bean, general manager of the Royal Festival Hall, step forward to make an announcement. That always meant something had gone wrong. But what was he saying? 'Due to circumstances beyond our control' – pause for maximum effect – 'tonight's concert will take place exactly as advertised.'

From that moment, the audience happily anticipated the unexpected. It was quick to get to its feet for the loud, attention-getting drum roll of the National Anthem, only to subside sheepishly back into its seats when it realised it was the opening of a fanfare by Francis Baines.

Malcolm Arnold entered to conduct the first item, *Grand Grand Overture,* which he had written specially for the occasion. With him he brought three vacuum cleaners and a floor polisher, which had important solo roles. The piece was naturally dedicated to former President Hoover. Before he could begin, there was disruption at the back of the hall as a busker dressed in shorts, raincoat and hat ran down the aisle playing 'The Irish Washerwoman' on his fiddle; no ordinary busker, but the distinguished violinist, Yfrah Neaman.

Only after this interruption could the *Grand Grand Overture* begin, though, having begun, Arnold seemed reluctant for it ever to stop. It worked itself up to false ending after false ending, as if he was determined to exceed the length of all Beethoven's codas played one after the other.

In among the orchestral players, the beaming tuba player was having the time of his life. He was Gerard Hoffnung and the Hoffnung Music Festival was his brainchild. Most people knew him best as a cartoonist from his drawings in *Punch*, the *Daily Express*, *Lilliput* and other papers, and from his books of cartoons. His collections *The Maestro, Hoffnung's Musical Chairs, Hoffnung's Acoustics* and others have run into many impressions since they first appeared in the 1950s.

Hoffnung's visual imagination was surreal. A hippopotamus opened its mouth in a giant yawn to reveal its teeth were an immaculate Bechstein keyboard. Molluscs bubbling quietly on the seabed turned out to be an amorous pair of cymbals. And how else would tortoises make music than by treating their upturned stomachs as drums? His visual jokes for the evening included obtaining an Alpenhorn almost ten feet long, mounted on a crag at the back of the platform.

Hoffnung's drawing was by no means his only talent. Having taught himself the tuba, he developed into a very competent player. He had a quick-witted, idiosyncratic sense of humour, which he displayed as a panellist on the BBC show *One Minute Please.*

Hoffnung was convinced there was much humour in classical music that went unnoticed and the festival was his attempt to highlight music's comic potential. He was able to call on many contacts, who were pleased to join in for the fun of working with him, even though they knew that involvement might be time-consuming, demanding and not overpaid.

After the *Grand Grand Overture* came Donald Swann's version of Haydn's 'Surprise' Symphony, including a septet of stone hot-water bottles. The purpose of Dennis Brain's hosepipe became clear when he played an adapted version of Leopold Mozart's Concerto for Alphorn and Strings. It emitted 'a faint but musical sound like a distant bugle call', *The Times* reported next day.

One of the greatest successes was the *Concerto Popolare* by Franz Reizenstein, a representation of the age-old battle seen to exist between conductor and soloist. The orchestra launched into the thunderous opening bars of Tchaikovsky's First Piano Concerto, only for the pianist to respond with the start of the Grieg Piano Concerto.

This notion was not so far-fetched as it might sound. In one 'proper' concert consisting of two piano pieces, the conductor gave the downbeat for Liszt's *Todtentanz*, while the soloist simultaneously launched out on Rawsthorne's First Piano Concerto. At another concert of two Beethoven piano concertos, the conductor, thinking they were beginning with the Fourth Concerto, which commences with a piano entry, nodded politely to the soloist to begin. The soloist, thinking they were playing the Third Concerto, which begins with the orchestra, nodded back to indicate he was ready when the conductor was. The nodding went back and forth for some time until the orchestra could bear it no longer and burst out in giggles. The intrepid pianist in *Concerto Popolare* was Yvonne Arnaud and she received the soloist's customary bouquet, a collection of vegetables.

Other works on the programme included a setting of Sir Walter Scott's ballad *Lochinvar* and *Variations on a Theme of Annie Laurie* by Gordon Jacob, scored for many weird instruments such as contrabass serpent (a genuine instrument used by Handel), hecklephone and hurdy-gurdy. There was the *Geographical Fugue* by Ernst Toch in which the choir had to cope with a text consisting of difficult place names such as Titicaca. As encore, they had to repeat the whole text at double speed. *The Times* liked the work but was unhappy that it was 'mainly swamped by the audience's amusement'. The final piece was Resphigi's *Feste Romana*, played by an orchestra of over one hundred players plus the thirty-six trumpeters of the Royal Military School of Music with all the gusto they could manage.

Public response to the concert was so enthusiastic that EMI issued a recording in time for Christmas and Hoffnung made plans for a second concert. This took place two years later and was modestly entitled The Hoffnung Interplanetary Music Festival. One reviewer described it as 'the greatest musical joke of all time'. Two more concerts were due to take place in November 1959, but Hoffnung died in September of that year, aged only 34. With the involvement of Hoffnung's widow, Annetta, Hoffnung concerts continue to take place around the world and some of the works he premiered have become famous in their own right.

A DISASTROUS FIRST
PERFORMANCE

LONDON, FEBRUARY 1958

The world premiere of the English composer Michael Tippett's Second Symphony has gone down as one of the most notorious fiascos of recent musical history. Hardly two minutes into the piece, the performance broke down and the distraught conductor, Adrian Boult, turned to the audience and graciously took the mishap onto his own shoulders, announcing, 'Entirely my mistake, ladies and gentlemen.' In the very public inquest afterwards, it began to appear that it was not Boult's mistake, but that of the leader of the BBC Symphony Orchestra, the highly experienced Paul Beard.

Tippett's method of writing for the violins could be unorthodox. Rhythms often suggested themselves to him in shapes, which sometimes ran across barlines. Beard thought this notation was unduly complicated and had rewritten some of the bars, about a dozen in all, in a more conventional manner. It was a technical adjustment only and had no effect on how the music sounded.

Tippett objected to the rewriting, recalling in his autobiography that he had pointed out to Boult and Beard that the changes would create more problems than if played as originally written. 'And so it turned out,' he wrote. The myth grew up, still current today, that this disaster was all due to Paul Beard. The 2005 Tippett centennial exhibition in the British Library displayed the score of the symphony with Beard's reworkings and a caption to that effect.

162

Now, working from his own tape of the broadcast performance, the conductor, musicologist and writer, Jonathan Del Mar, who has conducted the symphony on several occasions, has been able to reconstruct exactly what happened. The story appears to be very different and, thanks to Del Mar, can be made public for the first time.

Tippett's Second Symphony was one of a number of new orchestral works commissioned by the BBC to mark the tenth anniversary of the Third Programme (now Radio Three) in 1956. The composers were given reasonable notice of their deadlines, the plan being that one piece would be premiered each month starting in October 1956.

The commission was a good opportunity for the public rehabilitation of Tippett, a controversial figure who had been a communist during the 1930s. As a committed pacifist and conscientious objector, he was imprisoned for three months during World War II. This did not prevent him composing, although his scores could not reach the outside world due to prison restrictions. However, he managed to evade these when Benjamin Britten came to give a concert. He and Britten swapped scores and Britten carried Tippett's out with him as though it was his own.

Tippett accepted the commission on condition that there was no time limit. This was sensible of him, as works of symphonic scale aren't always finished to schedule. Sir William Walton's First Symphony is a famous example. Walton began work on it in 1932 with a first performance date of April 1933 in mind. However, progress was not as swift as hoped and these plans were cancelled. Eventually the first three movements were completed and were performed on their own in December 1934, while he waited for inspiration for the fourth. It was not until late 1935 that the last movement made its public appearance.

The BBC accepted Tippett's conditions and Tippett kept them in touch with progress, writing in July 1956 to apologise for the delay. The BBC had run into problems with its ambitious project, with both the Tippett and a work by Petrassi that also was not going to be ready on schedule. Other works had to be shuffled around to fill the gaps.

The tenth anniversary celebrations came and went without Tippett's symphony appearing. Eventually he and the BBC agreed to a first performance date of 5 February 1958 at London's Royal Festival Hall.

The BBC must have been mightily relieved when Tippett wrote in November 1957 to say the work was at last finished. But with less than three months to the first performance, much remained to be done. The orchestral parts had to be printed and proofed, and the new piece rehearsed. The orchestra would be working to a tight deadline.

The score was awaited with some anxiety. Tippett's work was regarded as exceptionally complex and likely to present technical problems needing extra attention. Some of his previous compositions had drawn criticism from their performers. The day before the first performance in 1955 of his opera *The Midsummer Marriage*, an article had appeared in the *News Chronicle* headlined, 'This Opera Baffles Us Too, Say Singers'. Later that year, the Dennis Brain Wind Ensemble said that his new Sonata for Four Horns was impossible to play as written and transposed it down a tone. The following year, his new Piano Concerto was declared unplayable by its intended first soloist, Julius Katchen, although a replacement, Louis Kentner, carried through its first performance as planned.

Once the score arrived, Boult supported Beard's proposal to rewrite the violin parts. Tippett's caveats were very forcibly overruled, to the extent that he was told the symphony would not be performed unless the changes were made. Tippett was unimpressed by Boult's lack of authority over Beard, especially when Boult allowed Beard to play a violin solo in the scherzo slower than the speed indicated. Boult was regarded as inexperienced in conducting new music, and had been far down the list of preferred conductors for the performance.

The new symphony was the final work of the evening. With Del Mar's help, we can chart the course of disaster with accuracy. The performance broke down when the flute got lost in a difficult passage and emerged with a big solo a bar too early, possibly brought in by Boult, raising the question of whether the conductor was also lost. The clarinet followed the flute, the oboe followed the clarinet, and very soon the entire woodwind section was a bar out with the strings. A colossal trumpet entry came in with the strings; the horns were counting with the woodwinds and came in together with the cellos and basses, instead of a bar later. By now, the orchestra had been torn apart for over twenty bars and Boult had no alternative but to throw in the towel.

He must have done so very reluctantly. It was a humiliation for any orchestra, let alone one of the prestige of the BBC Symphony Orchestra. To make matters worse, the performance was being broadcast. After a few seconds' pause to gather their wits, they started again and this time got it right.

Afterwards, some critics felt that the orchestra was not up to playing such difficult contemporary music, leading the Controller of BBC Music to defend it in a letter to *The Times*. The orchestra was 'equal to all reasonable demands', he said, implying that Tippett's were unreasonable. Tippett did not leap to defend the players, however, and a coolness developed on both sides. He withdrew from conducting the symphony at the Proms later in the year, but was invited to attend rehearsals, on the amazing condition that he did not approach within forty feet of the platform. Tippett agreed, but insisted that Boult should come to him when there was some point to discuss, rather than he to Boult.

And the fuss about Beard's rewritten violin parts? A colossal red herring, according to Del Mar, because at the end of the disputed passage the violins were completely together in the right place at the right time. Furthermore, he says, the passage where the hapless flute got lost was written with the same complex notation that Beard had insisted was unplayable for the violins. And he completes Beard's vindication by pointing out that every orchestra since has followed his practice and rewritten the same bars in the same way.

LA DONNA É MOBILE

LONDON, JUNE 1961

Even for committed supporters of avant-garde music – often
called 'squeaky-door music' by unsympathetic professional
musicians – it is sometimes hard to know what has value and
what has not. But from time to time, an invisible boundary is
crossed and someone feels obliged to stand up and declare that
the emperor has no clothes on. The late Susan Bradshaw, a
highly regarded pianist, teacher and writer, and called the
'conscience of composers', did so very effectively on at least
two occasions.

Bradshaw's associations with avant-garde music were very
strong and went back to her days as a student in the 1950s
when she upset the musical faculty by performing Bartok's
Sonata for Two Pianos and Percussion, considered very
advanced at the time. Since then, she had become recognised
as one of the leading proponents and performers of modern
music.

In the late fifties and early sixties, there was a fierce debate
in musical circles about what was legitimate music with
musical value and what was concocted twaddle without any
qualities. This debate came to public notice as a result of
two performances on the Third Programme on 5 June 1961
of *Mobile* by the unknown 22-year-old Polish composer,
Piotr Zak.

In a negative review in *The Times* the next day, Jeremy Noble
described *Mobile* as being written for 'electronic tape and two
partially improvising percussion players'. Donald Mitchell in

166

the *Daily Telegraph* talked about 'a succession of whistles, rattles and punctured sighs'.

It took two months for the truth to come out. There was no such composer as Piotr Zak. The whole thing was a hoax involving Bradshaw and Hans Keller (writer, musicologist and the BBC's Chief Assistant, Chamber Music and Recitals).

The furore reached the popular press. Keller later described on the Third Programme how he and Bradshaw had produced *Mobile* in a studio, bashing about on percussion instruments and more or less anything that came to hand. They then ran it through an echo chamber, and went to Howard Newby, the controller of the Third Programme, to see if they could get it broadcast. Newby, who was the first recipient of the Booker Prize in 1969, is reported to have approved the hoax.

Keller and Bradshaw defended themselves by saying it was to prove their point. How can something be called music if there is no way of differentiating the good from the phoney? Possibly it was also to have some fun at the expense of the experts, who thereafter regarded Keller and Bradshaw with much suspicion.

A few years later, Bradshaw was at a concert in London that contained a work by the American composer LaMonte Young. Young was grouped with Philip Glass, Steve Reich and others as a minimalist composer. Among his compositions were a piece for dragging chairs and one called *The Second Dream of the High-Tension Line Stepdown Transformer*.

Young had dedicated a piece to the philosopher and composer Henry Flynt called *42 for Henry Flynt*, the total content of which, in one performance, was a gong struck 42 times identically. Young left the choice of instrument and the number of repetitions entirely to the performer, so the number and the sound were variable from performance to performance.

On this occasion, the performer was the experimental composer, Cornelius Cardew, very well known to Bradshaw. He had been a fellow student and one of her co-performers in the Bartok piece mentioned earlier. Cardew announced that the number of repetitions for this performance would be 292 and sat down at the piano. Whatever people felt about the unexpectedly large number they kept to themselves. Cardew then revealed the manner of his performance. Raising one forearm above the keyboard, he poised it, then brought it down on the keys with an ear-shattering crash of discordant notes. The audience sat aghast, realising that they would have to listen to this cacophony another mind-numbing 291 times. But the conventions of concert behaviour are strong and it looked as though people were prepared to suffer in silence.

As the forearm slams continued to resound remorselessly through the chamber, Bradshaw was unimpressed by the musical value of the experience. Possibly she did some quick sums. *42 for Henry Flynt* lasted for about a quarter of an hour, so this version could take nearly two hours!

It isn't known quite what number Cardew had reached when Bradshaw decided she had heard enough. Getting up from her seat in the front row, she leaped onto the platform. Before Cardew could react, she dragged him off his piano stool and instantly terminated the performance. The applause was heartfelt, prolonged and, no doubt, full of relief.

KNOWING THE SCORE

WHITEHAVEN, CUMBRIA, SUMMER 1964

The virtuoso Russian cellist Mstislav Rostropovich, who died in 2007, was invited by the impresario Anthony Phillips to play in a music festival at the Rose Hill Arts Centre, near Whitehaven, Cumbria. Rose Hill is a private house with a small professional arts centre in the garden, somewhat along the lines of Garsington Manor in Oxfordshire, where the summer opera series is performed. The Rose Hill festival was set up by the businessman and entrepreneur Sir Nicholas Sekers, a silk manufacturer. Its object was to provide artistic nourishment in an area that at the time was somewhat short of cultural activity. Its theatre opened in 1959 and has an interior designed by Oliver Messel and described as 'a rose-red, silk-lined jewel box'.

Great artists were often invited to Rose Hill but it was a particular privilege for this northwestern audience that Mstislav Rostropovich would travel so far, not least because at the time he was in engaged in a Cello Marathon concert series with the London Symphony Orchestra. This consisted of thirteen concerts and included twenty new works, many of which had been specially commissioned. Taken all together, said Anthony Phillips, the LSO series constituted a very testing and terrifying event. Nonetheless, Rostropovich agreed to go to Rose Hill and play the piano to accompany his wife, the formidable soprano Galina Vishnevskaya.

Apparently Rostropovich is fond of playing tricks. Phillips had known him for many years, and knew this. All the same, he

169

was taken in when the artist said he was feeling somewhat cautious about undertaking this concert, in the middle of the vast LSO series, and when not playing his usual instrument. There was some extra tension because of the known perfectionism of Vishnevskaya. Rostropovich said, 'I won't have time to prepare the piece or rehearse it properly so I will need a really good page-turner. Will you do it for me?' Naturally, Phillips said that he would.

There was a slightly unusual beginning to the concert, in that Rostropovich brought his own score into the concert hall and placed it on the desk as Vishnevskaya took up her position. The programmed piece was Mussorgsky's *Songs and Dances of Death*. Phillips saw at once that the score was that of *La Traviata*. He did not know what to do. The audience was seated and ready, Vishnevskaya was prepared. Phillips tried to get the attention of Rostropovich without distracting the audience, but the maestro's concentration was wholly on the concert and he was resolutely focused within himself.

Rostropovich peered at the score of *La Traviata* and started to play the first of the Mussorgsky songs, perfectly, with great sensitivity, continuing to gaze at the score as though reading it. Phillips thought there was no point turning the score for the wrong piece, but after a time Rostropovich nodded to him, so he turned the page. This continued throughout the performance. As it was the wrong music, Anthony had no idea when he was expected to turn, and several times Rostropovich became quite fierce and nodded urgently to hurry him up. Any performance depends to an extent on the page-turner. If the musician does not know the piece by heart – which on the whole accompanists do not – the page-turner is crucial. If the page is turned too early or too late, it can wreck the performances of all the players. There is therefore tension attached to the performance of this essential role, and the trick could be seen as mischievous. It was a demonstration of the almost superhuman virtuosity of this great artist, however, that leaves the ordinary musician or concertgoer simply gasping in amazement.

Page-turning is perennially hazardous. In 1803, the first performance of Beethoven's Piano Concerto Op. 37 No. 3 in C minor was given at the Theater an der Wien. The page-turner was named Seyfried. He recalled:

> In the playing of the concerto movements he asked me to turn the pages for him; but – heaven help me! – that was easier said than done. I saw almost nothing but empty leaves; at the most on one page or the other a few Egyptian hieroglyphs wholly unintelligible to me scribbled down as clues for him; for he played nearly all of the solo part from memory, since, as was so often the case, he had not had time to put it all down on paper. He gave me a secret glance whenever he was at the end of one of the invisible passages and my scarcely concealable anxiety not to miss the decisive moment amused him greatly and he laughed heartily at the jovial supper which we ate afterwards.

MERRY PRANKS OF A MASTER PIANIST

DUNDEE, JANUARY 1967

When there is an unexpected glitch in a concert, some musicians will struggle to maintain their concentration, others will not let it affect them at all, and others will react in a way totally at odds with their public image.

In 1967, the distinguished conductor and pianist Daniel Barenboim was playing the solo part in Beethoven's 'Emperor' Piano Concerto in the Caird Hall, Dundee with the Royal Scottish National Orchestra under Alexander Gibson. During the performance, one of the pedals fell off the piano. Barenboim waited until a passage came along for orchestra only, then dived beneath the piano to fix it back on again. It didn't take him long, but obviously an impish thought struck him while he was doing the repair work for he didn't re-emerge.

Gibson, meanwhile, was busily conducting and keeping half an eye on the situation. To his horror, Barenboim's next entry began to approach and the piano stool was still empty. Unable to see what was going on, Gibson imagined that Barenboim had run into difficulties. He began to slow down the tempo of the piece to allow more time for the repairs. Short of stopping, there was not much more he could do. Eventually, no matter how much he slowed down, the moment of Barenboim's entry finally arrived. At that precise instant, Barenboim popped up from beneath the piano and took his cue as though nothing had happened, much to Gibson's relief, and the amusement of those of the orchestra who had spotted what was going on.

On another occasion, Barenboim was soloist in the Schumann piano concerto, and his great friend Zubin Mehta was conductor. Barenboim came onto the platform and sat down on the piano stool, but was dissatisfied with its height and started trying to adjust it, though with some difficulty.

The convention is that the conductor catches the eye of the soloist before commencing in order to check that he or she is ready. On this occasion, Mehta appears not to have registered that Barenboim wasn't totally prepared and gave the downbeat for the orchestra to play the very short sharp chord that is instantly followed by the piano's first entry. Barenboim just about managed to make his entry on time and the movement proceeded, with Barenboim feeling a bit aggrieved about the incident and also not too comfortable on his piano stool.

This much was clear, because at the end of the first movement he started fiddling around with the height, again without success, finally beckoning Mehta over to look at the problem. 'Look,' he appeared to be saying to Mehta, 'down there.' Mehta bent down to inspect. 'No, lower,' Barenboim indicated, so Mehta bent over even further, at which point, with Mehta doubled up by the piano stool, Barenboim launched into the start of the second movement. The second movement is like the start of the first, only it is the piano that gives the very brief introductory phrase, before the orchestra comes in. Mehta scrambled back to the podium to pick up the beat. 'Honours even,' Barenboim must have thought. There was no chance for the deciding rubber – the third movement continues straight on from the second.

THE PIANIST WHO CAME
A KROPPER

BANGKOK, MAY 1967

This incredible tale concerns the pianist Myron Kropp and a recital he gave in the chamber music room of the Erewan Hotel, Bangkok.

The recital got off to an unpromising start when Kropp arrived at the piano to find he had a stool to sit on rather than his preferred bench. Kropp liked a bench because his energetic style sometimes resulted in him turning sideways if he was sitting on a stool. He briefly left to search for a bench but, finding none, returned to the stage and began his recital.

The piano was a Baldwin Concert Grand, a fine instrument but no longer new and needing constant attention in a climate such as Bangkok's. In the humidity the felts, which separate the white keys from the black, tended to swell, causing an occasional key to stick and Sod's Law dictated that this is exactly what happened during the first section of Johann Sebastian Bach's Toccata and Fugue in D minor with which Kropp began his programme. Kropp managed to play through to the end despite the handicap. However, in the next section, annoyance started to get the better of him and he began to direct comments at the piano. Because he was facing the piano, the remarks were largely inaudible. However, during one of the louder passages, his energetic playing swung him round so he was facing the audience at exactly the same time as he passed some uncompromising comments. His language was reportedly so strong that one audience member sent his children from the room.

174

The situation worsened when someone began to laugh. The laughter was contagious and by the time the audience had regained its composure Kropp appeared somewhat shaken. Nevertheless, he swivelled himself back into position facing the piano and, leaving the fugue unfinished, commenced Bach's Fantasia and Fugue in G minor.

At this point, if nothing else had gone wrong, the situation might have remained manageable. Unfortunately the concert grand's G key in the third octave now also began to stick. Kropp did nothing to help matters when he began using his feet to kick the lower portion of the piano, rather than to operate the pedals.

Perhaps it was this jarring that caused the right front leg of the piano to buckle slightly inward, leaving the entire instrument listing at about a 35-degree angle. The audience gasped, for if the piano had actually fallen several of Kropp's toes and possibly his feet might have been broken. The audience were therefore somewhat relieved to see Kropp slowly rise from his stool and leave the stage. Assuming the recital was over, some began clapping, and when Kropp reappeared a few moments later it seemed as if he was responding to the applause. However, it transpired that he had left the stage to get a red-handled axe hanging backstage in case of fire, for that was what was in his hand. He began to hack at the left leg of the piano, possibly attempting to make it tilt at the same angle as the right leg and thereby correct the list. However, when the weakened legs finally collapsed altogether with a great crash and Kropp continued to chop, it became obvious that he had no intention of going on with the concert.

The demolition finally came to an end when ushers, hearing the snapping of piano wires and splintering of sound board, came rushing in. With the help of the hotel manager, two Indian watchmen and a passing police corporal, Kropp was finally disarmed and dragged off stage to disappear for ever.

So that is how Kropp came a cropper. If you thought as you read this story that it sounded too bad to be true, you were right. It is, in fact, a spoof review by Kenneth Langbell, who wrote a weekly satirical column in the English-language version of the *Bangkok Post.* It has amused many people since its first publication on 27 May 1967, though, understandably, not the piano manufacturers, who wrote to the newspaper to complain plaintively about the negative publicity stemming from the original article.

PROTEST AT THE PROMS I

LONDON, AUGUST 1968

During the Cold War, the arts were one of the few areas of relatively normal contact between the West and countries behind the Iron Curtain. There were many visits by Soviet musicians in that period and the tour to Britain in August 1968 of the State Orchestra of the USSR was just such an occasion. A substantial programme was arranged, with four Proms at the Royal Albert Hall, split by appearances at the Edinburgh Festival.

The first of the Proms was scheduled for 21 August. It was the orchestra's debut performance in Britain and there was no doubt it would receive a warm welcome from the promenaders. That is, until the world woke up that very morning to discover that overnight the Soviet Union and Warsaw Pact countries had invaded Czechoslovakia, overthrown the Dubcek government and brought the so-called Prague Spring to a tragic close.

The unprovoked invasion was condemned as an outrage in the West. Protests were instantly organised in London and elsewhere. Demonstrators burned the Red Flag and chanted pro-Dubcek slogans outside the Soviet exhibition in Earls Court. In the early evening, a 5,000-strong march led by Tariq Ali set out for the Soviet Embassy to protest. After that, aware of the concert that evening and who was playing, the demonstrators moved on the short distance to the Albert Hall, but were kept from getting within a hundred yards by the police.

It was in this heightened state of tension that the concert took place. As the audience began to assemble, it was clear that

177

a disruptive element was present, though no one knew what form any disruption might take. Some anticipated a physical protest such as throwing stink bombs or flour, or drowning out the music with catcalls.

In the context of the day's events, the music selected for the concert was highly embarrassing from the Soviet point of view. The two main pieces were Shostakovich's Tenth Symphony, written in the aftermath of Stalin's death, and Dvorak's Cello Concerto with the great Mstislav Rostropovich, who died in 2007, as soloist. Such a mix of Russian and Czech music was guaranteed to point up the day's events and was the last thing the Soviets wanted.

According to a close personal friend of Rostropovich, the cellist was saddened and angered by the invasion and highly nervous about the performance. Although personally very popular with British audiences, he knew that a Soviet musician playing a great Czech work might be taken as inflammatory.

The concert started with Glinka's overture to *Ruslan and Ludmila*. As the musicians filed on, the friendly applause with which the promenaders usually welcome an orchestra, especially one from overseas making its first appearance at the Proms, was drowned by loud cries of 'Freedom for the Czechs' and 'Hands off the Czechs'. The heckling continued for some time, though there was a large section of the audience that did not blame the Kremlin's foreign policy on the visiting Soviet musicians and refrained from joining in.

Yvgeny Svetlanov, the conductor, then rushed on. Wisely in the circumstances, he omitted playing his country's national anthem and launched into a furious account of the Glinka, which was played without interruption from the protesters. The shouting recurred, though, in the interval between the overture and the Dvorak. There is no doubt that Rostropovich was in a highly emotional state when he came on to play. In his book *The Henry Wood Proms*, David Cox says that he played with tears streaming down his cheeks, and many reports comment on his extraordinarily personal interpretation that evening. He did not play precisely Dvorak's markings but adapted them in a way that enabled him to express his deepest feelings through his instrument, turning the piece into a lament for what his country, to which he was deeply loyal, had done to another country.

Perhaps this was most clearly demonstrated at the end of the concert, when in a very unusual gesture – not an encore in the accepted sense – he returned to the platform and played a Bach sarabande with great intensity. He had played this piece recently as a memorial to a friend and the message was unmistakable.

By the end of the concert he had succeeded in showing where his feelings lay and those of many of his countrymen. If the piano in the slow movement of Beethoven's Fourth Piano Concerto quietens the angry orchestra 'like Orpheus taming the wild beasts' in a famous description, then Rostropovich did the same to the Proms audience that night.

Rostropovich continued to show the power of music to make personal and political statements. In 1989 he played Bach at the demolition of the Berlin Wall, and in 1991 flew from Paris to Moscow, entering the Russian Parliament building where Boris Yeltsin was trapped and playing to show his support. Possibly it was a coincidence, but still a moving one, that it was 23 years to the day since the Soviet Union's invasion of Czechoslovakia.

ENCORES FROM THE AFTERLIFE

LONDON, MARCH 1971

Wigmore Hall is one of the most prestigious recital venues in the world. Many thousands of concerts have taken place there but it is doubtful if any was more unusual than the one given by Rosemary Brown on 6 March 1971.

The programme of music by Bach, Liszt, Schubert, Schumann, Mozart, Debussy, Chopin and Beethoven seemed fairly standard concert fare. Except none of the music to be played had been heard before. This was extraordinary. The corpus of works by these famous composers is very well known. Sometimes a new manuscript of an existing work surfaces, but hardly ever a new, unknown piece. When one does, such as Bizet's Symphony in C and Schumann's Violin Concerto in 1933, and a Haydn Cello Concerto in 1961, it is the musical equivalent of striking gold.

So how did it happen that so many new works had suddenly appeared at the same time? The audience at the recital would have known the reason very well. Rosemary Brown, the organiser and piano soloist, claimed that the long-dead composers had personally dictated them to her from beyond the grave.

When Brown first came to public notice on a BBC television programme in 1969, she was a widow with two children, living in difficult circumstances in south London. Her musical knowledge was minimal. She had received piano lessons for a short period as a child but lack of money had forced her family to stop them.

On the programme, Brown said that her first contact was with Liszt when she was seven, though she did not then know who he was. He began to dictate compositions to her in her late forties when she was at home unable to work because of an injury. He also accompanied her shopping and was knowledgeable about cheap bananas. Knowing of her money problems, he prompted her to do the football pools and she won small but helpful amounts on two occasions, though Brown says he didn't actually give her any tips.

Through Liszt, Brown met Chopin. After that, word seems to have got around in Heaven, because many other composers sought her out as a conduit to the living world. She received symphonies from Beethoven, études from Chopin and songs from Schubert. Schubert told her that he had now completed the 'Unfinished' Symphony and allowed her to hear it. 'It is very, very beautiful,' Brown reported in her autobiography *Unfinished Symphonies*, without giving further information.

By the time of the concert, she had composed over four hundred pieces. Her rudimentary piano skills had improved over the years, and she could take down dictation and play with some degree of proficiency. She even demonstrated the process live on the programme. Liszt, she said, was present to encourage her.

The March 1971 concert was the first major public performance of any of these works. Her claims aroused considerable, if sceptical, interest in the media. *The Times* sent a distinguished critic, Stanley Sadie, to the concert to give an opinion. Sadie, as editor of *The New Grove Dictionary of Music and Musicians* until his death in 2005, held one of the most influential positions in music.

Though Sadie didn't question Brown's sincerity, he was unimpressed by the music. He used words like trite, static, predictable, banal, tinkly and sentimental, and inclined to the view that the works were not very good pastiche. About harp pieces by Bach, Schumann and Debussy, he commented dryly that it was curious how the composers had now taken to that particular instrument. As for the Mozart apparently composed for the occasion, 'It sounded like a work of his second childhood.' He concluded, 'When Mrs Brown produces something nearer a masterpiece, we must listen more attentively.'

Not everyone agreed with him. Brown found sympathetic interest from musicians of international repute such as Leonard Bernstein, John Lill, Peter Katin, Stephen Bishop-Kovacevic and André Previn. Bernstein said he would 'buy' just about all of it, except for one bar in a work by Rachmaninov. Rachmaninov seems to have taken the criticism to heart because Brown says he subsequently rewrote the bar.

Over the years, Brown continued to give similar concerts, but the music's credibility declined. None of the thousand or so compositions she transcribed became accepted as the masterpiece Stanley Sadie thought would be the litmus test of authenticity.

Scholars were not convinced either. In 1992 Professor Geoffrey Gibbs completed research on *Valse Brilliante*, supposedly dictated by Liszt, and identified Chopin's Scherzo in B minor as a clear source.

As well as music from beyond the grave, Brown claimed contact with the spirits of Bertrand Russell, Einstein, Bernard Shaw, Jung and others, and presented plays, poems, essays and philosophy purportedly written by them. She died in 2001, having gained personal fame and exposure for her claims, but not serious recognition.

She is not the only person to have presented works whose attribution is questionable. Early in his career the famous violinist Fritz Kreisler found that he was short of the type of music that he liked to play in his recitals and decided to write suitable pieces himself. However, that meant his name would appear too frequently on the programme as soloist and composer. He also suspected that no one would pay any attention to music written by himself. So he attributed the new compositions to little-known composers of the seventeenth or eighteenth century, such as Pugnani and Porpora, and said he had come across them in a monastery in Avignon in the south of France.

The critics were totally taken in. On one occasion he included a piece under his own name and one of his 'fake' pieces, only to be roundly ticked off by a reviewer for daring to present his own work alongside the genuine work of a master. Such comments amused him highly. He eventually owned up in 1935, greatly annoying the doyen of music critics, Ernest Newman of *The Times*, one of his leading supporters.

In 1948, Mikhail Emmanuilovich Goldstein, a Ukrainian composer and librarian of the Odessa conservatory, discovered a new symphony by the Ukrainian composer N D Ovsyaniko-Kulikovsky in the archives.

The new symphony, Symphony No. 21, dating back to 1809, looked genuine enough. Its subtitle 'For the Dedication of the Odessa Theatre' fitted in well with Ovsyaniko-Kulikovsky's connections with that theatre, where he had presented his serf orchestra.

Ukrainian and Russian musicologists were delighted to find such an early example of Ukrainian symphonic music. Learned dissertations were written and the symphony was performed in 1949 and recorded by one of the USSR's top orchestras. The record notes called the author 'a master' and promised that the obvious question – where were symphonies numbers one to twenty? – would soon be answered.

When the establishment had fully committed itself to the symphony's authenticity, Goldstein announced that he was the composer. He had perpetrated the hoax to disprove a critic's remarks that, as a Jew, he could not compose in true Ukrainian style. Goldstein didn't do himself any favours because the ensuing furore ensured that his other work has since been completely overshadowed.

Other composers who have written hoax pieces include Berlioz and Hugo Wolf. Wolf, best known as a composer of lieder, had a talent for imitating Schumann and set up a recital to perform a number of 'Schumann' songs. However, the master of ceremonies accidentally revealed the secret and the infuriated Wolf raced off the stage without ever performing them.

In 1931, there was great excitement when a recently discovered Mozart violin concerto was performed for the first time. It was Mozart aged only ten, but still a valuable addition to the corpus. As the manuscript was unfinished, its discoverer, the violinist Marius Casadesus, took it upon himself to complete it. Called the 'Adelaide', it was swiftly accepted into the official Mozart canon, given a Köchel number and recorded by the great Yehudi Menuhin. It was not until 38 years later, during a row over royalty rights, that Casadesus admitted it was entirely his own work.

At a prom in October 1929, the first performance took place of an orchestrated version of Bach's Toccata and Fugue in D minor by a young Russian, Paul Klenovsky, a pupil of Glazunov. It required extraordinarily large numbers of woodwind, horns, trumpets, trombones and percussion and made a terrific impact on the audience. It was subsequently played at many concerts and was still so popular a few years later that a publisher tried to track down the composer with a view to publishing the piece. However, he was unable to find any trace of Klenovsky. He went to Sir Henry Wood, who had been the conductor that night, and asked for his help. To the publisher's astonishment, Wood said there was no such person as Klenovsky. He himself had written the music under the assumed name because he was getting tired of the criticism in the musical press that his own compositions were over-orchestrated. He had taken a good deal of ironic satisfaction from the repeated hearings of the very heavily overorchestrated Toccata and Fugue, knowing that if it had gone out under his own name, it would have been played only once.

Occasionally the reverse happens, and musicologists declare a piece to be spurious when it is in fact genuine. Experts scathingly dismissed part of a Mozart piano concerto in this way, only for Mozart's autograph score to turn up a little later to embarrass them.

Provenance is a tricky area and even the most famous names can make misjudgements. In the middle of the nineteenth century, 49 German folk songs were published under the title *Old German Love Songs*. The collection was edited by one of the pre-eminent composers of his or any other era. Later, it was discovered that the songs had been written contemporaneously by a schoolmaster. Even the great Johannes Brahms could be taken in.

THE FORGOTTEN FOUR MINUTES

LONDON, JULY 1976

A few days after the seventieth birthday of the composer Elisabeth Lutyens, a big celebration concert was held at the Purcell Room in her honour. As well as her own music, the programme included music by composers whom Lutyens admired such as Debussy, Schumann and Robert Saxton.

Lutyens herself had written a new piece for the occasion, a quartet called *Mare et Minutiae*, to be played by the highly respected Medici Quartet, led by David Robertson. As was fitting, Lutyens was asked to introduce her new piece and say something about her music in general. She requested that Malcolm Williamson, who had studied with her and was now Master of the Queen's Music, should also take part in the discussion. The organisers were agreeable, but since Lutyens and Williamson were known to be on the garrulous side once they started talking about music, they decided that the very experienced critic, writer and broadcaster John Amis should act as moderator to keep the show under control.

The first performance of *Mare et Minutiae* was the highlight of the evening and the audience of friends and admirers of Lutyens listened with great attentiveness. The piece was beautifully played by the Medici Quartet and, with a loud flourish, finally reached an ecstatic climax. There was a loud burst of applause from the audience and the delighted Lutyens rose to acknowledge the reception.

It was at this point that John Amis noticed Robertson, leader of the Medici, urgently trying to attract his attention. 'John,'

Robertson whispered, 'that wasn't the end. There's still another four minutes to go!'

Amis sidled up to Lutyens, who was still taking bows. 'Lizzie, Lizzie,' he muttered, 'it's not finished yet.'

Still graciously smiling as she took the applause, Lutyens whispered back through clenched teeth, 'It had bloody well better be!' Amis relayed the message back to the quartet and the last four minutes were quietly forgotten.

Later Lutyens was asked how it was she didn't know there was still more to come. 'Oh, well,' she said carelessly, 'composing is like doing yesterday's *Times* crossword. As soon as I finish a piece, I forget it.'

In 1981, another concert was planned at St John's, Smith Square for her 75th birthday, but sadly this had to be cancelled for lack of funds, possibly a euphemism for poor ticket sales. Lutyens's uncompromising music, though much appreciated by her peers, never made a popular breakthrough. Her birthday did not go unmarked though. The same week the BBC included two of her works in a concert, and there was a celebration concert for her at the Wigmore Hall.

A BAD BLOW ALL ROUND

LONDON, JUNE 1977

Advertisements for alfresco concerts always look so tempting. A summer evening's picnic under the trees in some delightful park listening to Dvorak or Tchaikovsky drifting across a lake sounds perfect. And what could be nicer than a trip down the Thames to the accompaniment of Handel's *Water Music*? The idea appeals to our romantic instincts, so we stifle our doubts about the weather or the organisation and turn up, hoping for the best, but sometimes getting the worst.

In 1977, as a contribution to the Royal Silver Jubilee celebrations, Imperial Tobacco Company (ITC) sponsored a series of concerts that it called the Thameside Festival. Various elite indoor venues were chosen, such as the Banqueting House, Whitehall, Hampton Court Palace and St George's Chapel, Windsor. There was one outdoor setting, St Katharine's Dock, near the Tower of London. Conductors and soloists were of the highest calibre, among them Janet Baker, Jessye Norman, Simon Rattle and Itzhak Perlman, with the English Chamber Orchestra as permanent orchestra.

St Katharine's Dock was advertised as a 'rugs and cushions' concert, which had a nice informal ring. The programme, conducted by Charles Mackerras, was entirely Handel and included the *Water Music* and the *Music for the Royal Fireworks*, naturally accompanied by fireworks (in Jubilee year fireworks were like chips and came with everything).

ITC decided not to venture onto the Thames proper, but placed the orchestra on a barge, which it set afloat in the centre of the dock.

With tickets at only £1, the concert caught the public imagination and some six thousand people arrived, many more than expected. The roads were jammed with cars and the start, scheduled for eight o'clock, was put back to allow everyone to get in.

ITC executives present may well have had their minds elsewhere. The same day the company had proudly launched a new tobacco substitute called New Smoking Materials (NSM) and was anxious for news of its acceptance. NSM was claimed to be a major advance in tobacco safety and ITC was optimistic of capturing a substantial portion of the healthy-smoking market.

Finally, 45 minutes late, the concert got under way. At least, the crowds on the quayside assumed it had, as they could see Mackerras's vigorous gestures and the orchestra playing with might and main. But only frustrating snatches of sound ever reached them. A strong breeze was blowing Handel's joyous music away from the quayside and across the river. Fed up with the long wait and the rapidly chilling evening, people's patience ran out. A lengthy queue of dissatisfied customers formed, asking for their money back. Soon the roads were jammed with cars heading back the way they had only recently come.

One way and another it was a bad Thursday for ITC. A report on the fiasco in *The Times* made poor PR, and, more importantly for the company, the new tobacco substitute flopped. Early in October ITC announced the line would be discontinued and that 100 million of the new cigarettes would go up in smoke.

The Thameside Festival organisers obviously hadn't learned about the pitfalls of concerts on the Thames from a similar incident a year earlier, amusingly reported in *The Times* diary.

The concert promoter Arthur Martin was more ambitious than ITC and organised a flotilla of craft to proceed down the Thames from Tower Pier to Hammersmith. Once again there were delays, as punters turned up in such numbers that there weren't enough boats to take everyone. The flotilla set off untidily 45 minutes late. The orchestra, the Little Symphony of London, conducted by Arthur Davison, was on its own boat, the *St Mawes Castle*, which had loudspeakers that were supposed to relay the sound across the water.

Passengers on the surrounding boats could see by the conductor's gestures that the orchestra had begun to play, but most could hear little or nothing. Either a strong wind blew the sound in the wrong direction, or a power boat came roaring past, or the noise of the engines, as the boats tried to keep up with the orchestra, drowned out the music. The orchestra's boat was doing its best, sometimes circling the bridge piers to give the other boats a chance to catch up.

Acoustics were better under bridges, except when a train happened to be passing overhead. Even so, some people did not hear a note the whole trip. Even the promised refreshments were a disappointment – sandwiches, not the expected banquet. Only the orchestra had a thoroughly enjoyable evening, according to Darell Davison, the son of the conductor, a cellist in the orchestra that evening and now its conductor.

Of course, we only hear of the disasters. There must be examples when everything has gone perfectly, such as the first performance of the *Water Music* in 1717. It was played as George I and his court proceeded by barge to Chelsea; then again, by royal command, after supper at Chelsea; and yet once more on the way back to Whitehall at three in the morning. And you can bet supper wasn't just sandwiches.

RACE AGAINST TIME

GLOUCESTER, AUGUST 1977

1977 was a very busy year for the Australian composer Malcolm Williamson – too busy. It was the Queen's Silver Jubilee and, as Master of the Queen's Music, he was much in demand to produce music for various celebrations marking the occasion. One by one the commissions mounted up until he was stretched to breaking point. Completing each score to meet the date of its premiere became a constant race against time.

As the year began, he was already working on three substantial compositions simultaneously. A mini-opera for children was due in June, his *Mass for Christ the King* was to be premiered in August, and his Fourth Symphony was scheduled for December. To add to his busy schedule, an American tour was planned for July.

Unanticipated demands made his workload even heavier. He was asked to set the *Jubilee Hymn*, with words by his literary counterpart, Sir John Betjeman, the Poet Laureate. The BBC was producing a programme on the House of Windsor and wanted a six-movement suite to accompany it. Benjamin Britten had died the previous December and Peter Pears asked for an organ piece for his memorial service. The conscientious Williamson felt obliged to accept all these requests, but they put him under enormous time pressure.

He was also under financial pressure. Prestigious as these projects were, they did not pay very well and Williamson, with a family to support, supplemented his income by writing film scores. His was the scary music behind many horror films, such as Hammer Productions' *The Brides of Dracula* and *The Horror of Frankenstein*. In Jubilee year he was balancing the books by writing the score for *Watership Down*. All in all, he had the equivalent of three years' work to do in one.

Under all these pressures, Williamson caused a sensation at a press conference in March by attacking the Arts Council, complaining bitterly that he had asked for a £5,000 commissioning fee for the Mass and been offered exactly nothing. He had been able to undertake the work only because money had been forthcoming from other sources. Johnson Wax promised £2,000 but payable after completion, and there was £1,000 from the Royal Philharmonic Orchestra (RPO), who were to perform the piece, but that was a loan. With proper funding, he said, he wouldn't be forced to take extraneous, commercial work and his commissions would be finished on time. The press loved the story and it got wide publicity. But it changed nothing as far as Williamson was concerned.

In June, the first of the three major commissions took place as scheduled, as 17,000 Merseyside schoolchildren performed *The Valley and the Hill* before the Queen in the streets of Liverpool. Williamson had had so many ideas it turned out to be twice as long as expected, not unusual with him. Still, one down, two to go.

Now he could concentrate on completing the *Mass for Christ the King* to be performed at the Three Choirs Festival in Gloucester Cathedral on 25 August. It was the most important of a number of new works commissioned for the 250th anniversary of the festival.

John Sanders, the organist at Gloucester and responsible for preparing the performance, had been keeping a close eye on progress and was becoming increasingly concerned as the vocal score and the orchestral parts failed to appear. At last, the vocal score – or at least parts of it – arrived, so the choirs could begin rehearsing to a piano reduction in the usual way. It was not until two weeks before the performance that the choir had the complete vocal score in their hands.

But there was still no sign of the orchestral parts. Sanders kept putting back the orchestral rehearsals, confident that the

RPO would need little time to master the music. Finally, he set up a rehearsal date in London as late as he dared, only one week before the performance. Williamson promised the parts would be ready, but when Sanders arrived for the rehearsal there was no sign of them. He was forced to rehearse Elgar's *The Dream of Gerontius* instead, which the orchestra knew backwards anyway. The rehearsal was interrupted halfway through by the arrival of Williamson's assistant, laden with orchestral parts. It was only two-thirds of the work, but at least they were able to make a start.

Sanders returned to Gloucester, still short of several movements and with only a few days to go. Surreally, day by day, parts of the score began to drift in sent by train, as if, even at this late date, Williamson truly believed it was not a lost cause, though it was clear to Sanders that only a partial performance was possible at best.

Even on the day of the performance, Williamson arrived with still more sheets, then hurried off to continue work. The choir and orchestra rehearsed desperately, once in the morning, then again in the afternoon right up to shortly before the performance, trying to cope as more sheets sporadically reached them. With performance time only minutes away, Sanders was forced to make some cuts. Out went the Gloria and Credo, also a responsorial psalm requiring the involvement of the audience. The Agnus Dei was performed with organ accompaniment in place of the orchestra. Though there were inevitable imperfections in the performance, the critics sensed that the Mass was an unusual work of potential and looked forward to hearing the completed version.

In July the following year, Williamson appeared at another press conference, not to take issue with the Arts Council, but to flourish the finished score of the Mass. The long-suffering Three Choirs and RPO therefore had sufficient time to prepare for the first complete performance, which took place on 3 November 1978 in Westminster Cathedral. The Queen, as dedicatee, was present, the first time a British queen had stepped foot inside that cathedral for four hundred years.

Williamson had one more major composition to complete in

1977, his Fourth Symphony, commissioned by the London Philharmonic Orchestra (LPO) and also dedicated to the Queen. Its first performance was planned for 8 December. Originally an eighteen-minute work, it had grown to half an hour. Williamson disappeared to the Camargue, where he worked late into every night, but it was still incomplete early in the week of the performance. Three movements were playable and it was agreed to play these before the Queen and the Duke of Edinburgh. However, the next day Williamson changed his mind and vetoed any performance, saying it would be improper to play it only in part. Instead of the symphony, the LPO played Elgar's *Cockaigne* overture.

On the day of what should have been the first performance, Williamson held yet another press conference where he set out the train of events that had resulted in his failure to complete two important commissions during the year. He even had a good word for the Arts Council. In March he had felt 'total disgust' towards it, but now he thanked it for its great support during the year.

Exhausted by the events of 1977, Williamson turned down all new commissions for 1978, took a sabbatical and finished both the Mass and the symphony. The symphony was not as lucky as the Mass. By the time Williamson died in 2003, it had never received a performance.

A FISHY TALE

CHATHAM, OCTOBER 1977

In 1977, the Philharmonia Orchestra took the significant step of finally buying back its original name, sold by its founder Walter Legge in 1964 when he disbanded the orchestra as his own property. A relaunch using the restored name was organised by the managing director Gavin Henderson, and a series of concerts was arranged. Conductors included top-rank names such as Carlo Maria Guilini, Riccardo Muti and Andrew Davis.

It was all looking very promising until Henderson discovered that conflicting engagements meant that Davis had to pull out of his two concerts at the Royal Festival Hall. Conductors with the quality necessary for the Philharmonia were often booked three or four years ahead and Henderson could find no one suitable to replace Davis at short notice. He was almost at his wits' end when he remembered that there was an internationally known conductor who had exactly the right pedigree and was likely to be available. That was the good news. The bad news was that he was Russian, Yevgeny Svetlanov, and would need permission to leave the Soviet Union.

Henderson knew this was by no means a foregone conclusion. Soviet artists were still being denied exit visas, as was to happen to Svetlanov himself in 1984. However, there had recently been a slight thaw in the Cold War, and the desperate Henderson had little choice other than to try and exploit it. He arrived in Moscow and immediately became embroiled in the bureaucratic fun and games characteristic of cultural contacts between the Soviet Union and the West. One day he would be told that all was being arranged, only to be informed the next that it was impossible. This went on for ten days until Henderson got fed up and announced that he was going back to England. 'Such impatience after only ten days,' the bureaucrats must have thought, but at least it stirred them into action. Suddenly they announced they would meet his request. Henderson's hopes rose. Only the conductor they proposed was not Svetlanov. '*Niet*,' said the fed-up Henderson, 'Svetlanov or no one.'

Miraculously his tactics worked and Svetlanov was given an exit visa. It was a terrific coup for Henderson and the orchestra, and the good news swiftly circulated through British musical circles. Svetlanov was arguably the doyen of Russian conductors. The benefits began to pour in as EMI beat the doors down with recording contracts.

Svetlanov finally arrived in London and was conducted to his hotel. He took one look at it and announced, 'Hotel disgrace! I go airport.' Henderson hastily arranged for an alternative. Svetlanov was not happy with that either, nor the next, nor the next. 'I go airport,' he threatened with increasing menace. 'It's terrible,' his English interpreter said to Henderson, 'he means it this time, he's got a car.' It took twelve hotels before Henderson found one that was acceptable.

The next day he took the conductor to meet the orchestra at Chatham, where a concert had been organised at the Central Hall, as a warm-up prior to the Festival Hall. The hall, even Henderson admits, was not totally satisfactory. The conductor's changing room was little better than a shed. The platform was so small that there was no room for four of the violinists and they had to be dropped.

When Svetlanov came onto the platform, he immediately registered the small string section and was appalled. Furiously he began to rehearse the first item, the overture from Glinka's *Ruslan and Ludmila*, taking it at a hectic pace. Russian orchestras were used to playing it at high speed, but the Philharmonia struggled to keep up as Svetlanov whipped the pace along, shouting unintelligible instructions and conducting with such frenetic energy that he snapped his baton. Angrily he left the platform and sat in his 'dressing room' (the shed), demanding his car.

Seeing Svetlanov's terrible mood, Carl Pini, the orchestra's leader, tried to mollify him, but without success. Someone else had a better idea and offered him vodka. That did it. 'I haf never been so insulted,' Svetlanov shouted. 'Bought by a vodka!'

'It really is the end,' the interpreter reported urgently to Henderson. This time Henderson thought so too. All he could see were unfulfilled engagements and financial and artistic disaster for the orchestra. He was deep in these gloomy thoughts when one of the violists, Ken Cayzer, came up. Henderson, anticipating yet another problem, thought Cayzer's timing could have been better, but Cayzer insisted on speaking to him. He handed over a photograph. Henderson saw it was a picture of him, the violist, holding a large fish. 'Give the maestro this,' Cayzer said.

Henderson didn't like to think how Svetlanov would react if he walked in and gave him a picture of a fish, but what had he got to lose?

Very tentatively he approached Svetlanov and gave him the picture, explaining that it was at the request of a member of the orchestra. Svetlanov looked at it and, to Henderson's surprise and relief, broke into an enormous beam and kissed him heartily on both cheeks.

Some twenty years earlier, Svetlanov had been in London to conduct the LPO, of which Cayzer was then a member. There were a couple of free days in Svetlanov's schedule and he expressed the desire to go fishing. A message was sent round the orchestra, 'Anyone fancy a couple of days' fishing with the maestro?' There is such a wide range of hobbies and interests among orchestral players that there was every chance someone would be a fisherman. Svetlanov had got on famously with Cayzer and had never forgotten the incident.

The concert that night marked the beginning of a long and fruitful relationship between Svetlanov and the Philharmonia. Suddenly the orchestra could do no wrong. At one point in the march that is the third movement of Tchaikovsky's Sixth Symphony (*Pathétique*), he even stopped conducting, simply nodding his head in time as the orchestra played. It was his way of saying, 'You are a good orchestra.' The orchestra wholeheartedly returned the compliment. The audience at Chatham never knew how close it came to missing a sell-out concert and what it owed to a picture of a fish.

THE CONCERT THAT WENT WITH A BANG

LIVERPOOL, SUMMER 1978

On a hot Sunday evening in Liverpool, the Royal Liverpool Philharmonic Orchestra (RLPO) was playing at the Philharmonic Hall in aid of a charity for people with learning disabilities.

The full house had enjoyed many popular pieces and there was something of a carnival atmosphere with the audience clapping along with the *Sea Songs* in best Last Night of the Proms tradition.

As so often, the grand finale was Tchaikovsky's *1812* overture, complete with spectacular cannon and mortar effects. Under the control of operators kitted out in Napoleonic War uniforms, two authentic old-style cannons that might have come off HMS *Victory* had been mounted at the back of the orchestra behind the brass section, and were aimed imposingly over the audience.

Cliff Bibby, one of the first violins, thought they looked rather too powerful for an enclosed space, and was somewhat surprised they hadn't been tried out during the rehearsal. Orchestral players are always a bit wary of the *1812* and can tell plenty of light-hearted stories about special effects coming in at the wrong place, or more loudly than planned, or not at all. After the rehearsal, he went up to one of the management team to check.

'Oh, no,' replied the operator he spoke to, 'we do this all the time. We only use a very small charge.' Reassured, though not entirely convinced, Bibby let the matter drop.

The cannons at the climax of the *1812* go off singly at regular intervals, following cues from the conductor. So when Anthony Ridley, the conductor for the evening, gave the cue, the operator of the first cannon lit the fuse. But whoever had loaded the cannon had got the wrong mix of wadding, paper and gunpowder. Totally unexpectedly, a sheet of flame and sparks shot out of the cannon's mouth. The noise, funnelled towards the audience by the hall's special acoustic shell, was so incredibly loud that it half-deafened the orchestra, which very nearly ground to a halt but somehow managed to continue, albeit in a growing cloud of smoke and cordite.

In the auditorium, the audience, equally stunned, cringed in their seats, knowing that the second cannon was about to go off. When it did, the effect was the same as the first. It was too much for one lady violist, who leaped out of her seat and ran from the platform screaming. Later, she recalled that she remembered starting the overture, but the next thing she knew she was back in the bandroom being ministered to, having thrust her viola into the hands of a colleague as she ran off. When she got home, she sat in the garden till midnight, 'a shivering wreck', trying to recover. Since then, she has had special dispensation from the orchestra from playing in the *1812*. She even avoids listening to it.

Those immediately in front of the cannon suffered worst. The bass trombonist was sitting with his head between his hands. More seriously, a tuba player was knocked off his chair by the blast and was so shaken that he was unable to continue playing, though in the confusion no one noticed. He was so badly traumatised that at the end he could not move from his chair and had to be led off the platform. The audience, in a jovial mood up to then, had gone deathly quiet. The cloud of cordite had drifted into the auditorium and was settling on people and all the surfaces. A lady in the front row who had come in wearing a white dress went out wearing a grey one.

The operators of the cannon, seemingly completely unaware of what was going on, started preparing for their second salvoes. As Bibby graphically puts it, 'I saw the buggers were reloading!'

The piece somehow staggered to the end. A lot of the orchestra were furious. When the conductor left the stage, Allan Travers, the leader, swiftly followed him. But Ridley, entering into the spirit of the evening, had gone off to collect a comic mask, which he put on and returned to the platform. His vision now restricted by the mask, he did not see Travers and they bumped into each other, probably the first time that a conductor returning to take a bow has met the leader coming in the opposite direction. Tempers continued to flare in the bandroom. When the person who had organised the cannons walked through, one of the horn players had to be physically restrained from assaulting him.

Next day the *Liverpool Echo* reported the story under the headline 'Orchestra Brings the House Down'. The repercussions, so to speak, were far-reaching. Players went off for hearing tests, checks were done on the building structure to make sure it wasn't damaged, and the RLPO apologetically issued vouchers to the orchestra to pay for their cleaning bills and brought in an army of cleaners to wash down the walls.

Later, Bibby found that there had been some pre-rehearsal tests of the cannons. They were so loud that the management asked for them to be toned down. Somehow or other the adjustments were insufficient (probably nothing to do with visits to the pub in the break before the performance).

FROM HIGH SOCIETY TO HIGH SECURITY

BELGRAVIA, LONDON, DECEMBER 1985

Arne Richards, musical director of the Oxford Concert Party (OCP), has played gigs in very varied locations, including a grand house and a high-security prison. The sense of satisfaction he got from performing in two such contrasting venues was very different from that he had anticipated.

In December 1985, he and guitarist Bill Lovelady were asked to perform a recital at a de luxe residence in Belgravia. Richards was instructed to hire 'the most beautiful harpsichord in London' with no expense spared, so he dutifully hired a wonderful seventeenth-century Ruckers harpsichord. It was delivered to the client's flat and tuned twice the same day in a special seventeenth-century tuning. Richards and Lovelady practised a Vivaldi concerto and some of Lovelady's own compositions, and Richards went over the Handel and Scarlatti sonatas he was going to play on the harpsichord. They were told that a rich Iranian woman owned the flat and that the recital was in honour of a mystery royal guest.

On the day of the concert Richards and Lovelady arrived at the flat and rehearsed in a large reception room with chairs set out for the recital. After finishing their preparations, they enjoyed smoked salmon and champagne while waiting for the audience to assemble.

The guests arrived in incredible cars, the women dripping with jewellery. Eventually, and much later than the agreed starting time, their hostess told them that the guests of honour had arrived. As the special guests entered the room, Richards recognised Prince and Princess Michael of Kent with a large entourage.

Richards and Lovelady were asked to begin their programme, which they did. To their dismay, people talked all the way through the Vivaldi concerto and the pair gradually realised that no one had any intention of listening.

Richards's normal custom was to announce the music and talk a bit about the pieces before playing them. However, the audience was making such a racket that he launched straight into the first Scarlatti sonata without introduction. The audience was now talking so loudly he could hardly hear his instrument. The two musicians conferred and decided to abandon the original programme and just improvise, even playing some jazz and boogie-woogie.

The 'concert' ended and the pair were thanked and told 'how beautifully' they had played.

Lack of audience attention is an occupational hazard for musicians. After a concert on one of his grand American tours in the mid-nineteenth century, Louis Moreau Gottschalk in his *Memoirs of a Pianist* pithily summed up the situation. 'The concert was deplorable this evening. Complete silence. I correct myself. Silence when I entered and when I went out, but animated conversation all the time I was playing. But happily we conducted things briskly, and despatched over eight pieces in twenty-five minutes.'

Equally happily, Richards and Lovelady collected a large fee and a mention in the Nigel Dempster column in the next day's *Daily Mail*.

Should the situation recur in the future, they might like to take a tip from Wieniawski, the nineteenth-century Polish violinist. In a similar situation in London, he converted the piece he was playing, Raff's *Cavatina*, into 'God Save The Queen', knowing that the dignitaries would immediately have to stop talking and stand to attention, which they did. However, he did not take into account that the unmusical lot resumed chatting as soon as he reverted to the Raff. Though he repeated the same trick a few more times, and got the same response, they never took the hint, but only wondered why there was a piece that contained so much of the National Anthem.

The French composer Erik Satie also had his problems with audiences. For a concert in an art gallery in Paris in 1920, he came up with a new form of music that he called *musique d'ameublement*. He designed it as the musical equivalent of furniture or wallpaper, which very quickly ceases to be noticed, and gave strict instructions to the gathering to consider it of no importance and to ignore it. But, perversely, as soon as the ensemble of clarinets, trombone and piano began to play, everyone stopped looking at the pictures, sat down and began to focus on the music. Satie was in despair. 'No, no,' he cried, 'don't listen! Walk about, talk, go on talking!' Clearly he and the Richards-Lovelady duo had each other's ideal audience.

Some years after performing for royalty, Arne Richards had another experience, which turned out to be equally eye-opening.

In 1992, the OCP, of which Richards is musical director, won a contract to perform in prisons throughout the UK and Ireland. The OCP is well known for its wide repertoire of classical and non-classical music and its involvement in educational projects.

After the concerts, which always proved to be highly success-ful, the group were able to talk to the prisoners and it became apparent that prolonged and personal contact was really needed. As a result, OCP started offering four-day projects, often involving men who had no experience of practical music-making, as well as some who did. The ground-breaking project was followed by the Home Office, including the then Home Secretary, Jack Straw.

In July 1996, Richards and his group spent a week at HMP Whitemoor, a high-security prison that houses some of the most dangerous criminals in the country. OCP had directed several successful projects there in the past. Just after their previous concert, there had been an IRA breakout, before which a pound of Semtex high explosive had been smuggled into the prison. As a result, security on this visit was higher than ever. The band had to go through extremely exhaustive hour-long searches, and have their fingerprints and mug shots taken. They watched nervously as their priceless instruments – two violins, viola, cello, double bass, harpsichord and accordion and thirty or forty exotic percussion instruments from different parts of the world – were also electronically searched.

Each morning they spent two hours with one group of twenty men, followed by two hours with a different group in the afternoon, culminating in two separate performances on the final day. The groups were kept separate because the morning group consisted of vulnerable prisoners including sex offenders, who had to be kept apart from the main prison.

As always, the men were encouraged to explore the sounds of the instruments, and over a period of time they became confident enough with themselves and with each other to improvise. Using songs, music and poems written by the inmates, interspersed with OCP's own repertoire, it was possible to put together an hour's programme to perform to an audience of inmates, prison officers, tutors and other staff.

'Michael', a group member from the main prison, was a notorious gangland celebrity. OCP were unaware of this until after the project, but he had a reputation within the prison of being extremely antisocial. He was particularly taken with the ocean drum – a large bodhrán-type drum containing seeds that makes sounds like rain or the swishing of the sea. He played this throughout the sessions and made a considerable contribution to the music.

Because of his status as a career bank robber and hard man, many officers and inmates came to see him perform at the final session. People simply couldn't believe that he was capable of joining in any group, let alone participating in a concert on stage.

After the performance, a buoyant Michael approached Richards. 'Arne, that was terrific – I really enjoyed the whole week – when are you coming in again?'

'Well, Michael,' Richards paused – 'I suppose it does depend upon the funding.'

Michael thought for a moment. 'Well, I suppose I could

probably arrange some funding . . . on the other hand, the last time I did that, I got twenty years!'

The next time Richards saw Michael in Whitemoor, he was about to be released. He told Richards that as a direct result of the OCP project he had taken up painting for a living.

BRASSED OFF II

NORTHAMPTON, FEBRUARY 1991

The second of our three brass-band travel stories concerns the famous Brighouse and Rastrick Band.

In February 1991, Roy Newsome, one of the best-known and most highly respected figures in the world of brass bands, was invited to guest-conduct the band, which was travelling down from the Huddersfield area. The sell-out concert was to take place at Spinney Hill Hall, in Northampton, and contained many favourites, such as Suppé's *Poet and Peasant* overture, Debussy's *Girl with the Flaxen Hair* and some rousing Tchaikovsky, the finale of his Fourth Symphony and the ever-popular *1812* overture.

Newsome arrived in good time for the 7.30 p.m. start, but as the appointed time drew near there was no sign of Brighouse and Rastrick. It wasn't until shortly before starting time that a call was received from the band saying their coach had broken down on the M1. They assured the organisers that the coach company had organised a replacement and they would do their best to get there as soon as possible.

One of the concert's organisers did a bit of lateral thinking and raced off in his car to the breakdown point, his idea being to collect the music and the music stands, and bring them back to the hall so they could be set up in advance and thus save time when the band arrived. He duly located the band, collected the music and stands and set off back to Northampton.

Things were looking better for the band too, when not one but two replacement coaches turned up, one from as far away as Huddersfield. They transferred their instruments and set off for Spinney Hill Hall. The concert was going to be late, but only by half an hour, and the band changed into their concert uniforms on the way to save time.

In the meantime, some six or seven hundred people were waiting patiently for some entertainment. The organisers managed to use up some time by spinning out the raffle for twenty minutes or so, but they were becoming more and more desperate as the delay lengthened, to the point of offering money back to those who wanted to leave.

When the band finally arrived, the bandsmen poured out of the coach and prepared to rush straight onto the platform. But they were told to save their energy. The driver who had gone to collect their music and stands had not yet reappeared.

It was Roy Newsome who stepped heroically into the breach. Seated on a tall stool, 'looking a bit like Dave Allen', he says, he told banding stories for well over an hour to entertain the audience.

When the music and stands eventually arrived, the man who had gone to fetch them explained, shamefacedly, that he had run out of petrol. So much for lateral thinking. It was not until nine o'clock that Roy Newsome finally raised his baton and the band launched into Sousa's 'Stars and Stripes For Ever'.

Speaking of his ad-libbing performance, Newsome admitted he had never done anything like that before and had surprised himself. 'It was strange,' he says, 'how one story triggered off another and I was able to keep going.' He enjoyed the experience, but not enough to take it up as an alternative career.

AN ALARMING CONCERT

CHICAGO, OCTOBER 1991

The Chicago Symphony Orchestra (CSO) is by common consent one of the world's great orchestras. It has been associated with legendary composers such as Richard Strauss, Sergei Rachmaninov and Igor Stravinsky. Its eminent music directors include Fritz Reiner, Rafael Kubelik, Sir Georg Solti and Daniel Barenboim.

In 1991 the orchestra decided to celebrate its hundred years of existence by re-creating exactly the first concert it had ever given back in 1891. As part of the celebrations, it invited its two living former music directors, Kubelik and Solti, to share the conducting duties with the current maestro, Daniel Barenboim.

Prior to the concert the CSO gave a dinner for four hundred of its most generous donors. As a mark of appreciation, each donor was presented with a gift, beautifully wrapped in a box. After dinner, the contented donors proceeded into the concert hall, taking their box with them. They had not got around to unwrapping the gift and were therefore unaware that it was an elegant, specially marked desk clock with an alarm, all set to different times and, crucially, some of which were switched on.

The programme opened with a Wagner overture. During Beethoven's Fifth Symphony which followed, there was an occasional annoying bleep, attributed to someone's thoughtlessness in not switching off his watch bleeper, but as the concert progressed, more and more clocks came to the time where their alarm was due to go off. During the first item after the interval, Tchaikovsky's First Piano Concerto, the bleeping became a major annoyance. Solti, the conductor, and Barenboim, who was soloist, struggled to keep their concentration and fought against their growing irritation.

Henry Fogel, executive director of the CSO, couldn't figure out what was going on until it occurred to one of his staff that the noise might be the alarm clocks handed out at dinner. They dashed out into the lobby and tested one of the clocks. It was the same sound. They looked at each other in a different kind of alarm. Inside, like a ticking bomb, were almost 400 clocks, many of which were likely to go off throughout the rest of the concert. Solti and Barenboim would go berserk. In fact, Solti was already so disconcerted that at the end of the first movement of the Tchaikovsky he started to address the audience, clearly intending to take them to task for not having switched off their bleepers. This was, of course, totally unfair so Fogel decided to take matters into his own hands. He walked out onto the stage and took the brave step of interrupting Solti. Solti, a Hungarian with excellent English, told Fogel afterwards, 'I thought I was losing my mind. First I hear beeping, then you walk out on stage and interrupt me – I thought I was in a loony bin!'

Fogel told the audience about the four hundred randomly set alarm clocks. After they had stopped laughing, they dutifully took them outside to the ushers, who kept them in the lobbies until after the concert. After that, the programme continued without incident, a memorable centennial evening made more memorable for the wrong reason.

HOVE TOO

HOVE, SUSSEX, MAY 1993

Is it good karma to call one's band Attacca? John Williams believed so during the early 1990s when the band was assembled and set out on its somewhat headlong musical career. It was a small ensemble and the idea was to perform mostly new works and arrangements of light classics and ballads. This kind of repertoire would play well, as they say, in town halls and smaller venues, to a general rather than specialised audience.

Thus, when they were booked by the Brighton Festival to give their debut performance one Saturday evening in Hove Town Hall to a capacity audience, there was no reason to anticipate anything out of the ordinary.

Rather the reverse, in fact. The audience would be drawn mostly from the town of Hove, a byword for respectability. This is the town, after all, that preserves its reputation so fiercely from its raffish neighbour Brighton to have earned the nickname 'Hove actually'. The phrase is not only apocryphally the residents' answer to the question, 'Do you come from Brighton?' but also genuinely the name of a pub. Hove, bastion of calm; Attacca, players of light summer music. The scene was set.

The programme included the first performance of a work by the Australian composer Peter Sculthorpe. The usual checks were made in advance. Would they need a piano? Yes they would, but the one in the hall would be all right. On arrival, however, the musicians realised that the piano in the hall wasn't good enough. The organisers telephoned everywhere for a better piano and eventually located one at Steinways. However, it could not be delivered to Hove Town Hall until 6 p.m., which meant they would not have time to rehearse. John Williams decided to postpone the start of the concert by about an hour.

When the audience began to arrive they were told this and responded predictably: some took it well, others became very angry, then they all went off to the pub to wait it out. It was an unusually hot evening, which always makes people more fractious.

The heat and anxiety had ratcheted up the tension for the musicians too. As the day progressed the Town Hall had become progressively hotter. By the time the piano arrived the temperature was tropical, and the musicians opened the doors to let in some air; pretty soon, the members of the audience, who were waiting outside, began to surge in.

Another problem now presented itself: the tickets did not distinguish between balcony and stalls, so people didn't know which seats they should have. According to Gavin Henderson, now principal of Trinity College of Music, then artistic director of the Brighton Festival (including Hove, actually), 'People were pounding over seats, climbing over each other – and pretty soon, fights began to break out'. In time a marvellous peacemaker came forward and begged for calm; somehow the audience was placated, everyone was seated, and the band began to play.

A curious lighting system was in place in Hove Town Hall that night: big stage lights had been set up behind the auditorium, lights of such extraordinary wattage that they generated incredible heat. They were directly behind the back rows and people who were sitting there soon began collapsing. Some actually fainted, and there was a smell of burning or, at any rate, singeing hair. Another fight broke out, and the police and an ambulance were called. With the heat the musicians were dreadfully dehydrated but there was no water to drink in the building. In the confusion, somehow the roles of policemen and ambulancemen were reversed, with policemen tending to the injured, while ambulancemen tried to bring the unruly people to order.

By this time, according to Gavin Henderson, people were beginning to find it funny, which is something. Of course the audience were recompensed with tickets and vouchers. Strange to relate, however, Attacca did not thrive after that evening and was soon disbanded. The musical term *attacca*, after all, means 'moving straight on'.

KARLHEINZ STOCKHAUSEN TAKES TO THE AIR

AMSTERDAM, JUNE 1995

HELICOPTER STRING QUARTET (1992/93)
for string quartet,
4 helicopters with pilots and 4 sound technicians
4 television transmitters, 4 x 3 sound transmitters
auditorium with 4 columns of televisions and
4 columns of loudspeakers
sound projectionist with mixing console / moderator
(ad lib.)
The duration is circa 32 minutes.

The idea for the piece that resulted from this specification came to the avant-garde composer Karlheinz Stockhausen in a dream, and he put it first to Professor Hans Landesmann of the *Salzburger Festspiele*. It was 1991, and Professor Landesmann had commissioned a string quartet from Stockhausen, who had at first refused on the grounds that the string quartet was an eighteenth-century form. He said that in a composing lifetime of 45 years he had not written symphonies, sonatas, piano concertos or, for that matter, violin concertos, for the same reason. These forms were felt to be restricting, formal, obsolete. Every inappropriate thing.

However, the Arditti Quartet was expected to play the world premiere of the new piece in 1994, and in the light of this Herr Stockhausen's dream might be considered a stroke of luck. He described it in minute detail in a 98-page illustrated booklet that accompanied the recording, quoted on the othermusic.com website.

I heard and saw the four string players in four helicopters flying in the air and playing. At the same time I saw people on the ground seated in an audio-visual hall, others were standing outdoors in a large public plaza. In front of them, four towers of television screens and loudspeakers had been set up: at the left, half-left, half-right, right. At each of the four positions, one of the four string players could be heard and seen in close-up.

Most of the time, the string players played *tremoli*, which blended so well with the timbres and the rhythms of the rotor blades that the helicopters sounded like musical instruments. When I woke up, I strongly felt that something had been communicated to me which I never would have thought of on my own. I did not tell anyone anything about it.

The composer later explained that after the dream he developed the *Helicopter String Quartet* as the third scene of one of a cycle of music dramas that he had been composing since 1977.

A performance is staged in this way: the moderator explains to the audience what is to happen, the players walk to the helicopters – or are driven there, followed by video cameras, which transmit to the television monitors. From their embarkation into the helicopters until they disembark, each string player and his helicopter is transmitted via camera, television transmitter, three microphones and sound transmitters to his own group of monitors for the audience. As it was envisaged, each string player was to be constantly audible and always visible in close-up – face, hands, bow, instrument. Behind each player, the earth would be seen through the glass cockpit of the helicopter.

The original score was to last eighteen minutes, later expanded to twenty-one minutes, with the ascent, descent and landing to take five minutes each. Detailed instructions were given about the flight paths and heights of the respective helicopters.

The whole scheme was sent to Professor Landesmann at the end of 1993 and, to the surprise of the composer, he approved it in principle. Next, negotiations between the *Festspiele* and the Austrian Army (for the helicopters) took place. Permits had to be obtained. Irvine Arditti was contacted, who suggested using taped helicopter sounds instead, which did not find favour with Stockhausen.

However, the planned performance, which had been scheduled for 1994, did not please the Green Party and they blocked it. Their view that the flight would be environmentally intolerable was held responsible for the extraordinary fees asked for the use of television and radio equipment by the general director of Austrian broadcasting.

So the project moved to Holland, where Jan van Vlijmen, the director of the Holland Festival, obtained the necessary permits and sponsors and scheduled three performances of the piece in Amsterdam on 26 June 1995. The piece was rehearsed in four separate rooms, with Stockhausen listening from a control studio. The players came into the studios to listen. Many more technical tests and rehearsals took place until in June 1995 the technical equipment was set up in a specially fitted auditorium, and the final rehearsals began, with four helicopters. The three flights finally took place at 4.30 p.m., 6.30 p.m. and 8.30 p.m., for different audiences.

The work was recorded by Dutch radio and is in their archive. Karlheinz Stockhausen dedicated it 'To all astronauts'. Richard Hawley, director of the Lichfield Festival, describes the idea of divorcing the audience from the music, and the players from each other, as 'really nice', and finds special praise for the fact that 'you couldn't come away whistling the tunes'. And on 19 January 2001 Stockhausen was awarded the German Music Edition Prize in the category of Scores of Works of the Twentieth Century for the score of the *Helicopter String Quartet*.

A SHOW OF HANDS

OSLO, APRIL 1996

The well-worn phrase 'The show must go on' is not exclusive to the acting profession. Mariss Jansons was conducting *La Bohème* on 25 April 1996 when he had a heart attack, but as he slumped from the podium his hands kept on conducting. Jansons sank lower and lower until his hands were all that were visible to audience and musicians as he fought for his life. He conducts without a baton, as a malign growth on his thumb has prevented him from using a baton for some years. Those hands make compulsive viewing: sometimes the palms are face up to the orchestra, as if in supplication for a good performance; sometimes they sweep across the stage as if trying to levitate the violins over to join the cellos.

Jansons was conducting the Oslo Philharmonic, the orchestra he had taken from near obscurity to become an international force. Its managing director ran to the stage and shouted, 'Is there a doctor in the house?' If there had been any need of market research for concerts this might have provided a pointer, for in answer to the question about a third of the audience stood up.

The Latvian-born maestro is acknowledged as one of the world's finest conductors and his achievement since taking over the Oslo Philharmonic in 1979 is often mentioned alongside that of Sir Simon Rattle with the City of Birmingham Symphony Orchestra. He has lifted the orchestra and himself to international prominence, developing a rare relationship between maestro and musicians, devoting enough time to build

216

up a formidable music ensemble. Music critic Norman Lebrecht says, 'He is possibly the most inspiring conductor alive, one of the mystic few whose mere presence seems to transform the sound that players make.'

In the same year as the heart attack Jansons and the Oslo Philharmonic were invited for a week-long residency at the Musikverein, the ornate home of the Vienna Philharmonic. His wife was frightened; his doctors were furious. Five nights conducting exhausting programmes by a man whose arteries, two Harley Street consultants confirmed, were too frail for bypass or transplant, and who had a defibrillator in his chest (a machine that detects an irregular heartbeat and adjusts it with an electric jolt). Naturally, he did it, and it was a success.

Jansons's father was the conductor Arvid Jansons, head of the Riga State Opera. It was he who suggested Jansons junior to the Oslo Philharmonic. Mariss Jansons studied in Russia, then Vienna, where he was spotted by Herbert von Karajan, who invited him to work with the Berlin Philharmonic. The Soviet authorities, fearful of another sixties' defection, forbade it, and he became assistant music director of the Leningrad Philharmonic. His home is still in the city (now St Petersburg). Before his heart attack he used to drive between there and Oslo.

When asked about the night of his heart attack, Jansons answered rather oddly. 'It was terrible, really terrible,' he said, adding, 'It was very exciting'. He was, of course, talking about the music. 'I like enormously this opera. I conducted and everything went fantastically and seven minutes before the end I suddenly felt terrible pains in my left arm and heart and I knew immediately it was very serious. The question was what to do now. I must save my emotional energy. So I decided I will do very small movements. If I conduct normally then it's the end.

'Stopping was not an option. I felt worse and worse and worse. I had no strength and it was completely dark in my eyes and I said to the orchestra leader, "I feel very badly." Then I don't remember anything. The musicians told me afterwards that I still conducted.' He paused, considering the unthinkable as if for the first time. 'If I had stopped conducting immediately, perhaps it would have been better.'

He did not conduct for six months after the heart attack, and the Proms was one of many performances he had to miss. Those who see him in his concerts abroad may be witnessing a conductor in an exploration that is as much spiritual as musical. 'Being so close to death has brought an extra dimension, more subconsciously but a little bit consciously, too. I think I get deeper as a musician. I like more quiet music now. I like slower tempos like the Beethoven Second. The slow music and slow tempos is much more difficult. If you can fulfil the slow tempos then you have more to say. Many people take faster tempos because they don't have to say anything. You are afraid it will be boring, particularly when you are young. But now I am not afraid of this.

'My wife says I am crazy and I must do less. "It's better you live longer," she says, "not think about how the concert is exciting." I see this, too. But at the same time I'm an artist and it's my life. The doctors in Russia always said I had some problem. But I didn't believe. My father died from a heart attack and I wasn't careful enough, and the age between fifty and fifty-five is always a most difficult time for men. Age, heredity and cholesterol, I learned a lot in the recovery clinic in Switzerland. Those three things are so important.'

CONCERT IN A CAVE

LANZAROTE, MAY 1997

The Almira Quartet was based in the Midlands industrial city of Birmingham, but often played in other towns and countries. They toured most summers with Welsh Opera, as part of the touring orchestra. They enjoyed this travelling as much as many musicians do, which is to say, very much indeed.

One memorable summer they travelled to the Jameos del Agua cave system on the Canarian island of Lanzarote to play in a most unusual concert hall. This particular concert was rendered strange enough by its setting, but also contained a bizarre moment of contact with wild creatures.

The concert hall is in a tube-shaped volcanic cave at the edge of the sea, part of a cave system formed by a sideways volcano coming from the Monte de la Corona. This erupted three thousand years ago and somehow blew the rock out horizontally, creating interconnecting chambers. The complex series of galleries was developed by the artist César Manrique in 1968 and its name derives from the fact that a *jameo* is formed when a tunnel ceiling collapses, revealing volcanic passages. The underground sequence includes a restaurant/café, and the concert cave offers a near-perfect acoustic. At the foot of it is a large stage that extends into Jameo de la Cazuela, the next volcanic bubble, and the latest to be made accessible to the public. Eerie lighting illuminates its stalactites, and in the rock pools you can see the tiny, almost circular, blind albino crabs that are the symbol of the island.

Seating for the audience is on raised platforms and the stage is close enough to the rock pools for the little crabs that live there to be visible from the corners of the players' eyes. At the rear of the stage there is a further cave, which is netted and open to the elements, having a hole in its roof. Birds fly into it and thence into the recess behind the stage, where they can be watched flying around during the concert.

The second pool in the cave complex is also notable, as it has some extraordinary chemical content that turns the water an almost surreal shade of luminous turquoise, and is apparently under a conservation order so strict that even the Spanish royal family may not set foot in it. The crabs, according to violinist Simon Chalk, look like pure white barnacles under this water as they settle on the rocks in the crystal water of the pool.

This was the destination for the Almira concert tour that took place in May 1997, in which the programme was Haydn's String Quartet Op. 76 No. 5 in D major, followed by a piece for solo piano (with a grand piano cleverly manoeuvred onto the stage), Bartok's Sixth Quartet (his last), and lastly the Schumann Piano Quintet in E flat. The cave was at its capacity of six hundred and the concert was to be televised, although the crew from the Canarian television station didn't turn up to videotape it until halfway through the Haydn piece.

Apart from the disruption caused by the arrival of the video crew, the strange part was that as the concert progressed, the albino crabs edged out of the shallow pools towards the musicians and began nibbling their feet. The viola player that night was David Aspin, whose polished black concert shoes took some of the nibbling. He believes they did it from curiosity rather than hunger or aggression, or indeed critical comment. But whatever the cause, it was certainly one of the more exotic audience responses the Almira had encountered.

ENCORE TO START

BIRMINGHAM, JULY 1997

Nigel Kennedy is one of the world's most famous violinists, with a reputation that can fill any concert hall. He is also something of a maverick. He sometimes expresses preferences that could almost be set alongside what is referred to as diva demand – those wishes of grand performers that are satisfied by concert managers to keep them happy. These often take the form of a certain kind of wine or, for operatic divas, a particular scent in the dressing room. For Kennedy, the wish list is said to include champagne in the dressing room and, more quirkily, a square of red carpet to stand on while playing.

It is often the preference of Kennedy not to rehearse with the orchestra, arriving in the evening at the time of the concert instead. During rehearsals his part is played in by the first violin. This practice does not always find favour with the orchestral players, who have of course already tuned up, and is believed to be not much admired by Sir Simon Rattle, the conductor who brought the Birmingham Symphony Hall and the City of Birmingham Symphony Orchestra to world prominence during his long tenure. Rattle was principal conductor and adviser from 1980 to 1990, and music director from 1990 to 1998. He is a highly disciplined man who demands dedication from his players, and he and Kennedy frequently perform together.

In the summer of 1997, Kennedy was engaged to play Elgar's Violin Concerto with the CBSO at the EMI Centenary Concert at Birmingham Symphony Hall. The building had

221

been opened in April 1991 and was – and is – considered to be acoustically exemplary. Rattle had left the CBSO and Birmingham by this time, and had moved to the Berlin Philharmonic. Like Kennedy, he had been invited to return because he was an EMI artist, and the CBSO had often been recorded by the company. It had been their idea to give a concert with two of their most famous performers appearing in the hall that was so much admired for its acoustic and recording properties.

The Elgar was followed by Vaughan Williams's *The Lark Ascending*. They were to play it on the evening of 5 July and record it a couple of days later, a frequent practice for the CBSO and EMI when they worked together. According to his habit, Kennedy arrived on the concert platform at the time of the concert, having not rehearsed with the orchestra. He surveyed the concert hall, which was packed to the roof with an audience in gala clothing and gala mood. Because of the anniversary and the importance of the occasion, many local grandees had come. The violinist took a spontaneous decision.

'I think I'll play the encore first,' he said, and without reference to conductor or orchestra began a virtuoso solo piece of Bach lasting nearly ten minutes. There is some confusion of recall as to whether the piece was the well-known *Chaconne* or the E major Prelude. Whichever one it was, according to a member of the concert hall staff, 'The Maestro was not terribly impressed' by the decision to play it, and neither apparently were the members of the orchestra, sitting with their hands in their laps. It had happened at least once before that Kennedy had pre-empted the opinion of the audience and played an encore first. Who knows what was running through his mind as he worked his way through this unscheduled Bach?

The audience, however, was ecstatic, and applauded him to the rafters. The concert then continued according to the programme, and a couple of days later the Elgar and the Vaughan Williams were recorded for posterity.

PROTEST AT THE PROMS II

LONDON, AUGUST 1998

Late-night proms at the Royal Albert Hall are often used to showcase new music, as on 10 August 1998, when the programme consisted of recently written works by prominent British composers such as Thomas Adès, Colin Matthews and Marc-Antony Turnage. The orchestra was the Birmingham Contemporary Music Group under Sir Simon Rattle.

The audience was sparse, but those who did attend included a number with a professional interest in the contemporary-music scene, such as Sally Groves, head of contemporary music at the long-established music publishers, Schott.

The first work was *Coursing* by Oliver Knussen. It had only been under way for a minute or two when the audience was shocked and bewildered by the sound of personal alarms going off in unoccupied boxes on either side of the hall. As they looked up, startled, they were further stunned to see hundreds of leaflets floating down towards them.

Given some of the effects used in avant-garde music, it wasn't totally out of the question (though unlikely) that this was part of the performance. However, a quick look at the leaflets made it clear that they contained anonymous attacks on a number of leading figures across the music scene, in particular Rattle and Groves. Rattle, known for his independence and encouragement of ground-breaking musical initiatives, was, in summary, accused of being an untalented Establishment lackey; Groves of being part of a 'devious, sleazy cabal' controlling the publication of new music.

The interruption not surprisingly stopped the performance in its tracks and a search was launched for the perpetrators. They had apparently hidden in the boxes before the performance, carried out their plan and then disappeared into the night, unidentified, possibly a couple of young composers with a grudge.

Eventually Rattle restarted the Knussen piece and conducted for the rest of the evening with 'consummate professionalism'. The concert was very successful and at the end the audience, bearing in mind Rattle's and the players' ordeal, cheered them with added enthusiasm.

Some reviews in the next day's newspapers described the protest in unflattering terms and felt that the protesters could have found far better targets for their grievances. 'If only they had struck in the early evening prom,' said Richard Morrison in *The Times*, referring to *And: the Feasting at its Height* by Sofia Gubardulina. The colon in the title – a warning sign of bad music – particularly irked him. The *Sunday Times* felt the same about a piece by the Russian composer Rodion Schchedrin. Both writers slightly gave the impression that there was nothing wrong with setting off alarms and flooding the arena with leaflets as long as the activities weren't aimed at music of which they approved.

THE THOUSAND-YEAR REVERBERATION

LONDON, JANUARY 2000

This concerns a concert series in the most expansive sense of the word: Jem Finer's work *Longplayer* is destined to play for a thousand years. It began on 1 January 2000 at Trinity Buoy Wharf Lighthouse in East London and will play continuously until its completion on 31 December 2999. You can hear it at a listening post at the Lighthouse on the first weekend of every month (this should build up to a concert series of 12,000), and the sound travels across the River Thames.

From time to time there are special events and talks at the Lighthouse to consider the electronic piece in different ways. The work was envisaged by Finer as 'a reaction against the transient indulgence of the forthcoming millennium celebrations'. It is based on a twenty-minute recording of Tibetan music stored on computers, though it can also be performed by living composers using Tibetan bowls.

The manipulation that creates the thousand-year loop is described as: 'Six copies of the same gramophone record on different turntables all spinning at different speeds with different bits playing at the same time.' This process alters the pitch of the sounds, and Finer set the pitch shifts to create precise intervals between the samples. These are octaves, fifths and fourths, which are common to folk songs and classical music. Every two minutes the musical sequences have to return to the start point. The sound it makes is described as chiming and humming.

225

Finer's musical background was with the Pogues in the eighties and nineties; he has a degree in computer science, has taught photography and mathematics, and is artist in residence at the astrophysics department of Oxford University. No doubt that is why he speaks of 'the pure physics of music'. Of the Tibetan prayer bowls and gongs he said, 'You can play them in different ways: you can make them vibrate by drawing a stick around their edge, you can hit them, you can put water in them and bring out new overtones.'

The Trinity Buoy Lighthouse is not the only listening post; there are others around Great Britain and in Brazil and India. The company that originally produced it is called Artangel. Its director Michael Morris said at the outset, 'There is a wonderful sense of unity created by people in different parts of the world listening to the same piece of music, as the years unfold.' Other participants in its creation were ambient music inventor Brian Eno; John Kieffer, Director of Music at the British Council; sound artist Joel Ryan; and composer David Toop.

The artist Polly Gould described the impression created by listening to *Longplayer* as 'intense', and said it was experienced as 'a visceral reverberation in one's own body'. The screens of the computers that generate the sound show the sound waves in coloured undulations. In general, current art writers regard the piece and its performance as both conceptual art and political philosophy. Kodwo Eshun said of *Longplayer*, 'Its contained simplicity masks demonic multiplicity.' A concert on the Internet was part of the planning, as was a form of franchising, to maintain the finance.

HEARD INSTINCT

Musical animals are normally confined to the pages of scores. Composers have always been particularly drawn to birds and birdsong. Larks ascending and cuckoos in spring come to us courtesy of Vaughan Williams and Delius. Quails, nightingales and cuckoos pop up in Beethoven's 'Pastoral' Symphony. Rimsky-Korsakov wrote *The Golden Cockerel* and about bumble bees. Quadrupeds include a barking dog in Elgar's *Enigma Variations*, various cats in Hans Werner Henze's opera *The English Cat*, and *The Cunning Little Vixen* in Janacek's opera. Sheep can be heard bleating in Richard Strauss's *Don Quixote* and characters in Tchaikovsky's ballet *The Nutcracker* include a mouse king and attendant mice. Below sea level swim Schubert's *Trout* and Debussy's *Goldfish*. The largest musical zoo is Saint-Saens's *Carnival of the Animals*, followed not far behind by Ravel's *L'Enfant et Les Sortilèges* with its menagerie of cat, dragonfly, bat, owl, squirrel and frogs.

As for animals themselves, it is thought that some can appreciate or respond to music. According to one report, cows give higher milk yields when listening to Haydn's string quartets. But animals *playing* recognisable music crosses a different boundary and implies a creative intelligence that human beings don't usually attribute to them. There are stories of dogs and seals that purport to sing, but they are in the realm of circus sideshows. The songs of humpback whales have been included in the music of American composers Alan Hovhaness and George Crumb, but that is hardly a conscious contribution by the whales. Yet there is one group of animals that appears to display musical ability such as keeping in rhythm and playing tunes.

The Thai Elephant Orchestra performs near Lampang, a town in northern Thailand. It was established in 2000 by two Americans, Richard Lair, a conservationist, and David Sulzer, a neurologist, who works and composes under the name David Soldier. Lair is affectionately known as Arturo Tuskanini.

The orchestra consists of a dozen elephants that give regular concerts to visitors to the Thai Elephant Conservation Centre and even issues CDs. The elephants play on a variety of specially adjusted percussion and wind instruments, such as gongs, harmonicas, the *renat* (similar to a xylophone) and slit drums. Because the instruments are indigenous, the music also sounds local, like a gamelan orchestra. Observers report that the music is not just random banging. The elephants sway back and forth and play in time and choose all the notes and rhythms. According to Eric Scigliano in the *New York Times*, 'the players improvise distinct metres and melodic lines, and vary and repeat them.' Like any good orchestra, they practise every day. Some of them also paint, and sales of their paintings raise funds for the centre.

Elephants are a very significant feature of Thai cultural life but their numbers are sadly depleted. A century and a half ago there were over 100,000, but today the figure is thought to be about 2,700 domesticated elephants, with a further 1,500 in the wild. Continued financial support is needed to safeguard their future, and a portion of the profits of the concerts is fed back into the conservation centre. So the elephants are to a certain extent providing for their own future.

As well as Thai music, the orchestra has expanded into the classical repertoire with a recording of part of the first movement of Beethoven's 'Pastoral' Symphony. Perhaps Beethoven would have included a trumpet part if he had known. The orchestra's first CD sold five thousand copies and is believed to be the first instrumental CD issued by non-humans. The orchestra does not yet undertake overseas engagements because of difficulties packing their trunks.

CAUGHT WITH HIS TROUSERS DOWN

BLOIS, FRANCE, JULY 2001

One of the main pleasures of Harrow Choral Society's 2001 tour of the Loire Valley was the chance for the eighty-strong choir to sing in three of the beautiful cathedrals of the region. The first concert was in Blois Cathedral, parts of which dated back to the tenth century. So, musically speaking, did its organ. While many older organs had been modernised with electronic technology, the organ at Blois still relied on the traditional, laborious method of manual stops.

Because the choir's organist Bernard Barker could not simultaneously play the music and also adjust the huge array of stops by hand, two helpers from the choir were roped in at the last minute. Unfortunately neither could read music, so Barker set up a rudimentary system of cues. When a page needed turning he would nod. To show when a stop needed pulling out or pushing in, he stuck Post-its on the stops with corresponding stickers on the music. The idea was that when the assistants saw the sticker in the score, they would adjust the appropriate stop.

It was a hot July evening. In the confined space of the organ loft, Barker, in evening dress, was rapidly becoming over-heated, so he decided to remove his trousers. There was an added complication. The choir and the organ were situated at opposite ends of the nave, so Barker, hidden high up in the organ loft, wasn't able to see the cues of the conductor Simon Williams.

229

To get round this, the choir had brought with it a TV camera, which it focused on the conductor, thus enabling Barker to see Williams on a screen in the organ loft. The reverse was not true, however. Williams would not be able to see Barker and he needed to know when Barker and his assistants had altered the organ stops between movements so he could start the next section. To indicate when the organ was ready it was agreed that Barker would cough. Because it would have to carry across some fifty yards, the cough would have to be loud and distinct.

It was perhaps inevitable that most of the things that could go wrong did. Responding to a hearty cough from behind him in the pause between two of the movements, Williams brought down his baton. The expected response from the organ did not materialise. The cue was in fact from a member of the audience with a nasty summer cold.

Up in the organ loft all was not going according to plan either. The Post-its idea wasn't really working. If you couldn't read music, as the helpers couldn't, you hadn't the slightest idea when a Post-it point had been reached. The desperate Barker was reduced to a range of sniffs and grunts for cues, making sure at the same time that they didn't confuse the conductor by sounding like a cough. Add his frustrated expletives when a cue was missed or the wrong stop adjusted, as well as the anxiety of his sweating helpers in case they made another mistake, and it can be seen that the organ loft was a long way from being the tranquil environment associated with the making of beautiful music.

The audience, if it noticed the difficulties, didn't let them spoil its enjoyment, and the concert received a standing ovation. Barker was summoned to the front to take a bow. Exhausted and trouserless, he opted to stay in the organ loft, and bowed to the audience from there, although in a somewhat inelegant crouch. He had discovered that the balcony rail of the organ loft was lower than modesty and dignity demanded.

THE PHANTOM CLOCK

DARTINGTON, DEVON, AUGUST 2001

One of the many musical hats worn by Gavin Henderson is artistic director of Dartington International Summer School, which is set in idyllic Devon countryside by the River Dart.

As Henderson was planning the Dartington programme for 2001, he must have been struck by the mild coincidence that a recital to be given by the pianist Joanna MacGregor contained Sir Harrison Birtwistle's *Harrison's Clocks*. The work was inspired by the book *Longitude* by Dava Sobel about the struggle of John Harrison, the eighteenth-century clockmaker, to invent clocks that would keep perfect time at sea. His eventual success solved the thorny longitude problem. Those same clocks were now on display at the National Maritime Museum in Greenwich, literally yards from Trinity College of Music where Henderson, wearing another of his hats, happened to be principal.

This coincidence was no longer in Henderson's mind by the time he sat down in the Great Hall, Dartington, to hear MacGregor's recital. MacGregor was the dedicatee of *Harrison's Clocks*, with exclusive performing rights for a limited period, and was going to make a recording of the piece while she was there. Birtwistle, the composer, was also present, so it was a special event for Dartington, and Henderson was looking forward to the performance with great expectation.

The piece had not been going long when Henderson became aware of a loud and distracting sound, as of a clock ticking. Other people found it annoying too and the message reached Henderson, 'Can't you stop the clock?'

231

'But there is no clock in the room,' indicated the bemused Henderson. He looked around for another source but could find nothing obvious. It might have been something like a rope slapping against a flagpole, except Dartington's flagpole had no rope. Even more eerily, some people heard it and some didn't. Birtwistle's wife noticed it, but Birtwistle himself, sitting next to her, did not. Henderson found enough people, about twenty, who had heard it to know it wasn't a figment of his imagination.

Fanciful and light-hearted explanations were offered, such as the spirit of Harrison joining in, but at the end of the day, and despite further investigation, Henderson found no satisfactory explanation and left it as an unsolved mystery. Over the next few days, every time there was a performance in the hall, he kept his ears open for the phantom ticking, but never heard it again.

Later in the week, MacGregor was back playing in the hall, again with Birtwistle present. Henderson could hardly believe it, but once again a clock was heard loudly ticking. He is not a believer in the paranormal, but found it hard to think of an alternative explanation. Perhaps John Harrison, maker of timekeepers *par excellence*, was showing his admiration of the excellent timekeeping by Joanna MacGregor.

BRASSED OFF III

SADDLEWORTH AND THAMESIDE, LANCASHIRE, JUNE 2003

The ultimate travel test for brass bands is the Whit Friday contests, which date back to the 1880s, and are held in villages in the Saddleworth and Thameside areas near Manchester. Bands travel from village to village, perform a test piece and are judged on it. A band must enter at least six contests, usually more, because its best six positions are totted up to decide its score. The winner is the band with the lowest cumulative score.

Speed is of the essence in order to get to as many contests as possible, and give yourself the best chance of a good score, so everything is thought through in great detail. Routes are planned that will avoid other coaches. Seats in the coach are carefully allotted. Those with the heavier instruments, such as tubas and euphoniums, sit nearest the front so they can get off first, as it takes longer for them to get to the contest ground. A runner with booking fee clutched in hand is delegated to jump down from the coach as soon as it arrives at each stop and sprint off to register with the contest controller and get the earliest possible place in the running order.

For the Whit Friday contests in June 2003, the Grimethorpe Colliery Band, one of over sixty bands taking part, had prepared with its usual meticulous care. They had already played a few contests, and were about to set off for the next, when the driver announced that he had reached the limit of his allowed driving hours. This was no problem as bands always carry a relief driver. That day it happened to be a younger, inexperienced driver who had never driven with the band before. But, though he had been on the coach at the start, somehow he wasn't on the coach now.

Then someone remembered that he had got off at the first stop, saying he'd never heard the band play before and wanted to listen to it competing. Someone else recalled seeing him relaxing on a bench outside a pub with a drink. It dawned on everyone that, due to his inexperience, he didn't know that as soon as a contest piece was finished, everyone hurried back to the coach and drove off to the next contest. The coach had left without noticing he wasn't on board.

For a band with the worldwide reputation of the Grimethorpe, this was a disaster. Word would quickly get around and they would be a laughing stock. 'Has anyone got a coach-driver's licence?' the secretary asked, more in desperation than hope. As noted elsewhere about orchestral players, there is a wide range of non-musical skills among bandsmen and, unbelievably, someone had. Whether he had his licence with him to prove the point wasn't looked into too closely. The day was saved and, by the end of it, Grimethorpe had achieved a highly creditable third place. The winners were Fodens Richardsons with five firsts and one second. But perhaps the real heroes, and beating even the Grimethorpe for determination, were Ebury Brass, a collection of players from various Guards bands, who earlier that morning had been many miles away in London, playing in the Queen's Birthday Parade.

MARATHON MAN

LONDON, OCTOBER 2003

Homage to Beethoven can take many unusual forms. In 2005, the BBC devoted a week to broadcasting every note he had ever written. In December 1988, the American conductor Lorin Maazel conducted all nine symphonies in ten hours, splitting the workload among three orchestras.

For Julian Jacobson, Beethoven had long been a passion. As a pianist and professor of music at several important colleges of music, it was natural that he had learned a good number of the piano sonatas over the years. In 1989, he set out to learn them all. By 2000, he had given a number of complete cycles, spreading the performances out over a few weeks.

The following year he had an audacious thought. Would it be possible to play all 32 sonatas in one day from memory? It was not a *Guinness Book of Records* attempt. Anyway, though he did not know it at the time, Gary Goldschneider, an American, had accomplished that feat in the 1980s. Jacobson was convinced that it would be fascinating for an audience and for him to follow in a single day how Beethoven's style had developed over 27 years. He would dedicate the experience to a cause close to his heart, raising funds for WaterAid, a charity dedicated to providing clean water supplies to the world's poorest people.

With this motivation, he spent a year thoroughly revising and working on every sonata. By the beginning of 2003 he felt ready to book a hall, and chose the beautiful church of St James's, Piccadilly, venue for many recitals.

The performance was scheduled for Friday 31 October. The unusual challenge had attracted a good deal of publicity. BBC Radio 4 asked to interview him on *Today* at 8.15 on the morning of the concert itself in the church, and hoped he wouldn't mind giving a little taster by playing a few bars of the 'Moonlight' Sonata. With the concert due to start only an hour later, it wasn't ideal timing, but Jacobson knew it would generate good publicity for WaterAid and agreed.

The car that would take him to the church arrived just after six, a very early start for what was going to be a long day. With all his concentration focused on Beethoven, it was disconcerting for Jacobson to hear his driver humming Handel's *Messiah* all the way to Piccadilly; he managed to get lost too, so by the time Jacobson reached the church for the interview, he had already used up a lot of nervous energy.

Musically he felt very well prepared. However – like marathon runners, who do not train by running full marathons – he had not had a full dress rehearsal, so wasn't totally sure about his stamina. He was also concerned about his right hand, which had seized up for a short time a few weeks earlier.

The interview passed off without incident and at a quarter past nine he walked to the piano and sat down. Immediately there were a couple of problems he hadn't anticipated. Recitals in the church normally took place at lunchtime when the sun was high in the sky, but this early in the morning it was beating down on him from the upper windows, directly into his eyes. Very soon he had an overpowering headache. Among the sparse audience, there was also a woman praying – reasonable enough in a church – but doing so in a distractingly audible voice.

Jacobson recalled saying to himself early in the performance, 'This is the stupidest thing I've ever embarked on!' For a split second, he considered calling the whole thing off, but decided to press on for as long as he could. He coped with the first three sonatas and then took a short break, when he swallowed a couple of painkillers. This cleared his headache, but it wasn't until 12.20, when he finished the morning session with the 'Pathétique', that he felt confident enough to think he could achieve his goal.

The audience built up gradually throughout the day and reached two hundred during the long afternoon session, which ended at six o'clock. If people came out of curiosity, they stayed to admire Jacobson's playing, according him a standing ovation for the 'Appassionata' that ended that session.

Jacobson was pleased with his progress. Except for one small slip, which probably went unnoticed, his memory had been perfect. His concentration was good too, though sometimes, when he began a new sonata, he found it hard to move from the mood of the last movement of the previous sonata: to keep on schedule, he wasn't allowing himself the longer breaks that are usual during recitals. Most importantly, his hands weren't giving him any problems. He was on schedule too. Allowing for breaks, he was aiming to finish at ten o'clock.

After a short break came the titanic 'Hammerklavier'. Because of its scale, he dedicated an entire session to this one piece. It was also the only sonata for which he used a score. As he began the last session at nine, there were only three sonatas to go, Opuses 109 to 111. As he played the final chord, it was a magical experience for Jacobson to hear the church clock begin to strike ten, exactly as he had planned. Elated, he stood to take another standing ovation, having achieved what is probably the musical equivalent of climbing Mount Everest single-handed without oxygen.

Adrenaline still pumping, he raced off to a pub, downed three quick pints, then moved on to a Lebanese restaurant for further celebrations. Exhaustion did not hit him until after lunch the following day. Due to go to a party that evening dressed as Beethoven, he felt that he and the great composer had spent enough time in each other's company for a while and went in mufti. Satisfyingly, he raised more than £6,000 for WaterAid at the church, and donations sent directly to the charity from people unable to attend substantially swelled that amount.

A year later Jacobson repeated the feat at the Elliott Hall in Harrow, northwest London. Will he do it again? All being well, you may be able to catch him at a fringe event at the 2012 London Olympics.

THE GRANDEST LEG-PULL?

LONDON, JANUARY 2004

Erik Satie's mammoth composition *Vexations* was performed on 17 January 2004, or at any rate from 6 p.m. on 17 January until noon on 18 January. A full performance can take anything between 17 and 24 hours. This version was played at the Barbican in London by a relay of thirty pianists, some of them professional musicians, some not. The latter group included Roger Wright, controller of BBC Radio 3, Chris de Souza and Paul Guinery of Radio 3 and Alan Rusbridger, editor of the *Guardian*. In the former category was the conductor Malcolm Hicks. There was also Yoko Ono.

The performance was part of a BBC Symphony Orchestra weekend that concentrated on the work of composer John Cage, whose best-known work, the 1952 piece *4'33"*, contains no notes, only silence. Cage championed the inclusion of *Vexations* on this occasion as well as at its first performance, which was in New York in September 1963, when ten pianists worked in shifts. The programme note proposes that Cage's interest in the work elevated it from 'a forgotten footnote in Satie's biography to the status of a legendary work'.

Vexations is made up of a sequence of slow-moving chords played 840 times and is written on a single page of music. It has an eighteen-note bass line that is harmonised with chords in the right-hand part. The programme explains that the bass line is repeated and re-harmonised with an inverted version of the previous harmonisation. The effect is said to be hypnotic. Erik Satie proposed that 'to play this motif eight hundred and forty

238

times it would be advisable to prepare oneself beforehand, in the deepest silence, by serious immobilities'.

The 2004 interpretation took eighteen hours and involved playing through the night. It was played in the Barbican Conservatory to an audience that may have consisted of 1,009 people, although no one has an accurate figure as the organisers counted the audience members with a clicker as they entered the Conservatory, but they were not ticketed and the event was free, so it is at least possible that some people left and re-entered. Possibly they could have left and re-entered several times, to gain greater effect. The attraction could be hypnotic. Or perhaps they shared the feelings of John Cage when he first heard the piece in New York in 1963.

John Cage's response to this premiere performance, quoted in the programme for the BBC Symphony Orchestra's 'John Cage Uncaged' concert series in 2004, was that *Vexations* was:

> . . . very different from the thought of [the repetitions] or the realisation that they were going to happen. For them to actually happen, to actually live through it, was a different thing. What happened was that we were very tired, naturally, after that length of time and I drove back to the country. I slept an unusually long period of time and when I woke up, I felt different than I had ever felt before. And furthermore the environment that I looked out upon looked unfamiliar even though I had been living there. In other words, I had changed and the world had changed.

This extraordinary listening experience had waited seventy years from its composition in 1893 for its first performance in 1963, perhaps proof that the truly avant-garde is too much for its contemporary audience. However, the biographer of Erik Satie, Alan Gillmor, admitted, 'It may be one of Satie's grandest leg-pulls'.

EAT YOUR INSTRUMENTS – THEY'RE GOOD FOR YOU!

LONDON, JUNE 2004

It is traditionally difficult to get children to eat their vegetables, but if this afternoon is anything to go by they're perfectly happy to listen to them, for the Purcell Room is satisfyingly full of parents and children come to do just that.

The First Vienna Vegetable Orchestra is making a repeat visit to London's South Bank, two performances yesterday, two today. There is a wide-ranging programme from classical to dub, all of it played on instruments carved or concocted from vegetables, supplemented by a few kitchen utensils such as knives for grating sounds or mixers.

Although the orchestra of nine musical enthusiasts takes its vegetable music very seriously, it acknowledges that there is a playful element in the concept and is not above making the odd joke about canned music. In fact, puns seem to crop up without trying, so let's immediately give the chop to a couple of the worst. No, they don't play Beethoven's 'Grocer' Fugue, and yes, they've heard the one about the Greens Room. Don't even ask about their Chopin Liszt.

Behind the scenes it looks like the kitchen from hell. Early yesterday, courtesy of a sponsor, the orchestra received a restaurant-sized delivery of aubergines, cucumbers, tomatoes, peppers, celery, cabbages and pumpkins, as well as eight hundred carrots, an unusually large quantity, for reasons to be explained later.

Since then they've spent hours chopping, carving and

240

hollowing out with drills and knives. Sound quality depends on freshness so they leave making the instruments to as near concert time as possible. A tomato, the sole non-vegetable, needs no preparation time, but it takes a quarter of an hour to fashion a cucophone from a cucumber with a carrot mouthpiece and red-pepper bell, and half an hour to hollow out a carrot and make a carrot-recorder. By the time they've finished, there are celeriac bongos, leek violins, radi-rimbas, leek drumsticks for bashing the pumpkin bass drum, radishers and much more.

The concert starts with a short piece called *ditlaka*, traditional African music for horn flutes, but here played on carrot flutes. As the sound of the average cucumber or carrot doesn't carry very far, amplification is added. Some pieces, like *ur-gem-ix* and *steuck*, sound like electronic music. Some are improvised, such as a duet for a real trumpet and cucophone. Others are borrowed from the classical repertoire such as *Stravimprovsky*, an adaptation of Stravinsky's *Rite of Spring* (Rite of Spring Onions, surely), and the final piece, Strauss's *Radetsky March* (Raddishsky March?). Vegetable instruments don't have a long life, so the Stravinsky, fifteen minutes long, presents particular problems. The whole concert lasts about the length of a three-course meal.

What does the orchestra sound like? It has been compared to whale songs or Andean flutes and, less complimentarily, to creaks and squeaks. However, the audience is very satisfied and demands seconds. The encore, *Automate*, is a concerto in which eighteen tomatoes are smashed, a very juicy piece, but surely they've missed a trick by not including something by the late-sixteenth, early-seventeenth-century Italian composer, Gregorio Zucchini?

Usually at the end of a concert, the orchestra's cook swiftly turns the instruments into a vegetable soup, which is distributed to the audience. Not today though, as UK Health and Safety regulations don't permit it. Instead, each member of the audience is given a carrot flute, the reason for the mass delivery. The children go off clutching them and, who knows, maybe more in tune with eating their veg.

BEATING UP THE FESTIVAL HALL

LONDON, JULY 2004

The annual Rhythm Sticks Festival within the South Bank Arts Centre, London, takes place in July. It's a celebration of percussion – the rhythmic beating, shaking or rattling of drums, tablas, bodhrán, timpani, timbales, congas and all other percussive items. The instruments come from Australia, India, Japan, Africa, America, the Middle East and Europe, and if that list of countries and continents does not represent the whole world, it very nearly does.

In 2003 the celebrated percussionist Evelyn Glennie was invited by the organisers to compose a new work for the tenth anniversary of the event, which was to fall in the following year.

Miss Glennie is noted for innovation and she surpassed herself, creating three performance sessions in which members of the public played the Festival Hall itself. They played the walls, stairs, tables, chairs, banisters and counters, maintaining a compelling rhythm that held the audience and stopped all passing visitors in their tracks. *Bang on the Hall* concluded in the ballroom area, where there was a lighting rig and a platform. There the community musicians played tubing, tins, jerrycans, furniture, pillars, cleaning signs, bits of lighting rig, water-cooler bottles . . . pretty much anything percussive that could be struck, was struck. The event, which concluded the week-long festival, involved up to forty percussion participants at any given time and the event was 'absolutely packed'.

When Evelyn Glennie was approached for the commission, she decided not to simply compose and formally play a work. She wanted a community project. 'What I like about Rhythm Sticks is that it fuses together all the elements of percussion, but it also involves the audience across all age groups, and brings together many diverse groups from the local community,' she said.

Two groups took part, one with a musical background, the other without. Many of the percussionists were in the category of elders, and initially they had to be persuaded. 'When we went to meet them for the first time they were a little uncertain about the idea of percussion,' recalls organiser Daisy Sutcliffe. 'We ate tea and cake together very politely, and then we gave them all sticks. By the end of teatime they were playing on the cups and saucers, tables and tea plates – anything that came to hand. It was wonderful.'

Composer/choreographer Tim Steiner worked out the route around the building that enabled the foyers and their contents to be transformed into a battery of percussion, and disco groover MJ Cole created an environmental dance soundtrack from sounds recorded off the building itself, so that the rhythms of the players had a strong subliminal backing. Evelyn Glennie said of Cole, 'He dazzles his audiences in whatever performances he lends his creative touch to'. Rehearsals took place in the adjacent Queen Elizabeth Hall. The performers learned rhythms, dance movements and the disciplines of playing together.

On the day of the performance, members of the audience were expecting the percussion event but did not know quite what form it might take. They sat waiting in the cafeteria of the Festival Hall. There were other people in the cafeteria who knew nothing about it. Members of the percussion groups sat in the cafeteria too, informally, and with their sticks hidden. One of the group leaders wore a necklace of groundnuts to signify that the participants were all nuts; she also brought with her Jem the dog, who barked in time. One by one and table by table they began to play. Then they got up, and began to walk their choreographed route. They played the building, including a staircase, for about ten minutes, gathering audience members as they did so, until they arrived at the stage, where they played for twenty minutes. The audience number grew on one occasion to more than a thousand.

Soon afterwards the Royal Festival Hall closed for refurbishment.

Percussion postscript: Twice a year, the New Zealand Symphony Orchestra tours small towns. The places they visit do not have good concert halls, indeed they may not have concert halls at all. In October 2003, the NZSO played in Gore, a town at the foot of the South Island, which had no concert hall and had never had a symphony orchestra performance. The concert was scheduled to be played in the St James Theatre, a newly refurbished cinema, and by the time the orchestra arrived it had been sold out for weeks. During the interval the audience bought snacks as if they were at the pictures, and returned to enjoy Beethoven's Sixth Symphony with their ice creams. By the slow movement the audience had reached the cones, and the unbridled crunching created a percussion accompaniment. In the loud parts the crunching got louder, to match the piece.

THE SWAN AND THE FIREMEN

BIRMINGHAM AIRPORT, OCTOBER 2004

Members of the Orchestra of the Swan, based in Stratford-on-Avon, have the distinction of being the official musicians in residence at Birmingham Airport, where they play four or five times a year. What strange idea is this? It may even be a first worldwide. They give impromptu performances of some of the greatest repertoire for chamber orchestra, and among the favoured airport composers are Mozart, Elgar, Vivaldi, Handel, Tchaikovsky, Holst, Britten, Leroy Anderson and Tippett.

The music-making is intended to soothe the passengers, but of course it must compete with the background noise of a busy international airport. This venue joins some other very unusual musical locations for the ensemble, ranging from factory floor to hospital ward. Orchestra leader David Curtis points out that there are more than six thousand employees at the airport, and millions of passengers pass through it every year.

Music has been played in the airport's arrivals area, corporate headquarters, departure lounge and duty-free shop, but the prize for the most extraordinary location was awarded unopposed to the airport fire station. In October 2004, members of the orchestra gave a twenty-minute concert of Elgar and Mozart to the duty fire crew, who were in full firefighting gear and standing ready for action all the time the music was played. During the performance of Elgar's wistful Serenade for Strings and Mozart's Divertimento K156 the orchestra faced the extraordinary possibility that at any time their audience could be called away to put out a fire and possibly even to save lives.

It happens that many members of the Birmingham Airport fire crew are themselves competent musicians: there are some excellent keyboard and guitar players among them. The Orchestra of the Swan hopes to join up with them for a performance at some point. Perhaps the programme might include a performance of *Firebird*, *Music for the Royal Fireworks*, or maybe the piece specially written for a fire crew by Charles Ives, entitled *The Gong, the Hook, and the Ladder*.

The orchestra also considers the tastes of younger passengers in its music-making, and from time to time gives workshops that include a specially commissioned set of musical postcards. These are short, simple pieces that children can be skilfully taught to rehearse and perform in as little as five minutes. If a flight is delayed at Birmingham Airport the whole work can be performed in half an hour, hence the title *Around the World in 30 Minutes*. The workshops take place in the departure lounge, where apparently there is always an empty shop space that can serve as a concert hall. Parents watch, or sometimes join in. The instruments are brought along by the members of the orchestra and are always from the percussion section.

And how did this marvellous aeromusical arrangement come about? The orchestra had for some years enjoyed financial support from the airport through a board member who also supported the work of the musicians, and after a time they met the airport managers with a view to expanding their involvement. They wanted an imaginative idea that would link the Swan and the airport. They batted around the subject for some time before coming up with the idea, and what could possibly be more imaginative than the airport residency? A serious flight of fancy.

WHAT A TURN SHE GAVE

LEYTONSTONE, LONDON, MAY 2005

As we have seen earlier, page-turning is a critical activity, and you do it neither too early nor too late. Indeed, you must do it at precisely the right moment. Those who undertake this work are often musicians, since although they are waiting for the nod from the performer, they must be able to anticipate it by following the score. Sometimes musicians who are part of a concert event or a competition turn pages for other participants.

Kathryn Mosley is a pianist who plays in quartets and small ensembles, sometimes accompanies other players and singers, and also plays the organ in churches. The working life of a musician who is not a full-time member of an orchestra contains many variations, and it was in one of the less obvious roles, that of accompanist at a singing competition, that she took part in the Leytonstone Arts Festival at the beginning of May 2005. The competitors were in an oratorio class; the competition took place in St John's church in this northeast London suburb. Partway through the programme Kathryn was asked to step in for another pianist who had suddenly dropped out. She agreed, although she had not rehearsed with the singer, whose entry consisted of two arias from *Messiah*. The time before the performance was only enough for accompanist and singer to talk about the ornamentation. This caused Kathryn a little concern.

The pressure was stepped up somewhat when they were also called upon to perform earlier than had been listed in the programme, because the previous performer, on being called to sing, said that she couldn't yet as her accompanist was in the loo. The adjudicator said to Kathryn and the singer, 'Could you start, please?' and they agreed that they would. They were to begin with 'Rejoice Greatly' and continue with 'I Know that My Redeemer Liveth'.

A few bars into the second aria, an unknown woman appeared from the side of the stage and sat down on the piano stool beside Kathryn as she played. Kathryn was very alarmed. She glanced at the intruder, not understanding what was going on, but carried on playing. (It is worth noting that page-turners do not usually occupy the same stool, and such proximity is far too close.) She darted glances at the person to try to work out who it was and what it was all about, and from time to time she also looked anxiously towards the audience to check for any signs of reaction.

At the end of the page that Kathryn was playing, the stranger leaned forward and turned it. It is usual for musicians to nod for page-turners, and after this Kathryn thought she'd better do so, to ensure that the stranger knew when to turn. In other words, she had to go on as if she wanted it done. So throughout the piece Kathryn nodded for the pages to be turned, and the stranger turned them. When the last page had been turned, the unknown page-turner got up and walked off the stage.

It turned out that she was the other accompanist, she who had been in the loo. She had walked back on stage mistakenly and, finding herself in the spotlight, so to speak, had taken it into her head to turn the pages. There was no appreciation from the pianist for this action, however. She said, 'It was a spoiled performance, I didn't want her, she put me off'.

There is more than one way for a page-turner to be put off: Anthony Phillips, who turned pages for the great cellist Mstislav Rostropovich, recalls turning also for the composer Olivier Messiaen, who gave him his own, original score. This was quite an ordeal for the turner as the score was covered with the composer's drawings and symbols, and directions about emphasis, so it was almost impossible to read the music among all the hieroglyphics.

Some page-turners achieve distinction in their chosen

profession. Ruth Spelke has legendary status and her biography, as it features in programme notes, can be found when the browser turns their attention to virtual musical matters:

> Tonight's page-turner, Ruth Spelke, studied under Ivan Schmertnick at the Boris Nitsky School of Page Turning in Philadelphia. She has been turning pages here and abroad for many years for some of the world's leading pianists. In 1988, Ms Spelke won the Wilson Page Turning Scholarship, which sent her to Israel to study page turning from left to right. She is winner of the 1984 Rimsky Korsakov *Flight of the Bumblebee* Prestissimo Medal, having turned 47 pages in an unprecedented 32 seconds. She was also a 1983 silver medallist at the Klutz Musical Page Pickup Competition: contestants retrieve and rearrange a musical score dropped from a Yamaha. Ms Spelke excelled in 'grace, swiftness, and poise'.
>
> For techniques, Ms Spelke performs both the finger-licking and the bent-page corner methods. She works from a standard left-bench position, and is the originator of the dipped-elbow page snatch, a style used to avoid obscuring the pianist's view of the music. She is page-turner in residence in Fairfield, Iowa, where she occupies the coveted Alfred Hitchcock Chair at the Fairfield Page Turning Institute.
>
> Ms Spelke is married, and has a house on a lake.

And now it can be told: she's imaginary, and features on the Internet as a hoax.

ROLE REVERSAL

LONDON, MAY 2005

In something of a twist on the Biblical story, a concert performance of Handel's oratorio *Samson* in St George's, Hanover Square, as part of the 2005 London Handel Festival, was brought to a halt when not Samson but Delilah found herself imprisoned (though happily without also undergoing Samson's blindness and shorn head).

St George's, which was Handel's own parish church, is renowned for its fine acoustics, but doesn't have changing facilities, so performers change over the road in the premises of Sotheby's, the well-known auction house.

Samson is somewhat unusual in that Delilah (or Dalila, as Handel calls her) doesn't appear until after the interval. So when the rest of the cast went off to sing Part One, Claire Ormshaw, the soprano singing Dalila, had a chance to be on her own and run her eye over the score, read a book or do a crossword.

Some half-hour before her first entrance, Ormshaw judged it was time to cross to the church, so gathered up her score and strode confidently to the dressing-room door. But though she turned the handle this way and that, she couldn't get out. To her horror, she realised she had been locked in, giving her an instant insight as to how Samson must have felt in the prison at Gaza.

After calling out, 'Hello?' hopefully for a quarter of an hour or so, it became clear that there was no one around to hear. Becoming increasingly more desperate, Ormshaw says she 'tried every door a hundred times, gradually banging harder and even trying to pick the locks', feeling vaguely ridiculous in her beautiful red gown and being caught on CCTV. Though the last thing a singer wants to do just before singing is yell, it was an emergency, so yell she did. Exhausted, she looked longingly across at St George's mouthing, 'Please help,' and tried whatever phones she could find.

Fifty minutes had now gone by. 'Hysteria had set in,' Ormshaw says, 'and no voice left.' It briefly crossed her mind to remove an expensive-looking painting from the wall and set off the alarm, but the thought of appearing on the front page of the *Metro* next day deterred her.

Over at the church, the second part was about to get under way. Ormshaw's absence wasn't noticed because her first entrance was from the back of the church, away from the other performers. After a grand build-up between Micah and Samson announcing Dalila's approach, the harpsichord gives the cue and Dalila starts her first recitative.

Missing a cue can happen, so when Ormshaw failed to make her dramatic entrance, Laurence Cummings, directing the performance from the harpsichord, did the usual thing and played the chord again. Still nothing. After a minute or two, someone slipped away to the vestry, where the performers gather at the church, to investigate. They came back, people expected things to happen, but nothing did. In the embarrassed silence, Catherine Wyn-Rodgers, singing Micah, who was in the pulpit, tried to break the tension and cracked a joke about nobody daring to say, 'How typical of a woman!' The minutes ticked by and the audience began to chat among themselves. No one knew what was going on or if the performance would continue.

Meanwhile, the search had spread to other parts of the church without success. That could leave only one place where Ormshaw might be, as Catherine Hodgson, the festival administrator, quickly realised. Dashing back to Sotheby's, she found the imprisoned soprano at her wits' end.

It didn't take long to work out what had happened. Security at Sotheby's is naturally very tight. Seeing the performers leave for the church, and unfamiliar with the score of *Samson*, the guards assumed that everyone had gone and, without checking both the dressing rooms, locked all the doors as part of the security precautions.

Though the explanation was simple, getting Ormshaw released was not, as the guards needed permission to open up the section she was in (or it was assumed she was in). This was a slow process, but eventually she was released.

Despite her stressful experience, and the unsatisfactory warm-up she had undergone, Ormshaw was allowed only a brief moment to recover. Cummings played the chord again, and Ormshaw finally made her entrance, looking and sounding so composed no one would have guessed she had been yelling her lungs out for the best part of forty minutes. 'Ironically,' she says, 'my first recitative was about a turtle being left alone!'

At the end of the performance, Cummings explained what had happened, adding that it had not been ruled out that one of the guards was an Israelite in disguise. But surely, if it was anyone, it must have been a Philistine.

AN UNPROFITABLE GIG

ABERGAVENNY, MAY 2005

British orchestral players are not as well paid as some of their Continental colleagues and are often keen to accept freelance work to aid their cash flow. With good diary management, it's surprising how many gigs can be fitted into one day.

In some of his spare time from playing first viola in the orchestra of Welsh National Opera, Philip Heyman runs the Athena String Quartet. Early in 2005, he got a phone call from a friend who also runs a quartet. He had been offered a gig for May, a wedding reception in Abergavenny, which he couldn't accept. He offered Heyman the chance to take it over, which he was happy to do.

Before contacting the client – let's call her Mrs Hughes – Heyman religiously checked WNO's advance schedule for that Saturday. If WNO had a daytime rehearsal or was away on tour, he wouldn't have been available. He found that there was a performance in Cardiff that evening, but that wasn't a problem as long as the quartet didn't get away too late.

So that was the first thing he checked when he phoned Mrs Hughes. She told him the reception would finish at 4.30. As Abergavenny was only about thirty miles away from Cardiff, that left plenty of time to get back and he accepted the gig and booked his colleagues.

Three months later, Heyman set out for the hotel to fulfil the engagement. He and the other members of the quartet arrived in good time and made themselves known to the hotel staff. They were taken outside and set up in a pagoda on the lawn out

253

of the breeze. Although the reception was due to start at 1.30, people didn't start drifting in until about two o'clock. 'Half an hour less to play,' the quartet members said to each other gleefully.

It was a lovely afternoon. Against a background of popping champagne corks, the quartet played a pleasant selection of lighter classics, such as Mozart's *Eine Kleine Nachtmusik*, Dvorak's *Humoresque* and Elgar's *Salut d'Amour*.

There is no precise etiquette on these occasions, but someone from the wedding party, usually the bride's mother, will normally come over at some stage, offer the musicians a few complimentary words and organise refreshments.

When no one did, the quartet, used to treatment that varied from thoughtful to thoughtless, shrugged it off. However, they could see that their contribution was well received, and when they took a break, they received appreciative comments.

The reception began to break up at four o'clock, again to the quiet satisfaction of the quartet. Another half-hour they didn't have to play and less time pressure for the drive back for the evening performance. Heyman got up and made haste to make himself known to the client and collect his fee, as customers can occasionally be forgetful.

As he had no idea which one was Mrs Hughes, he headed across to the bride and groom, who were tying up loose ends with the functions manager. 'Hope you enjoyed the music,' he said. 'Could you tell me which is Mrs Hughes?' There were blank looks all round.

Then the penny dropped with the functions manager. 'But the Hughes reception isn't until next Saturday.'

In hindsight, it all made sense to Heyman. He'd been so anxious checking for a possible clash with his WNO commitments that he hadn't noticed that he was looking at the wrong week in his diary. Once he'd entered the wrong date, the rest was inevitable, given that popular hotels are booked virtually every summer weekend for wedding receptions. When he had arrived, although the hotel wasn't expecting him, it had assumed that the client had hired him. The bride, a music student, thought that the music was a gracious gesture by the hotel. Which explained why no mother-in-law had come over to say hello or offer a drink.

Though the other members of the quartet did not press him, Heyman felt honour bound to pay them. Once his bewilderment wore off, he saw the funny side, and the story began to circulate on the musical grapevine.

A week later, the Athena Quartet reappeared at the hotel for the real Hughes reception. It poured down and they had to play inside. Otherwise everything went very well and they even got a mention in the best man's speech. They had to play the full three hours this time, but at least they were paid, and, yes, they made it back in good time for the evening performance. Heyman won't be making the same mistake again and, having paid two lots of fees for one engagement, would welcome a couple of gigs to make up the shortfall.

There was a pleasant coda a couple of months later. Heyman opened his post one morning to find a letter from the mother-in-law from the first wedding. Thinking about the incident afterwards, she realised she had unwittingly benefited from his mistake, and enclosed a token of her gratitude in the form of a much appreciated cheque.

If Heyman turned up twice, there was an occasion in June 1963 when the distinguished clarinettist Jack Brymer accidentally failed to appear at all. He arrived in good time at Claydon House in Suffolk for a concert of Mozart chamber music with the Prometheus Ensemble.

When no one else turned up, he checked his instructions again and realised he shouldn't have been at Claydon House but at Claydon Hall in Buckinghamshire over a hundred miles away. He drove as hard as he could but got trapped in Bank Holiday traffic and never made it. An orchestra with more than one clarinet player might have been able to cover up, but not a chamber ensemble. The Prometheus Ensemble had to repeat the G minor String Quintet K516 they had already played once in place of the promised clarinet quintet. Brymer was not invited back again.

SELECTED BIBLIOGRAPHY

Amis, John and Rose, Michael, *Words about Music*, Faber and Faber, 1989

Atkins, E Wulstan, *The Elgar-Atkins Friendship*, David & Charles, 1984

Bakewell, Michael, *Fitzrovia: London's Bohemia*, National Portrait Gallery Publications, 1999

Banfield, Stephen, *Gerald Finzi: An English Composer*, Faber and Faber, 1997

Bennett, Alan, *The Madness of King George*, Faber and Faber, 1995

Berlioz, Hector, *The Memoirs of Berlioz*, trans. David Cairns, Panther, 1969

Boden, Anthony, *Three Choirs: A History of the Festival*, Alan Sutton Publishing, 1992

Brocket, C W, 'Gottschalk in Madrid: A Tale of Ten Pianos', *Musical Quarterly* lxxv, 1991

Brown, James, *Oboists Telling Tales*, privately published by James Brown, 2002

Brown, Rosemary, *Unfinished Symphonies*, Souvenir Press, 1971

Brymer, Jack, *In the Orchestra*, Hutchinson, 1987

Cairns, David, *Berlioz* (2 vols), Allen Lane, 1999

Camden, Archie, *Blow by Blow*, Thames Publishing, 1982

Campbell, Margaret, *The Great Cellists*, Robson Books, 2004

Campbell, Margaret, *The Great Violinists*, Granada Publishing, 1980

Campbell, Margaret, *Henry Purcell: Glory of His Age*, Hutchinson, 1993

Carpenter, Humphrey, *The Envy of the World: Fifty Years of the BBC Third Programme and Radio Three*, Weidenfeld and Nicolson, 1996

Carse, Adam, *The Life of Jullien*, W Heffer & Sons Ltd, 1951

Chenevix Trench, Charles, *The Royal Malady*, Longmans, 1964

Cooper, Barry, *Beethoven*, OUP, 2000

Coward, Noël, *Noël Coward Autobiography*, Methuen, 1986

Cox, David, *The Henry Wood Proms*, BBC, 1980

David, Hans T and Mendel, Arthur, *The New Bach Reader*, rev. Christoph Wolff, W W Norton & Co, 1998

Elkin, Robert, *The Old Concert Rooms of London*, Arnold, 1955

Fako, Nancy Jordan, *Philip Farkas and His Horn*, Crescent Park Music Publications, 1998

Fénelon, Fania, *The Musicians of Auschwitz*, trans. Judith Landry, Michael Joseph, 1977

Finck, Harry T, *Musical Laughs*, Funk & Wagnalls, 1924

Fitzlyon, April, *Maria Malibran*, Souvenir Press (Educational & Academic), 1987

Flower, Sir Newman, *Handel: His Personality and His Times*, Panther Books, 1972

Forbes, Elliot (ed.), *Thayer's Life of Beethoven*, Princeton University Press, 1964

Gaines, James, *Evening in the Palace of Reason*, Fourth Estate, 2005

Gianturco, Carolyn, *Alessandro Stradella (1639–1682): His Life and Music*, Clarendon Press, 1994

Gottschalk, Louis Moreau, *Notes of a Pianist*, J B Lippincott & Co, London, 1881

Gray, Cecil and Heseltine, Philip, *Carlo Gesualdo, Prince of Venosa: Musician and Murderer*, Kegan Paul, Trench, Trubner & Co, 1926

Griffin, Miriam T, *The End of the Dynasty*, Yale University Press, 1984

Griffiths, Paul, *Olivier Messiaen and the Music of Time*, Faber and Faber, 1985

Hallé, Sir Charles, *Life and Letters of Sir Charles Hallé*, Smith, Elder & Co, 1896

Harding, James, *The Ox on the Roof*, MacDonald, 1972

Heyworth, Peter, *Otto Klemperer: His Life and Times* (2 vols), Cambridge University Press, 1996

Hoffnung, Annetta, *Gerard Hoffnung*, Gordon Fraser Gallery Ltd, 1988

Holland, Richard, *Nero: The Man Behind the Myth*, Sutton Publishing, 2000

Horwood, Wally, *Adolph Sax 1814–1894: His Life and Legacy*, Bramley Books, 1980

Jacobs, Arthur, *Henry J. Wood: Maker of the Proms*, Methuen, 1994

Kenyon, Nicholas, *The BBC Symphony Orchestra 1930–1980*, BBC, 1981

Lebrecht, Norman, *The Book of Musical Anecdotes*, Sphere, 1987

Lochner, Louis P, *Fritz Kreisler*, Rockliff Publishing Corporation Ltd, 1951

Macalpine, Ida and Hunter, Richard, *George III and The Mad-Business*, Pimlico 1991

Marek, George R, *Gentle Genius: The Story of Felix Mendelssohn*, Robert Hale, 1973

Martyn, Barrie, *Rachmaninoff: Composer, Pianist, Conductor*, Scolar Press, 1990

McKenna, Marian, *Myra Hess: A Portrait*, Hamish Hamilton Ltd, 1976

Meredith, Anthony and Harris, Paul, *Malcolm Arnold: Rogue Genius*, Thames/Elkin, 2004

Mitchell, Mark, *Vladimir de Pachmann: A Piano Virtuoso's Life and Art*, Indian University Press, 2002

Morrison, Richard, *Orchestra: The LSO: A Century of Triumph and Turbulence*, Faber and Faber, 2004

Newman, Richard with Kirtley, Karen, *Alma Rosé: Vienna to Auschwitz*, Amadeus Press, 2000

Nichols, Roger, *Mendelssohn Remembered*, Faber and Faber, 1997

Norris, Geoffrey, *Rachmaninov*, Dent, 1967

Olleson, Philip, *Samuel Wesley: The Man and His Music*, Boydell Press, 2003

Orledge, Robert, *Satie Remembered*, Faber and Faber, 1995

Ostwald, Peter, *Glenn Gould: The Ectasy and Tragedy of Genius*, W W Norton & Co, 1997

Poulenc, Francis, *My Friends and Myself*, trans. James Harding, Dobson Books, 1978

Richards, Sam, *John Cage as . . .*, Amber Lane Press, 1996

Rischin, Rebecca, *For the End of Time*, Cornell University Press, 2003

Robbins Landon, H C, *Handel and His World*, Weidenfeld and Nicolson, c.1984

Ryan, Thomas, *Recollections of an Old Musician*, Sands & Company, 1899

Scholes, Percy A, *The Mirror of Music: 1844–1944* (2 vols), Novello & Co and OUP, 1947

Scott, R H F, *Jean-Baptiste Lully: The Founder of French Opera*, Peter Owen, 1973

Shaw, Bernard, *London Music in 1888–89*, Constable and Company, 1937

Shaw, Bernard, *How to Become a Musical Critic*, Ed. Dan H Laurence, Rupert Hart-Davis, 1960

Shead, Richard, *Constant Lambert*, Simon Publications, 1973

Sherlaw Johnson, Robert, *Messiaen*, Dent, 1989

Spark, William, *Musical Memories*, W Reeves, 1909

Spiegl, Fritz, *Book of Musical Blunders*, Robson Books, 1996

Stein, Gordon, *Encyclopaedia of Hoaxes*, Gale Research Int. Ltd, 1993

Taylor Arthur R (ed), *Labour and Love*, Elm Tree Books, 1983

Tippett, Michael, *Those Twentieth Century Blues*, Pimlico, 1994

Walker, Alan, *Franz Liszt: The Virtuoso Years 1811–1847*, Faber and Faber, 1983

Walsh, Stephen, *Igor Stravinsky: Creative Spring Russia and France 1882–1934*, Jonathan Cape, 2000

Watkins, Glenn, *Gesualdo: The Man and His Music*, OUP, 1973

Wegman, Rob C, 'Who was Josquin?' from *The Josquin Companion* ed. Richard Sherr, OUP, 2000

Williams, Adrian, *Portrait of Liszt, by Himself and His*

Contemporaries, Clarendon Press, 1990

Wolff, Christoph, *Johann Sebastian Bach: The Learned Musician*, OUP, 2000

Yancich, Milan, *An Orchestra Musician's Odyssey*, Wind Music, 1995

Newspapers and Journals
Caernarvon & Denbigh Herald
Daily Telegraph
The Economist
Guardian
Independent
Musical Times
Musical World
New York Times
North Wales Chronicle
The Times
Sunday Times

Reference Works
New Grove Dictionary of Music and Musicians ed. Stanley Sadie, MacMillan, 1980 and 2001

The Concise Oxford Dictionary of Music, ed. Percy Scholes and John Owen Ward, OUP, 1973

The Concise Oxford Dictionary of Music, ed. Harold Rosenthal and John Warrack, OUP, 1972

Internet Articles
4BarsRest, *Whit Friday*, 2003

Barnhart, Francis, *The Siegfried Idyll: Jewel of the Wagner Romance*, 2004

Canadian Encyclopedia, *Toronto Symphony Orchestra*, 2005

Catholic Encyclopedia, *St Cecilia*

Conway, Paul, *Malcolm Williamson – a 70th Birthday Tribute*, 2001

Fogel, Henry, *An Alarming Incident*

Forman, Frank, *Notes about Nikolai Dmitrievich Ovsyaniko-Kulikovsky's Symphony No. 21 in G Minor*, 1993

Harrison, Paul, *Hildegard of Bingen,* 1997
Internet Cello Society, *Ennio Bolognini*
Lair, Richard, *Asian Elephants in Thailand,* 2004
Langbell, Kenneth, *A Humid Recital Stirs Bangkok,* The
   English Language Bangkok Post, 1967
Miller, Malcolm, *Thirty-two Sonatas a Day,* 2004
Nettheim, Nigel, quoting J Cuthbert Hadden's 1914 piece, in
   Pachmann, 2001
Wikipedia online encyclopedia
Wong, Audrey, *Music for St Cecilia's Day,* 1996